A HISTORY OF THE S·P·C·K

Thomas Bray

A HISTORY OF
THE S.P.C.K

by

W. K. LOWTHER CLARKE, D.D.

With an
EPILOGUE
by
F. N. DAVEY

LONDON
S · P · C · K
1959

First published in 1959
by S.P.C.K.
Holy Trinity Church
Marylebone Road
London, N.W.1
Made and printed in Great Britain by
William Clowes and Sons, Limited, London and Beccles

Contents

		page
	PREFACE	ix
I	INTRODUCTION	I
2	THOMAS BRAY AND HIS PROJECTS	5
3	BEGINNINGS	
	(a) The First Five Years	11
	(b) The First Secretaries	15
4	CHARITY SCHOOLS	19
5	EAST INDIA MISSION	59
6	LITERATURE	
	(a) Libraries	77
	(b) Publishing	80
7	THE ACTIVITIES OF THE SOCIETY 1704–1800	86
8	FOREIGN LITERATURE	103
9	OTHER ACTIVITIES	
	(a) French Proselytes	132
	(b) Georgia	134
	(c) The Scilly Mission	138
10	DISTRICT COMMITTEES	141
11	THE SOCIETY IN THE NINETEENTH CENTURY	
	(a) Progress and Policy	148
	(b) Education	156
	(c) Missionary Grants	162
	(d) Work among Emigrants	165

CONTENTS

12 NINETEENTH-CENTURY PUBLISHING AND BOOK-
        SELLING
        (a) Bibles and Prayer Books   170
        (b) Religious Tracts and Books   172
        (c) General Literature   181
        (d) Treatment of Authors   186

13 BUSINESS METHODS   188

14 THE TWENTIETH CENTURY, 1914–44   193

15 EPILOGUE   209

    APPENDICES:
        A. The S.P.C.K. in Ireland and Scotland   219
        B. Pitcairn Island   222
        C. List of Secretaries   224
        D. Some Trust Funds   225
        E. S.P.C.K. Bookshops   226

    INDEX   229

vi

List of Illustrations

Thomas Bray   Frontispiece

To face page

Some outstanding servants of the S.P.C.K.   16

"The Society acquired premises in Bartlett's Buildings"   17

"Members used their influence . . . in promoting Charity Schools"   50

"For the Better Preservation of Parochial Libraries"   51

The East India Mission: sketch map   *page* 76

"As faithful a translation as possible"   128

"The most important development . . . has been the opening of
bookshops"   129

"The new S.P.C.K. House in Northumberland Avenue"   154

"Grants to school and church building in the Mission Field
continued"   155

"The spiritual care of emigrants would continue"   182

"Literature . . . designed for special classes"   183

"250th Anniversary . . . celebrations were planned with imagination"   212

"The Society's headquarters was moved . . . into a church"   213

vii

Preface

IN A SENSE I began working for this book nearly forty years ago, when as Secretary of the S.P.C.K. I formed the habit of using the lunch hour for looking at the archives of the Society preserved in the strong room. This I did intermittently between 1915 and 1944. When in 1949 I was invited by the Society to write its History I began a systematic reading of all the documents. This took me five years. I originally intended to write a complete history, but the publication of two books on the early period, which is the most interesting, H. P. Thompson's *Thomas Bray* and L. W. Cowie's *Henry Newman*, led me to alter my plan. All that is worth recording in the years 1699 to 1743 will be found in them. I therefore decided to write a popular book of moderate length. I have said comparatively little about the missionary grants recounted in the History by W. O. B. Allen and E. McClure, written for the Bicentenary of the Society in 1898, because they were grants in aid of work for which other Societies were primarily responsible and belong to their history rather than to that of the S.P.C.K. I have found the mastering of a great mass of material preserved at the S.P.C.K. as much as I could manage and have not attempted to collect much illustrative matter from other sources. Also I have been compelled to rely on my notes and to abandon any attempt to check everything by a further consultation of the original documents, which would have postponed publication for several years. A few errors are inevitable, but I trust no serious ones will have crept in. I may have been inaccurate in one point. The Society's Reports deal with the events of a year, which is generally not the calendar year. Something attributed, say, to 1861 may have occurred in 1860 or the early part of 1861. An attentive reader will find occasional repetitions, a subject being referred to in its logical place and also in anticipation or retrospect. These I have decided not to eliminate.

W. K. LOWTHER CLARKE

1

Introduction

THE CONDITION of England and its Church at the end of the seventeenth century, when the S.P.C.K. was founded, will be sufficiently illustrated in the chapters that follow; but a short sketch may be acceptable here. Superficially it might seem that the Church of England in 1660 made a triumphant return, but the wounds inflicted by the Civil War and the Commonwealth were slow to heal. The Cavalier Parliament was more responsible than the Church for the reprisals on Dissenters, which do not seem to have done much harm to the Church. Theologically the Laudian School seemed to have come back in full strength, but there was a powerful undercurrent which was destined presently to alter the whole situation. One great weakness of the Church was that it returned to power jointly with the monarch, Church and King being at the time inseparable in the public mind, so that when in 1688 the problem "which King?" arose, it was not prepared to meet the difficulty.

Morally the age of the Restoration was deplorable, if we may judge by the indictment presented by responsible writers. While every age is open to such condemnation there are special reasons for believing that the accounts given of the latter part of the seventeenth century are approximately true. The Court of Charles II notoriously set a bad example, but even a good example might not have had much effect on the people generally, who had reacted from "the rule of the saints" and the attempt to equate sin and crime. The laws were not adequate for the needs of the time, and in the absence of police, as we understand the word, enforcement rested with the magistrates, who were subject to little control from above. This problem of law and its enforcement exercised the consciences of serious men and led to the foundation of the Societies for the Reformation of Manners (or Morals

I

as we should say), "An Account" of which was published in 1699. Their purpose is stated to be "for the effecting of a National Reformation". The Societies first attracted notice after King William III's Proclamation "for preventing and punishing immorality and profaneness" in 1691, though much work had already been done in East London. Later in that year the House of Commons sent an Address to the King asking him to enforce the laws and to see that the Proclamation be read at least four times a year after Divine Service. The Account of the Societies is "commended by 29 Lords Temporal, 9 Lords Spiritual, and 7 Judges". The plan, we are told, was conceived by five or six gentlemen of the Church of England, who formed the first Society, composed of persons of eminence, who themselves bore the considerable expense involved. A second Society of about fifty persons succeeded in closing about 500 disorderly houses. A third Society consisted of Constables, who consulted together on how to perform their oaths. A fourth comprised informers. "They were much reviled but have taken no advantage from their actions, all rewards having been appropriated to the poor." "There has been a great reduction in swearing, and many night-walkers have chosen to be sent to the plantations rather than work in Bridewell." Public opposition is now at an end. Magistrates are appealed to; "their negligence and unfaithfulness in their office is the great cause of the debauchery and profaneness of the kingdom". The Societies are a great kindness to the poor, who profit by the fines. A righteous nation will be protected by God. It is necessary to employ the secular arm now that the ecclesiastical power is weakened and "hath, to speak justly, lost its credit".

The Societies, in which Churchmen and Dissenters co-operated, died out about 1730, having been crippled by an adverse judgement in the Court of King's Bench. An attempt in 1757 by the followers of John Wesley and George Whitefield to revive them was a failure.

Probably the Societies to a large extent merely drove vice underground and the parallel movement of "Religious Societies" is of more permanent importance. Something of the kind existed in the reign of Elizabeth I, when pious people met for "Exercises" and "Prophesying"; also the German pietistic organizations were destined to influence the S.P.C.K. greatly. But the movement in its Church of England form seems to have been spontaneous. It originated in 1678 with the sermons of Dr Horneck, minister of the Savoy Chapel. A number of young men who listened to them banded themselves together to lead lives of devotion. They met weekly to sing psalms, pray, study, and relieve the poor. The movement spread until there were 39 Societies known in London and Westminster and many more in the provinces. At first great secrecy was observed, only the ministers knowing all the names. They were delated to the Bishop of London, who replied: "God forbid that I should be against such excellent designs." He could hardly have answered otherwise in view of a rule of life which included monthly Communion, daily prayers in many City churches, humble deference to their ministers, and silence under revilings. The personnel of the two kinds of Societies was largely identical. The two movements ran on parallel lines, the one being directed to public reformation, the other to the cultivation of the personal religious life. The latter provided a field from which the supporters of the S.P.C.K. were recruited, but the former probably played a larger part in the formation of the new Society, if only by reaction. Dr Bray must have seen the limitations of what could be done by coercion and have set out to find a more excellent way, that of education.

Church life in William III's reign was turbulent and beset with controversy. The Non-jurors' schism, the attempt at Prayer Book revision in the hope of achieving comprehension, the struggle between the Bishops and the Lower House of Convocation, the beginnings of the Arian Controversy—all these may be studied in George Every's book *The High Church Party*, 1688–1718. The reader who comes from this, or from any history of the period, to the S.P.C.K. records will be impressed by the absence of controversy in them. He will be led to admire greatly the serenity with which the first members settled down to "get on with the job". The fierce controversies of the day find no place in their discussions. Supporters of the Restoration settlement, and later of the Hanoverian kings, they co-operated with the Non-jurors. Many of them were ordinary parish priests, who paid the utmost deference to the Bishops. The piety of the Religious Societies is not represented in the minutes of meetings, for the S.P.C.K. was founded to do practical work, not to promote devotion—that was the indispensable foundation of their activities, too obvious to need mention. Seventeenth-century England has been well termed an "adolescent Society"; the early members of the S.P.C.K. are recognizably grown-up Englishmen such as we meet today.[1]

[1] For the later activities of the Religious Societies see p. 101, where references to them are collected from the S.P.C.K. records. It is enough here to say that Samuel Wesley on 9 December 1701 received a packet of literature from the S.P.C.K., which included a copy of Dr Woodward's *An Account of the Religious Societies in the City of London, etc., and of their Endeavours for the Reformation of Manners*. On 7 February 1702 he founded a Society consisting of himself and eight others. John, who was born two years later, must have been familiar from childhood with the institution, which provided a pattern for his own Methodist Societies.

2

Thomas Bray and his Projects

THOMAS BRAY was born in 1658 in a little farmhouse, still standing, in the hamlet of Marton, Shropshire, three miles from Chirbury, where he was baptized. The family was of good standing, though poor, and Brays had lived in the neighbourhood for generations. Thomas was educated at Oswestry Grammar School and at All Souls College, Oxford, where he was a "poor boy", supporting himself by menial services to the Fellows. He graduated as B.A. in 1678 and proceeded to the degree of M.A. in 1693; in 1696 he became B.D. and D.D. Soon after his ordination he attracted the notice of Sir Thomas Price, of Park Hall, near Castle Bromwich, who made him his chaplain. In 1682 he became also Vicar of Lea Marston, to which preferment he added in 1685 the Rectory of Over Whitacre. Soon after this he married, but his wife Elenor died in March 1689, leaving two small children, William and Goditha. His home was evidently at Over Whitacre, where his wife was buried.[1]

In 1690 Bray became Rector of Sheldon, then a village but now a populous suburb of Birmingham, which living he held until shortly before his death. The passion of his life—or one of his passions, for he had many—was the encouragement of clerical studies, with the purpose of qualifying the clergy to catechize effectively, and in 1696 he published the first volume of *Catechetical Lectures*; it ran to over 300 pages in folio and dealt with the first four questions and answers of the Prayer Book Catechism only. In the previous year Archbishop Tenison had issued Injunctions under the authority of the Crown,

[1] Bray married again in 1698 and had four children by his second wife, all of whom died young. Of the other two, William became a publisher and bookseller, Goditha married a prosperous upholsterer. This chapter is based on H. P. Thompson's definitive biography *Thomas Bray* (S.P.C.K., 1954).

calling for observance of the 59th Canon (on Catechizing the Young), so the time was ripe for the book, which made the author's fame. The book sold the better because it was not merely theoretical but was based on his own method of teaching young people. They were to read the discourses and discuss them with him and so form the nucleus of an instructed congregation, for whom a monthly or even weekly Communion would be necessary. This applied to those who took the third course, for those aged 13 and over, which was also published separately under the title *Short Discourse upon the Doctrine of our Baptismal Covenant*; there were two other courses, for children under 9 and for those of 9 to 13. The first edition of the complete book, 3,000 copies, was sold out and realized a profit of £700.

In the autumn of 1695 Bray seems to have moved to London, having appointed a curate to take charge of Sheldon, and to have begun to make preparations for visiting Maryland as the Commissary of the Bishop of London (Henry Compton). His mind thought largely in terms of books. Only poor clergymen were likely to go to America and they would be unable to buy the necessary books. In December 1695 he printed *Proposals for encouraging Learning and Religion in the Foreign Plantations*, by means of books, and started a public appeal, to which Princess (afterwards Queen) Anne gave £44. The Bishops had approved his scheme, saying that it "will tend very much to propagate Christian knowledge in the Indies", perhaps the ultimate source of the name S.P.C.K. In 1697 Bray published *An Essay towards promoting all Necessary and Useful knowledge, both Divine and Human, in all parts of His Majesty's Dominions, both at home and abroad*, also consisting largely of lists of books. The idea was to meet any possible objection that the Plantations should not be helped at the expense of the Home Church. The latter he believed could best be helped by the establishment of libraries in connection with a revived system of Rural Deaneries. He did not sail for Maryland until the end of 1699, by which time the S.P.C.K. had been founded.

The Bray papers, which are for the most part preserved in Sion College Library, show the antecedents of the Society. They include Bray's draft of "A General Plan or Constitution of a Protestant Congregation, or Society for the Propagation of Christian Knowledge". In its earlier form the phrase used was "the intended *Congregatio pro propaganda fide et moribus Christianis*". The Society was to be incorporated by Royal Charter; only so could it receive and invest money. It was to be composed as to two-thirds of London clergy of note, the rest to be "eminent for their work and affection to religion and the Church of England". The Archbishop of Canterbury and the Bishop of London were to be the leaders and to be represented normally by their senior chaplains *ex officio*. The functions of the Corporation were to consult together about promoting religion in the Plantations; to search out suitable clergymen to be presented to the Bishop of London for ordination for work there; to set up libraries in the Plantations; and to give financial assistance to the missionaries.

The difficulties in the way of the scheme proved too great, and Bray laid it aside. He had by this time accumulated a vast load of work, too heavy to be borne by one man, especially as he was about to leave England. So a little group of his friends, four in number, formed themselves into a voluntary society at a meeting held at Lincoln's Inn, in the room of Serjeant (later Mr Justice) Hooke, on 8 March 1699. It was very much Bray's Society and indeed, after the S.P.G. had been founded and when both Societies were functioning, he took a greater part in the counsels of the S.P.C.K. than of the S.P.G. The primary object was to enable Bray's work to be continued on a secure basis. On 8 June he submitted his accounts to the S.P.C.K., showing a deficit of £631 owing to him, liability for which the Society took over. For the first two years of its life it did the work which presently fell to the S.P.G. by recommending missionaries to Bishop Compton. During the years 1695 to 1701, Bray was responsible for sending 129 missionaries abroad.

Leaving for the present the names of the founders of the Society, let us follow the rest of Bray's career. The greatest achievement was the foundation of the S.P.G.—the Society for the Propagation of the Gospel in Foreign Parts—which completed his original design. In 1700 a scheme was considered by the S.P.C.K. for procuring a Charter, which would put the Charity Schools on a firmer foundation. The difficulties seemed to be very great, and this scheme also was laid aside. As it turned out, this had an influence on the history of education, since it helped towards decentralization and the management of schools by local trustees. But Bray, with his unique industry and skill, on his return from Maryland began to work for the establishment of a Chartered Society. The matter was already under consideration by a

Committee of Convocation, but Bray approached King William III directly, sending a petition signed by himself alone. The Archbishop and the Bishop of London no doubt supported it behind the scenes. The S.P.C.K., having received a donation of twenty guineas from the Archbishop towards the expenses, took over Bray's liabilities under this head and invited subscriptions. The Charter was signed, and on 16 June Bray received the Letters Patent, which he presented to the Society on 23 June. The Society then asked the Archbishop to summon the first meeting of the new Society (the S.P.G.), which was held at Lambeth Palace on the 27th. The foundation members were largely members of the S.P.C.K.

In 1708 Bray, who had meanwhile returned to Sheldon, from which he had been absent for eight years, left it again to become Rector of St Botolph, Aldgate (City of London), where he lived an exemplary life as a faithful parish priest. *Pietas Londinensis* (1714) describes the church as having daily Mattins and Evensong and many special Sermons or Lectures, and caring generously for the poor. Ralph Thoresby, the well-known antiquary, records a visit paid to the church in 1723:

"(May 15th) Walked to the pious and charitable Mr Bray's, at Aldgate, was extremely pleased with his many pious, useful, and charitable projects. . . . (May 26th) Walked to Aldgate, where Dr Bray preached excellently both ends of the day concerning the Ascension of Christ. Evening, he read prayers again to a considerable auditory, especially of young persons. The Charity children were catechized in Dr Wake the present Archbishop of Canterbury's Commentary upon the Church Catechism, which was distinctly read by them, for their own edification and the instruction of the auditory. I was extremely surprised at the prodigious pains so aged a person undertakes: he is very mortified as to this world."

Bray continued to write important books, keep up all his old interests (including Charity Schools and prisons), and give ceaseless care to individuals. Finally in 1729 he established "The Associates of Dr Bray".

This body developed out of a small trust founded to administer a legacy, to be devoted to the conversion and education of negroes in the Plantations, from D'Allone, a Dutch subject of William III, who died in 1723. They also administered a trust to help in the foundation of a new colony. When in 1733 Georgia came into being this work was taken over by the Directors of Georgia, the personnel of whom was largely identical with that of the Associates of Dr Bray; for many years the two bodies shared the same office and Secretary. The other work was that of continuing Bray's work for libraries, for which purpose new funds had to be raised. The Associates of Dr Bray still exist, and carry on their work of providing theological libraries for the clergy (and others) in co-operation with the S.P.C.K.

Bray died on 15 February 1730, and was buried in St Botolph's church. The writer of the memoir, published in 1746, entitled *Public Spirit illustrated in the Life and Designs of the Reverend Thomas Bray, D.D., late Minister of St Botolph without Aldgate*, describes the sentiments which he says must have filled the mind of this estimable man in these terms: "And now the Doctor, having happily lodged his principal designs in the hands of able managers, being on the verge of the grave, he could not but review his undertakings with complacency, and thank the good providence of God, which appeared, to lay such trains for their advancement. His conscience crown'd him with a secret applause, which was an inexhaustible source of comfortable reflections and joyful presages in his last minutes." For once the conventional eulogies of eighteenth-century inscriptions ring true. Few men have founded institutions which after 250 years remain so flourishing and true to the purpose of their originator.

We return to the inaugural meeting of the S.P.C.K. on 8 March 1699, and note the names of the founders, whose presence was due to their being personal friends of Dr Bray.

Lord Guilford was the son of Sir Francis North, who became first Baron Guilford. He was born in 1673 and educated at Oxford; though in no way outstanding, he was a useful man. Bishop Burnet says of him: "does not want sense, nor application to business, and his genius leads him that way". He was Lord-Lieutenant of Essex from 1703 to 1706 and became President of the Board of Trade in 1714.

Sir Humphrey Mackworth, the son of a Shropshire country gentleman, was educated at Oxford and called to the Bar in 1682, in which year he was knighted. He married an heiress and engaged in speculation, in particular the so-called Mines Adventure, formed to exploit coal and copper on an estate near Neath. It got into difficulties, but S.P.C.K. had already disposed of the share it possessed.

Mr Justice Hooke, an Irishman educated at Trinity College, Dublin, was called to the Bar in 1681. He became Chief Justice of Caernarvon in 1706. For the first three years of its existence the Society met in his room at Lincoln's Inn.

Colonel Maynard Colchester, of Westbury Court, Gloucestershire, was M.P. for his county, 1701–8, and Verderer of the Forest of Dean. The Dutch gardens of Westbury Court are said to have been laid out on the advice of John Evelyn. He had founded a number of Charity Schools before the S.P.C.K. came into existence. The monument to him in Westbury Church says that he was "a principal founder and supporter of the Societies for the Reformation of Manners and Promoting Christian Knowledge, by Charity Schools, of which he set up and maintained several at his own charges".

3

Beginnings

(a) THE FIRST FIVE YEARS

IT IS convenient to sketch the first five years of the Society's life separately, since the minutes of the meetings have been printed in a book edited by E. McClure under the title *A Chapter in English Church History* (1888). The descriptive sub-title is: "being the Minutes of the Society for Promoting Christian Knowledge for the years 1698–1705 together with Abstracts of Correspondents' Letters during part of the same period".

The first meeting of Dr Bray and his friends is recorded as follows:

8 March 1698-9

Present. The Rt. Honble the Lord Guilford, Sir Humphrey Mackworth, Mr Justice Hooke, Dr Bray, Col. Colchester.

1. Resolved that Col. Colchester and Dr Bray go and discourse George Keith, in order to be satisfied what progress he has hitherto made towards the instruction and conversion of Quakers, and to know what he designs further to attempt, under the conduct of God's providence and assistance, in order to redeem that misguided people to the knowledge and belief of Christ, and that they may report the same to the Society tomorrow morning.

2. Resolved that we consider tomorrow morning how to further and promote that good design of erecting Catechetical Schools in each parish in and about London, and that Col. Colchester and Dr Bray give their thoughts how it may be done.

3. Resolved that the Right Honble the Lord Guilford be desired to speak to the Archbishop that care may be taken that a clause be provided in the Bill for employing the poor, to have the children taught to read and be instructed in the Church Catechism.

11

4. Resolved that Dr Bray be desired as soon as conveniently he can, to lay before this Society his scheme of promoting Religion in the Plantations, and his accounts of benefactions and disbursements towards the same.

We see here two of the main passions of Dr Bray's life, the American Mission and the teaching of the Catechism. George Keith is an interesting figure. A Scotsman, he joined the Quakers and became a leader, and a friend and fellow-traveller of William Penn. He went to America, ending in Pennsylvania, where he was appalled by the unsatisfactory teaching of the dominant Quakerism and organized a rival group. He was put on trial and condemned, but in 1694 returned to England, where he wrote against the Quakers and was finally received into the Church of England and was ordained in 1700.[1] Keith had fuller knowledge than anyone else of the situation with which Bray would have to cope in Maryland, and the two men naturally came together. Bray's interest in Quakerism would be primarily in the American form which dominated Pennsylvania. From the point of view of Anglicans, Presbyterians, and orthodox Dissenters alike, the Quakers, with their reliance on the Inner Light, were dangerously weak on the authority of the Bible and the doctrine of the Atonement. Catechetical Schools (presently to be called Charity Schools) were the great interest of Colonel Colchester, and Lord Guilford being influential in political circles was a valuable man where legislation was concerned.

The first meetings were held at frequent intervals; during March 1699 there were five, on the 10th, 12th, 16th, 19th, and 20th. On the 10th there is a curious minute: "Resolved that this Society will endeavour to procure for Mr Keith some certification or recommendation which may protect him in his travels, and procure him some encouragement from the Justices of the Peace." That violence was expected is surprising and we suspect that the successors of the Antinomian sects of the Commonwealth period were averse to the open preaching of authoritative Anglicanism and were grouped with the Quakers in popular speech. Before the end of the month Hooke had been appointed Treasurer, decisions had been taken as to "what shall be entered in our books", and schemes had been drawn up for raising

[1] H. P. Thompson, *Into All Lands*, p. 23 f.

12

money for schools. Arrangements for the first publications of the Society were made on 10 March, Keith's *Narrative* and *Catechism* (in two forms). The estimate was accepted on 20 March, £12 being subscribed towards the cost by the members present.

On 5 April Sir John Philipps, Mr Yates, and Mr Martyn were invited to become members of the Society, evidently personal friends into whose fitness no formal enquiry was necessary. and Mr Chamberlayne and Mr Bromfield were also proposed. On 15 April the only business recorded was: "Ordered that Lord Guilford and Dr Bray be desired to enquire concerning Mr Bromfield and Mr Chamberlayne." It is reasonable to suppose that the basis of membership was fixed at this meeting. Mr Chamberlayne was elected at the next meeting. So the practice began of proposing a member and leaving an interval for inquiry before the second proposal. This applied even to bishops. The Bishop of Chichester was proposed on 4 January 1700, and elected the next day. Apart from these formal matters the business at the early meetings largely consisted of reports from Charity Schools, a subject which is treated in a separate chapter. However, on 11 May we have the first example of the foreign contacts that were to play so large a part in the Society's history. "The two Germans attended, and Mr Chamberlayne [an accomplished linguist] was desired to discourse them. The business of the two Germans was to give an account of the two Schools erected at Halle in Saxony, by Professor Francke, and who was afterwards chosen a Corresponding Member for those parts."

Great pains were taken in the composition of statements to be signed by all members of the Society. On 19 April 1699 this preamble was adopted for signature:

"Whereas the growth of vice and immorality is greatly owing to the gross ignorance of the principles of the Christian religion, we whose names are underwritten do agree to meet together, as often as we can conveniently, to consult (under the conduct of the Divine Providence and assistance) how we may be able by due and lawful methods to promote Christian Knowledge."

Early in 1701, 115 men, including seven diocesan bishops, had signed this statement.

A second document was concerned with Parochial Libraries in the Plantations, especially on the continent of North America, the signatories committing themselves to subscribe and to endeavour to obtain benefactions from their friends and acquaintances. In a third the signatories promised to subscribe for the purpose "of erecting Catechetical Schools" and to raise "Lending Catechetical Libraries in the several market towns in the Kingdoms" and to distribute "good books or otherwise as the Society shall direct", the annual subscription to be paid in quarterly instalments. When the S.P.G. was founded, the second document was dropped and in its place was put a promise to pay a lump sum on admission for the designs of the Society. This, which was confined to Residing Members, continued until the early nineteenth century.

Other documents that deserve mention are the first and second Circular Letters to the Clergy Correspondents and the Circular Letter to Lay Correspondents. The first letter, dated 16 November 1699, begins: "The visible decay of religion in this kingdom, with the monstrous increase of Deism, profaneness, and vice, has excited the zeal of several persons of the best character in the cities of London and Westminster, and other parts of the nation, to associate themselves in order to consult together how to put a stop to so fatal an inundation." It goes on to recommend the method of Charity Schools.

The second letter (8 February 1699) urges frequent meetings of the clergy, with the leave and direction of the Diocesan, with a view to mutual encouragement in their pastoral labours, and asks the readers to correspond faithfully.

The letter to the Lay Correspondents (11 April 1700) is specially directed to country gentlemen: "God has given them a greater proportion of temporal blessings than other men, and 'tis but reasonable they should show greater zeal in promoting his glory in gratitude for them; their estates afford them ability to do much themselves, and their dignity gives a force to their example to influence those about them."

The annual subscriptions of these early members seem generous, when the value of money is remembered. For example (the admission fee is added in brackets): Lord Guilford £20 (100), Bishop of Worcester £20 (10), Bishop of Chichester £10 (5), Bishop of Chester £10 (5), Robert Nelson £10 (20), Colonel Colchester £8 (10), William Hayley £5 (5). Dr Bray paid no admission fee but his annual subscription was £5, to be taken in copies of his books, "to be given to children as the Society think fit".

(b) THE FIRST SECRETARIES

The first Secretary of the S.P.C.K. was John Chamberlayne, one of the outstanding figures of his time. His father, Edward Chamberlayne (1616–1703), was the author of *Angliae Notitiae, or The present State of England*. When he died his son John took it over and brought out many editions, changing the name after the Union with Scotland to *Magnae Britanniae Notitiae*. The book is a kind of *Whitaker's Almanack* combined with a Social Survey and still provides interesting reading. John Chamberlayne was born in 1666 and in 1686 went to Trinity College, Oxford, being already the author of a published book. From Oxford he went to the University of Leyden, where he became an accomplished linguist, able to correspond in sixteen modern languages. He translated many books into English and as a curiosity published at Amsterdam the Lord's Prayer in 100 languages, a work to which the Bishop of Carlisle (Nicholson) contributed a prefatory essay. In 1702 he was elected Fellow of the Royal Society. He was Gentleman of the Privy Chamber to Queen Anne and afterwards to George I. On 31 October 1699 he was elected Secretary of the S.P.C.K., retiring from the office in March 1702 owing to pressure of other duties; but he continued to help the Society, among other things translating all foreign correspondence. In a letter written to the S.P.C.K. on 1 May 1712 he describes himself as Secretary of the Society for Reformation of Manners, and to the Committee for propagating Religion in India. From 1701 to 1712 he was Secretary of the S.P.G.

Chamberlayne was succeeded by another great man, Humphrey Wanley (1672–1726), who had been employed as his assistant from December 1700, at a salary of £40. Wanley was educated at St Edmund Hall, Oxford. He became a disciple of George Hickes, Dean of Worcester, who was deprived as a Non-juror, and was Assistant Librarian of the Bodleian. Robert Nelson procured him the post at the S.P.C.K. Hearne says he was "a very loose debauched man", which seems improbable, for his relations with the Society seem to have been happy. During this time he made translations of works of piety from the French and produced his greatest work of scholarship, the final volume of Hickes' *Thesaurus*. After leaving the S.P.C.K. in 1708 he became keeper of the Harleian Library. He was a great collector of manuscripts and the chief mover in the refounding of the Society of

Antiquaries, and as an Anglo-Saxon scholar perhaps the finest critic of manuscripts that England has ever produced.[1]

In June 1708 Henry Newman was appointed Secretary in place of Wanley, retaining his office till his death in 1743. His extensive correspondence, official and private, has been preserved, thanks to his practice of making drafts of his letters, from which his clerk made fair copies.[2]

Newman's grandfather in 1638 sailed to Boston, in the neighbourhood of which place he lived as a Puritan preacher for twenty-six years. His son Noah became a Congregational minister and had one surviving child, Henry, born in 1670. Henry was educated at Harvard College, where he devoted himself to French and Mathematics and for a time was in charge of the library. He decided to come to England and after an adventurous voyage reached London in 1694. Next year he entered into a business partnership with a merchant and in 1696 returned to Boston, going to Newfoundland in 1698. For some years we lose sight of him. When he first appears in the S.P.C.K. minutes it is on 13 May 1703, when he is appointed corresponding member for Newfoundland. By this time he had shed his early Puritanism and become a loyal Anglican. In June 1708 he succeeded Wanley, having frequently attended meetings in the intervening years, receiving it seems a salary of £60; he regretted that he could not, like the Treasurers, work for nothing.

Henceforward, till his death in 1743, he wholly identified himself with the Society. At first he lived in Whitehall, but in 1714 a benefactor put his room in the Middle Temple at the disposal of the Society, for the use of the Secretary, and Newman lived there till 1728, when the Society acquired premises in Bartlett's Buildings and the Secretary was housed there. His personal tastes were simple. Breakfast consisted of milk and water with a slice of bread and butter. Every Tuesday morning he visited St Dunstan's Coffee House and probably transacted a good deal of business as he met his friends. In later life he countered the scurvy which a sedentary life engendered by riding on Hampstead

---

[1] See D. C. Douglas, *English Scholars*, p. 120 f.

[2] I have read all the letters preserved at the S.P.C.K. many times and am proud to have introduced Newman to the reading public in my book *Eighteenth Century Piety* (1944). Dr L. W. Cowie has gone much further in his *Henry Newman* (1956). I have confined myself here in the main to the material used in my essay.

Joshua Watson

Robert Nelson

Bishop T. F. Middleton

Some outstanding servants of the S.P.C.K.

From a water-colour by T. Hosmer Shepherd

"The Society acquired premises in Bartlett's Buildings"

Heath, and finally he resorted to the automatic horse "as patronised by Princess Amelia and several people of quality".

Newman worked at the office from 9 to 2, except on Saturdays, and then went to dinner, generally with a friend. In a circular letter written on appointment he directed that all letters intended for him be sent to the Reverend Mr Shute's house in Bartlett's Buildings, i.e., the Treasurer's. His duty was to read all letters to the Committee and receive their instructions as to replies. He had to make a fair copy of the proceedings and abstracts of all letters received, and in a separate book to keep copies of all books and papers sent to members. He entered accounts in four different books. In 1713 he noted: "I design to look over my accounts once in half a year. N.B. Not to send letters abroad till they have been perused by friends on whose judgement I can depend". In 1713 a Committee of Inquiry found that Newman in five years four months had written 6,340 letters with his own hand, kept the accounts, made abstracts of all inward letters and fair copies of minutes, copied all important documents, managed the Parochial Libraries, and indexed letter and minute books. As a result he was given a gratuity of £50 and his salary was increased to £80, to rise to £100 after two years. He paid half the clerk's salary of 8s. per week and provided him with board and lodging until 1727, when he asked the Society to contribute 4s. a week. A housekeeper cost him £20 12s. a year plus her board, and he paid 10s. a week rent to the Society, which paid for the premises £54 including taxes. As we see elsewhere, Newman played a part in many good causes outside his usual occupations. Also he acted as guardian to the children of the Marquis Du Quesne.[1] With unfailing kindness he constantly carried out commissions for members of the Society. Thus in 1741 he took charge of Archdeacon Denne's watch and saw to its repair, and for Griffith Jones of Llandowror he bought three bottles of stuff for broken-winded horses. He frequently advised members on legal matters, after consulting legal friends.

One of his worries was to find a competent clerk. The problem was discussed on 9 December 1700, when a special Committee reported on the qualities required. He must have such familiarity with the Society's affairs as to be able to suggest suitable answers to the Board. He must be able to arrange minutes, etc., under the proper heads and to prepare

[1] The story is told in *Eighteenth Century Piety*, pp. 54–68.

answers. He must be a loyal Church of England man, thoroughly pious and in love with the work; and possess good handwriting. So far was this paragon from being procurable that Newman had to make do with an inferior article about which he wrote in 1716: "my man is incompetent. In my absence he either does nothing for want of sense to do it or does it all wrong."

Another clerk was Delagarde, who was discharged in 1734: "he was of little more service than as a spectator in the office ... fickleness and constant application to dramatic amusements disposed him to neglect my business." Delagarde was succeeded by Norman, who did loyal service until 1742.

As an example of the tasks that fell to Newman we may quote a letter written to the Bishop of London on 12 October 1727 (a previous letter to Lord Perceval had met with no success):

"Having a present made me of a good natured little black boy native of Jamaica a beauty of his kind but not christened I have accepted of him upon condition I may have leave to make a present of him to your Lordship in acknowledgement of your great tenderness to the souls of the whole race of negroes.

"If I have such leave by the bearer or otherwise, he shall be delivered at Whitehall or Fulham free of any charge to your Lordship...."

After Newman, Thomas Broughton (1743–77), Michael Hallings (1777–85), and Dr George Gaskin (1783–1823) became Secretaries. Portraits of Broughton and Gaskin hang in the Society's house, but none of the three emerge as personalities. Broughton had been one of the early Methodists who met at Oxford under John Wesley.

4

Charity Schools

EDUCATION SINCE THE REFORMATION

THE GRAMMAR SCHOOLS were the great force which maintained and advanced education in the sixteenth and early seventeenth centuries. The upheavals of the Reformation had in some cases crippled them, for certain educational endowments were lost by the dissolution of the chantries. But new resources were obtained and the schools with the Universities to which they led produced many prodigies of scholarship. Latin, and in particular its grammar, was the main subject. Boys were expected to come to school prepared for the classical discipline, having learned to read and write from private tuition or at private, "petty" as they were called, schools. Writing, and even arithmetic, were often taught by an outside master. The supremacy of Latin is easily explained: it provided a fixed objective standard of culture, it was an international language, and in it were written the best works of scholarship, at a time when English and other modern languages had not stabilized themselves. The Reformers had to believe in education for the masses of the people, since the Bible had been substituted for the all-embracing influences of the medieval Church as the seat of authority. But to put beliefs into practice was not possible at that stage. The many strange doctrines produced by uninstructed Bible-reading, often inimical to good government, must have made the governing classes hold their hand when educational advance was considered. In any case, new schools were a matter of local initiative.

For most children education took the form of initiation into the traditional lore of the countryside and the housewife, and into the practical arts of their calling. When exceptional men of the labouring class learned to read and expound the Bible they would enjoy great prestige among their fellows.

19

The Civil War caused less disturbance to the schools than might have been expected, and the Commonwealth Government had many enlightened ideas. It continued the State regulation of education, practised by the Tudor monarchs, among whom Edward VI, for example, made the use of Lily's Latin Grammar compulsory. Some money was available for schools from confiscated Church endowments, and the deprived clergy were not usually interfered with when they opened private schools or acted as tutors to the sons of the well-to-do. Much attention was given to the theory of education and plans were devised which came to fulfilment in the Dissenting Academies of the eighteenth century.

With the Restoration in 1660 came a strong reaction against Puritan ways, including the influence of the State in education. Endowments often had to be restored to their former ecclesiastical holders. The only State control of schools took the form of the licensing of all masters by the Bishop of the diocese, which was resumed, with some easing in Charles II's reign, when in 1670 by a legal decision the licence could be dispensed with in the case of the founder of a school. And all the time the duty laid on the parish to care for the children of the poor in workhouses made it impossible to lose sight entirely of the problem of education.

THE LATE SEVENTEENTH CENTURY

To the founders of the S.P.C.K. the religious and moral situation seemed deplorable, and so no doubt it was. For nearly 150 years religious changes had been forced on the people from above, and apathy was the inevitable result. After a century of religious wars, the popular interest began to shift to other things. Charles II in some ways seems to be the first modern Englishman, the first, that is, with whom we can imagine ourselves conversing without undue strain. The frivolity of the Court was tempered by a deep interest in natural science, and the coming of Deism meant that the old presuppositions were no longer unchallenged. If the masses, in London especially, were brutal and wicked, the absence of a police force to control the more flagrant expressions of self-aggrandizement largely explains it; by a rough kind of self-discipline, marked by occasional irruptions of authority, the population governed itself throughout the eighteenth century.

PRE-1699 CHARITY SCHOOLS

The founders of the S.P.C.K. with zeal and driving power developed an existing institution. All writers on the subject are agreed that there were a fair number of Charity Schools to serve as a model, but no accurate estimate is possible. A school at St Dunstan-in-the-West, Fleet Street, was founded in the reign of Elizabeth I. The Red Maids' School, Bristol, goes back to 1634, the Grey Coat Hospital, Westminster, for girls, to 1698. Colonel Colchester maintained schools on his Gloucestershire estates. A few examples from the S.P.C.K. correspondence may be given. Kent was said to be particularly well supplied with free schools. In March-April 1714 a correspondent wrote that Folkestone had no need of a Charity School, John Harvey having in 1667 founded one, which his son Eliab endowed later. A letter from Robert Banks of Hull (November 1709) describes a Charity School set up by Act of Parliament in 1698; the building, which cost £600, held 100 children, but at present there were only 45 boys and girls. It was a boarding school and provided everything for the children. Various village schools also are mentioned. Three bits of information show how conditions varied. In 1709 a Doncaster correspondent said that several local people were seeing to the education of poor children and would welcome being organized. Also in 1709 George Keith, Rector of Edburton (Sussex), wrote to say that the parish was too poor to contemplate a Charity School but most of the children could read, suggesting a substantial amount of private benevolence. By way of contrast may be quoted a letter from Bristol (2 July 1709): 232 children in the writer's parish are supposed to be looked after by the Guardians, only three of whom are receiving any instruction.

THE FIRST YEARS OF THE S.P.C.K.

By the first years the period 8 March 1699 to 1 June 1704 is meant, the minutes of which have been printed *in extenso*.[1] At the inaugural meeting the second item reads: "Resolv'd that we consider tomorrow morning how to further and promote the good Design of erecting Catecheticall Schools in each parish in and about London, and that Col. Colchester and Dr Bray give their thoughts how it may be done."

[1] E. McClure, *A Chapter in English Church History*, 1888.

As we have seen, Dr Bray in 1696 had published the first of four projected volumes on the Catechism, *Catechetical Lectures on the Preliminary Questions and Answers of the Church Catechism*, a folio of 334 pages on the first four questions and answers. We cannot doubt what he meant. Much as he in common with his contemporaries valued the practice of learning the Catechism by heart, he also used it as a *Summa*, a manual of theology to be explained to the young by Biblical illustrations, examples from everyday life, and so on. The course was in three grades, for those up to 9 years, from 9 to 13, and over 13. Clearly, too, religion was the primary object of the new schools, in which the children were to learn to read the Bible and Prayer Book. (Religion, of course, was interpreted in an Anglican sense; the schools were to be "little garrisons against Popery".)[1] As will be shown below, writing and arithmetic were of secondary importance. Also, the scholars were to be "conditioned" for their walk in life. The Grammar Schools led to the Universities and professions, for the abler boys. The new free schools were to be complete in themselves, and provide the knowledge needed by ordinary working-class people in a Protestant country; there was no idea of turning out an "educated democracy". The new knowledge was to be imparted to boys and girls alike on equal terms.

A study of the S.P.C.K. minutes yields a surprising result. Schools were by no means the most prominent item in the discussions; the Society raised hardly any money with which to back its advice or sweeten its demands; indeed it had no powers with which to carry through any educational programme. What actually happened was that a few men of high standing and great ability supplied a focus for the new movement. People were wondering what to do and gladly accepted the clear directions given by the Society.

In the opening minute we note the phrase "in each parish in and about London". The members were all residents in London, country subscribers being termed "correspondents". Progress could be made only by a small group of men who gave personal attention to what happened under their observation. This explains why the schools mentioned are nearly all in London; the first outside London seems to have been at Chester, reported by the Bishop on 14 April 1701. Each school was an independent entity, governed by trustees, responsible to the general body of subscribers. At the second meeting of the

[1] White Kennet in his Anniversary Sermon in 1706.

Society (10 March 1698) it was "Resolv'd that this Society will subscribe a Stock for Insurance of the charge of setting up schools for
promoting Christian knowledge and that Mr Justice Hooke do draw
up an Instrument of Insurance and a Form of Subscription for the
contributors in their respective Parishes." Insurance meant that a parish
was guaranteed any deficiency in the amount required to start a school;
the guarantee was very small, £5 or so, and was hardly ever called upon.
Preachers of the day drew out the spiritual meaning of the Joint Stock
Companies coming into existence: in this case you contributed your
money and received a dividend in the improved happiness and morality
of the poor.

The income of the Society was very small and the occasional large
donations reported at the meetings were for specific objects and did
not pass through the accounts. So independent were the parishes that
members of the Society were asked to inquire of their friends what new
schools were being opened. That the S.P.C.K. attained the position of
authority which it undoubtedly possessed was due to the influential
position of the original members, their scrupulous care not to dictate,
their comprehensive view of the whole problem, and the genuine
services which they rendered. A few minor points may be treated here.

There are several examples of co-operation with the parish authorities, whose financial support made possible the opening of schools;
also of Religious Societies, in London, who in whole or in part
supported schools. In January 1701 a clergyman named Coghan was
appointed Inspector of all the Charity Schools in or about London and
Westminster, no doubt with the consent of the various trustees, at a
salary of £20 a year.

Dr Bray in 1699 approached the Bishop of London, suggesting that
he should instruct all ministers of parishes where schools had been
opened to catechize the children, and this the Bishop promised to do.
In January 1700 it was "Order'd that the Dean of Chichester be desired
to apply to the Bishop of London for the easy licensing the masters of
the Charity Schools". "His Lordship answer'd it was very fit and
reasonable, and he would take care in it." This probably refers to
concessions in the matter of fees for licences, which some country
schools found a heavy financial burden and neglected to pay. Members
of the Society successfully used their influence with both Archbishops
to promote the interests of Charity Schools, and the existence of the

3

Society must have helped greatly in securing ecclesiastical recognition.

There are frequent references to "the agents". These were not members of the Society and seem to have been confined to London. A Mr Bridges is frequently mentioned in these early days. In July 1699 the agents are "ordered" to treat with a schoolmaster for a school to be set up in St George's, Southwark. In March 1701 they are "recommended' to keep a list of benefactors to the schools in the vestry of the Parish Church. Frequently they are "called in" at a stage in a meeting. Their expenses are defrayed from time to time; once at least they are entrusted with a small sum to disburse to needy schools. It looks as if they were appointed by the trustees of the London Schools, who would be too large a body to function effectively, and were recognized by the Society.

A significant minute appears under 22 April 1703. Mr Skate "reported that they are now about a general visitation of the Charity Schools,[1] and that they have found hitherto all things relating to them in very exact order, saving that in one school some of the trustees do cause their own children to be taught with the poor children; and that in some other schools one master will undertake to teach more than fifty children. Resolv'd that this Society will endeavour to obviate these two mischiefs by a proper application to the trustees." Class distinctions had to be preserved; and the Society in dealing with the trustees had no weapon save that of suasion.

THE YEARS 1704 TO 1715

The publication of Rules and Orders in *Account of the Charity Schools*, 1704, was a landmark. In itself it had no authority (formal directions by the Bishops came later in 1723), but no doubt it was generally accepted as a model to be followed so far as possible. Details will be found below in the fuller description of the schools. At an early date difficulties began to arise. Schools of this kind needed a stable and assured income, which was hard to maintain when the first enthusiasm wore off and founders and benefactors died. In 1708, Brentford reported that subscriptions had fallen from £120 to £50, to the great detriment of the school. Indeed there are frequent notes that a school

[1] In the London district where alone there was any attempt at centralized management.

is "decayed". The numbers of Charity children are given by Hatton's *New View of London* (1708) as 2,248 in 60 schools, 1,874 of them clothed. Annual subscriptions amounted to £536, collections to £1,434, and donations to £5,861, the last being a clearly precarious item. The total number of schools in the country and of children educated in them is a matter of guesswork. The Society kept no proper records and after 1723 repeated the previous year's figures. In 1714 the diocese of Lincoln had more than 200 Charity Schools, which by 1723 had increased to 268. The London figures show an average of 37 children per school. If the Lincoln figures bore the same proportion, we should get nearly 10,000 children. But the diocese was largely rural and the average number may have been smaller. There is also the difficulty that the boys and girls of a parish may have been reckoned as going to one school or to two. If Lincoln was a fair sample of the country, and if we reckon that the population of the huge diocese was about 10% of the whole population, the Charity School children at the peak of the movement may have approached 100,000. But this is only a guess. In any case, the figure was probably a good deal higher than that[1] given by the S.P.C.K. Reports, namely, 23,421.

In May 1711 various complaints reached the Society of the behaviour of Charity School children and teachers at the late election, a presage of the political difficulties that were soon to arise.

A few details are added here which were not to be conveniently fitted into the preceding pages.

1710. Correspondents were urged to arrange yearly meetings of masters in their neighbourhoods, to confer about school problems.

1711. Correspondents were recommended to encourage the holding of evening classes to teach adults to read.[2] Mr Chisleton, a surgeon living off Fleet Street, "offers to give his advice and assistance to any of the Charity children that shall come to any disaster where the use of a surgeon shall be necessary, except the children in such parishes where surgeons have a salary to take care of all the poor".

1712. 7 February. John Honeycott, master of Clerkenwell Charity

---

[1] Presumably the London figures are reasonably accurate. For the country the Society relied on correspondents for a county or smaller area, who would find great difficulty in collecting information. The figures were repeated for more than fifty years without variation.

[2] Only in Wales (see p. 58) did anything come of this.

School, the previous day acted Shakespeare's *Timon of Athens* with his boys, inviting outsiders by tickets signed by himself. Mr Nelson and others met the trustees and left to them the removing of the scandal; the Bishop of London was asked to recall Honeycott's licence. We sympathize with this bold pioneer but cannot think that he made a wise choice of a play for his experiment.

Coleshill, Warwick. "One child every morning at the sound of a bell comes to church and on his knees says the Lord's Prayer in the audience of an undermaster, who immediately rewards him with a penny. Every house or family knows when its turn comes to send a child, for they go in the order that their houses are situated in the town and do not fail whether they be rich or poor."

1741. William Short writes from Exeter to say that the Charity Schools are suffering from the competition of private schools opened to meet the needs of poor parents, who avoid the Charity Schools for pride's sake. No doubt a small charge was made.

1715 AND AFTER

The death of Queen Anne and the succession of George I in 1714 inevitably affected the Charity Schools, which had been founded and carried on by the definite Church party, largely Tory in sympathies. The victorious Whigs could not be expected to look with favour on the schemes of their opponents. The suspicions might have died down if it had not been for the ill-starred Jacobite rebellion of 1715. That some of the teachers were for the Pretender and a few were indiscreet in their conduct was doubtless true, but rumour magnified greatly whatever cause there was for complaint. Schoolmasters were called upon to attend Quarter Sessions to take an oath of loyalty.[1] Of the trustees generally, Mr John Chamberlayn wrote on 6 July 1716 that the Trustees of Charity Schools are "for the greater part what you call High Churchmen.[2] . . . The best thing that I think can be said to extenuate the misguided zeal of some, that during an epidemical madness they had their share of it involuntarily, and if they are used with candour perhaps they will soon come to their senses. . . ." The

---

[1] As for example in Gloucester, see A. Platts and G. H. Hainton, *Education in Gloucestershire*, p. 33.

[2] See p. 81 for the meaning of the term.

members of the Society who conducted its affairs were well known as supporters of the Hanoverian Succession, the new Archbishop (Wake) had favoured the schools when he was Bishop of Lincoln, and with his help the Society weathered the storm. In December 1716 it ordered that schools in disorder must be broken up and reported to the Bishop. In 1719 the Secretary wrote to Mr Jennings of Great Gransden (Hunts.) that teachers who refuse the oaths must be discharged, otherwise schools will be ruined. The Society could do little in this matter, for each school was a law to itself.

The final settlement was made by the Bishop of London (Gibson). On 21 June 1723 Henry Newman, the Secretary, wrote to him to say he is making "a list of the masters and mistresses in obedience to your command". The list was sent on 20 July, marked to show: (a) those "infected with the madness that prevailed in the latter part of the late reign; (b) those who took the contrary part; (c) people of quiet disposition or about whose character nothing is known; (d) those who have much altered since 1716." The Bishop's regulations were accepted by the rest of the episcopate and by the S.P.C.K., who circulated them to the trustees of London Schools, who also accepted them, and to those outside London through the Bishops with a recommendation to accept. The document founded on the Bishop's directions is termed "Rules for the good Order and Government of Charity Schools, drawn up by the Trustees of these Schools within the Bills of Mortality."[1] The Bishop of London's directions circulated in 1724 are to be observed. Especially: (1) children are not to be taught anything to "set them above the condition of servants, or the more laborious employments"; (2) the psalms to be sung are regulated; (3) children are to be taught allegiance to the present Government. Every teacher is to be a member of the Church of England, "of known affection to his Majesty King George, and to the Protestant Succession, as by Law established . . . a constant communicant, etc." The rest of the rules repeat what was the general practice of the schools. In November 1724 the Bishop of London held a meeting of London masters and mistresses at St Paul's Chapter House; a list was taken of those present. Later a deputation went from the S.P.C.K. to thank the Bishop for his directions to the Trustees.

After this, which was the culmination of a long controversy, quiet

[1] I.e., the London district for the list of deaths published periodically.

settled over the scene. Very little of interest appears in the Society's records. In the Annual Sermons the same themes recur. The creative impulse had died down and the Charity Schools had become an institution. The next forward move in the direction of popular education was to be made by the Sunday Schools. They were objected to as destroying cheap labour and competing unfairly with other schools, but for a time they taught multitudes to read and write, using one day in the week only. As it was Sunday, the Bible had to be the text-book, as it was largely in the Charity Schools. Most of the children worked for the rest of the week, so that manual occupations were not needed. Teachers, mainly women, were paid a small sum; employers were glad that the children were kept out of mischief; the novelty of the experiment and the numbers that attended made the schools attractive; and co-operation between Church and Dissent was possible, for the children often studied together and went on to church or chapel. The S.P.C.K. welcomed the new development, which in its turn as an educational instrument was weakened by political suspicion, in this case arising out of the French Revolution.

Let us in conclusion try to see the Charity School movement in the light of history. G. M. Trevelyan is eulogistic: "An age to which we owe the Charity Schools and the S.P.C.K. was not wholly absorbed in the quarrels of High Church and Low. In some of these better activities members of the two parties co-operated with each other and with the Dissenters." The able men at the head of the movement introduced the principle of democratic co-operation into the field of education.[1] But it would be better to say that they were carried along by a wave that would have flowed in any case, though they did contribute leadership. The historian of the movement[2] points out that the desire to establish social discipline was the motive that accompanied the desire to teach religion. "Expression of patronage on the one hand and of subserviency on the other . . . were the common form." On the other hand it was primarily a middle-class and Puritan movement, consecrating wealth to God, accepting social inequalities as his will, and with no idea of altering the social fabric. The utilitarian motive had to be stressed in order to get support. Again, other writers, going back to Mandeville, who saw in the movement the self-satisfaction

[1] *English Social History*, pp. 325-7.
[2] M. G. Jones, *The Charity School Movement*, pp. 4, 5.

gained by imposing one's will on others, find something repellent in the business-like ordering of charity, which, as traditionally in the Church, was looked upon primarily as beneficial to the soul of the giver. And at this stage, when middle-class wealth was increasing, it was particularly pleasant to salve one's conscience by contributing to the welfare of the poor.

All such criticisms are justified, from the point of view of those living in a different age with different forms of temptation. But as historical judgements they are beside the mark. In the eighteenth century commerce had not developed sufficiently to support a large lower-middle-class. On the other hand, a very large labour force was needed for the rapid advance in capital goods, such as docks, roads, factories, etc. Before the days of labour-saving machinery millions could not be other than humble labourers. The philanthropists of the time must not be blamed for seeing no way of making the poor richer and for devoting themselves to making their existence less brutish.

Miss Jones is inclined to blame the S.P.C.K. for allowing itself to be diverted from its original objective and abdicating its position of educational leadership. But there is no evidence to show either that education of poor children ever was its primary objective or that it had the power to lead the country. The initial impulse having been given, a voluntary body with virtually no funds at its disposal could not continue to influence the schools. Anything like centralized government by a central committee was impossible in view of the temper of the age and the lack of efficient communications.

THE ANNUAL SERVICE

The first suggestion of an annual service for the Charity children was made in 1703, when "it was recommended to the agents to discourse the trustees ... about this matter". The service was actually held on 8 June 1704 in St Andrew's Church, Holborn, when 2,000 children walked in procession, headed in most cases by their parish priest. Next year the Church of St Sepulchre, Holborn, was chosen, and the number grew soon to 4,000. To accommodate so many it was necessary to use every inch of space, and galleries were erected for the occasion. Much interest was taken in the service, which was increased greatly in 1713, when the Queen went to St Paul's to give thanks for the restoration of peace, and stands holding 4,000 children were erected in the Strand; the arrangements were repeated at the Accession of George I. The Society employed a singing master to rehearse the hymn sung by the children. A letter from the Reverend Maurice Wheeler (10 March 1712), Headmaster of Gloucester Cathedral Grammar School, proposed that the service be held at St Paul's Cathedral; it would be "the most blessed sight on earth during the present dismal decay of religion". Not until 1782 did this come to pass; in 1738 the meeting place was changed to Christ Church, Newgate Street.

The Society had to be circumspect in its plans, for the real body responsible was the Trustees of the schools, who acted through a small Committee called the "agents". The Society on 2 April 1728 agreed "to cultivate and preserve a lasting correspondence with the Trustees . . . and that they will cheerfully bear all the necessary expenses that shall be occasioned by the Anniversary meeting of the Charity Children within the Cities of London and Westminster and Bills of Mortality". A fortnight later it was "agreed in regard the weather in Whitsuntide is commonly very hot, and that most of the Lords the Bishops, the nobility, and gentry are generally out of town at that time of the year, the first Thursday in May be recommended to the Society as a more proper day for the Anniversary meeting of the Charity children". On July 30 a reply from the Trustees agreed to Thursday in Easter Week. In 1782 a Society of Patrons of the Anniversary meeting of the Charity Schools was founded, and the S.P.C.K. henceforward dealt with it. The expenses of the St Paul's service were considerable, as will be seen from the gift of £1,000 made in 1789 by King George III on his recovery from illness. The S.P.C.K.'s annual contribution was generally £50. Relations between the two bodies were harmonious, though early in the series the S.P.C.K. objected to the carrying of pictures of the Saints to which churches (St Andrew, Holborn, and St Paul, Covent Garden) were dedicated, and in 1802, the Patrons having substituted an anthem for the customary metrical psalm, the S.P.C.K. held a rival service at St Mary-le-Bow. The following year witnessed a reconciliation, the Patrons giving way. The 1811 Report contains the sermon by Professor Marsh, who states that the Society of Patrons has 1,000 members. At last in 1877 the service was discontinued. The Cathedral authorities declared that the storing of the scaffolding in the crypt might lead to a fire and in any case its erecting and dismantling involved the discontinuance of daily services for two months.

The Society's Annual Report was in early years, beginning in 1719, "published at the request of the Trustees of the said Charity Schools", so that these were clearly considered very important; and, as was to be expected then, the sermon stood out as the chief item. These sermons are monotonous reading, but something can be learned from them. An almost uniform characteristic is the apology for educating the poor, which the preachers feel obliged to make. We have already discussed the background of this, but a few extracts from the divines will illustrate it admirably.

1705. *George Stanhope*, Dean of Canterbury. (The dates are generally those of the Annual Report and the sermon is often that of the previous year.) "The yearly processions of these little eleemosynaries ought not to be compared with the Hypocrites' Trumpet sounded before them."

1706. *White Kennet*, afterwards Bishop of Peterborough. "Among all the delectable sights that can fill the eyes of man, I believe none is more entertaining, more ravishing, than what we have now before us and around us. A dear and precious sight! Some thousands of poor children, arm'd with their own innocency, adorn'd with your charity, and, above all, illustrated with the first rudiments of learning, virtue, and religion. What spectacle upon earth can come nearer to that of a multitude of the heavenly host! ... In some of our schools, you may see them on a Sunday evening at their quarterly exercises of letters and religion, in a most edifying manner. Some of them are spelling the hardest words with more exactness than many adult persons can do, who yet think themselves masters of the English tongue. Some are reading with such an emphasis and clear pronunciation, as may instruct, if not shame, those men and women who come to hear them. Others are making speeches, or holding dialogues, or by turns rehearsing some chosen parts of Scripture, or likewise reciting some particular clauses in the Acts of Parliament restraining vice and immorality."

1715. *William Wake*, Bishop of Lincoln, speaks of the sad state of England caused by the neglect of the children, "such wickedness as could hardly have been imagined in a Christian country". "How far we are to thank our old, inveterate enemies the Papists for this deplorable corruption both of principles and morals ... can be doubted by no one." However, instruction is not a panacea, for it can be rejected. He also speaks of "our daily prayers, our constant catechizings . . . carefully attended upon by the greatest number of pious and well-dispos'd Christians that perhaps has ever been known in any age."

1717. *William Talbot*, Bishop of Salisbury, refers to the prevalence of crime and in particular to the "hellish brothel houses", the existence of which is due to girls having never been taught an occupation.

1719. *Thomas Sherlock*, Dean of Chichester, afterwards Bishop successively of Bangor, Salisbury, and London. He urges the constant inspection of schools, neglect of which is an "abuse of one of the noblest charities of this age".

1739. *John Thomas* is one of those who refute Mandeville's *Fable of the Bees* (1714), which maintained that social virtue, such as prompted Charity Schools, is the political offspring which Flattery has begotten upon Pride; it praised ignorance: knowledge for the poor should be confined within the verge of their own occupations. But (says the preacher) the knowledge of God is needed in every station of life.

1756. *Thomas Hayter*, Bishop of Norwich. "These poor children are born to be daily labourers and, for the most part, to earn their bread by the sweat of their brow . . . to unfit them for their life would be injurious both to the children and to the Commonwealth." The Schools are charged with causing shortage of labour, but this is due to the number of idle attendants of the rich. He speaks of "that torrent of licentiousness, which threatens at present to overwhelm laws, our liberty, and our constitution itself".

1757. *Dr Samuel Nicholls*. "You see their innocent and orderly deportment; how decent in their carriage; how uniform in their gestures."

1766. *Joseph Tucker*, Dean of Gloucester. Children are "more apt to imbibe evil than good . . . this is a melancholy truth . . . they cannot become such pests to Society . . . as it is but too probable they otherwise would have been". They are said to be educated above their station. Perhaps some *are* conceited—"as a wen or excrescence (may grow) out of a positive and substantial good".

1785. *Lewis Bagot*, Bishop of Norwich. Charity Schools provide the catechetical instruction enjoined by the Prayer Book.

1791. *Samuel Glasse*. "It is hardly to be believed what benefit these schools would derive from the occasional inspection of the several parishes to which they belong."

1793. *Samuel Horsley*, Bishop of St David's. The Society still has to face the objection that it makes worse hired servants. In free governments it is necessary to have "some considerable improvement of the understanding". Only despotisms can safely neglect the education of the poor.

1830. *James Henry Monk*, Bishop of Gloucester. "Callous indeed must be that heart, which does not expand with rapture at witnessing such an almost heavenly scene of innocence and adoration, and sympathize with the interesting condition of those who now *offer unto God thanksgiving, and pay their vows unto the Most High*." That a sentimental approach to the spectacle of the children was not confined to Bishops is shown by William Blake's lines:

"'Twas on a Holy Thursday, their innocent faces clean,
The children walking two and two, in red and blue and green."

LOCAL MANAGEMENT AND FINANCE

The S.P.C.K. *Account of Charity Schools* describes the method of starting a school. Four or five persons met, expressed their design in a few lines on a roll of parchment, and then put down their names for subscriptions, headed by the minister. Preliminaries before the school was opened generally took seven or eight months. A body of trustees had first to be formed; it usually consisted of the Vicar and churchwardens of a village, the Vicar always being one if he was a subscriber, with representatives of the subscribers. In a town the scheme was often on an inter-parochial basis, all the Vicars being trustees plus representatives of the subscribers. The trustees had to find school buildings, appoint teachers, inspect the schools, often clothe and feed the children; above all, they had to find the money with which to carry on. The practice was to draw lots for the first nominations and afterwards to take turns among themselves. In managing the school they were left to their own devices except for the suasion exercised by the S.P.C.K., which was gladly received, and for the authority of the Bishop. Canon 77 of 1604 was still in force, by which every teacher had to be licensed by the Bishop. As Canon 79 shows, Grammar Schools were mainly in the framers' minds and only masters are mentioned, no

33

reference being made to the education of girls. Probably licences in many cases were neither sought nor enforced, though some Bishops took a great interest in the movement. In suitable cases an attempt was made to interest the civic authorities. Thus the movement was inaugurated at Exeter by a sermon preached in the Cathedral by the Bishop before the Mayor and Corporation, urging them to set up schools. At Beverley in 1710 the Corporation gave £100 to equip a school. This, indeed, was the favourite way of helping, if help was given at all. The Corporations do not seem to have become annual subscribers. But the parish, as responsible for "pauper" children, often came to an arrangement with the trustees; thus about 1700, the Grey Coat School, Westminster, had 130 children on the parish account. And the secular authorities often took some of the burden of apprenticeship charges off the shoulders of the trustees.

The trustees generally began well so far as money went, for the new ideas were popular; the difficulty was to continue. The various sources of income will now be illustrated.

1. *Subscriptions and endowments.* The London Schools were best off; St Andrew, Holborn, had a subscription list of £291 in 1715 (for 160 children), St Giles-in-the-Fields £250 (for 165). At Oxford £150 p.a. was raised in 1708, at Shrewsbury £70. Endowments varied greatly. Cambridge at the beginning of the century had 260 children at free schools, which had small endowments, dating from before 1699. Liverpool in 1744 had an endowment "let out" to the Corporation, which paid 5% interest. Land was the usual form of endowment. Dr Colebath of Orwell (Cambs.) settled an estate bringing in £40 p.a. for the village school. There were many complaints that endowments were lost, and the S.P.C.K. kept on urging that they be inscribed on a board set up in the church; the Archdeacons gave similar instructions. This, and not ostentation on the part of our forefathers, was the origin of the many eighteenth-century lists of benefactions. Later in the century 60% of the Charity Schools in Gloucestershire are said to have had endowments.

2. *Legacies.* Dr South, of Oxford, was reported in October 1709 as having bought land to make his charity to Islip perpetual, £10 p.a. for teaching and £20 for apprenticing children. In 1744 a new school at Ely received a legacy from a Mrs Needham producing an income of £80. However, it was one thing to receive a notice of a legacy,

quite another thing to get the money. The Society often took up cases with the help of its legal members. A £2,000 legacy at Thetford had to be referred to Parliament. To apply to the Commissioners for Pious Uses was a "remedy as bad as if not worse than the disease". (Letter from Worlington, Suffolk, 23 January 1712.)

3. *The Parish Church.* The "Communion money" (alms at the Sacrament, which at this time generally was administered once a month) was a common source of income; the Cambridge colleges generally gave all this money to the Schools. Charity Sermons were a great help: St Margaret's, Westminster, on one occasion collected £163 15s. 7d. This method was appropriate in London, where famous preachers could be procured. Elsewhere "retiring collections" were made. The Society in 1711 warned against overdoing this practice, the frequency of which defeated its aim. In some places a collecting box was put in the church, perhaps carrying the effigy of a Charity Child.

The preaching of a Charity Sermon at a distance from the place to which the collection was to be devoted was not thought advisable. On 3 August 1718 the schoolmaster of St Ann, Aldersgate, took some children to Chislehurst for a sermon. When the collector came to Mr Farrington (one of the Justices) he was seized on the pretext that the money was intended for the Pretender. In 1719 the case was tried before Sir Littleton Powys. The point was that the money was devoted to a distant parish and that the rubric did not sanction the collection of money for other than parochial objects. The Judge wrote to the Lord Chancellor: "This case . . . is of a vast extent, and mighty consequence to the King and his people, and at which the very legislature itself may take great umbrage". Such collections had to be authorized by briefs (Royal Letters) or be taken for bodies which had charters of incorporation.

4. *Other methods.* Sometimes the ladies of a parish agreed to take full responsibility for a girls' school. At Ewhurst, Surrey, palls were bought and hired out at funerals for 2s. 6d. or 1s., the proceeds going to the school. At St Katherine-by-the-Tower the collectors of land tax gave their poundage to the school; there and elsewhere those responsible for street lamps gave their profits. A young lady at Newland (Glos.) gave part of her winnings at cards to the cause. Public examination of children was another idea; at Aldgate School £10 7s. 8d. was collected on one such occasion.

5. *The clergy.* There are perpetual references to the sacrifices made by the clergy. The Bishop of Salisbury (Burnet) in 1708 was subscribing £50 p.a. to Broadhinton School. The Bishop of Worcester in 1707 offered to give £1 to meet every £9 subscribed to set up Charity Schools in the towns of his diocese. The parish clergy were constantly either paying the whole cost of a school or maintaining some of the children.

6. *Other examples.* Winlaton (Co. Durham) was unique. There, 400–500 ironworkers gave ¾d. a week for the school, to add to the employer's contribution. Scarborough had its own method (letter of Robert North, 27 November 1741). "A Society for education was founded twelve years ago. The admission fee is 5s., weekly subscription 2d. We began with 9 members. Fines for being late or absent, Charity Sermons twice a year, and casual contributions have enabled us to maintain 26 boys and 14 girls clothed and taught, and we have over £300 of invested funds."

Several references to Religious Societies have been found. A letter of 26 April 1714 mentions that a Society in London has the care of a school. Another, dated 15 January 1712, states that a Religious Society has created a School at St Neots. It was founded in 1709 and by April 1710 had 70 members, all young men, who met on Sunday mornings to read *The Whole Duty of Man* and sing psalms; also on Tuesday and Friday evenings. They constantly frequented public worship on Saints' Days. On 27 January 1719 a letter from the S.P.C.K. to Thomas Burnett said that the Societies were under suspicion of disaffection. "They have been put under such regulations by the authority and wisdom of His Grace of Canterbury as have put it out of their power to propagate their disaffection." Oaths of allegiance are insisted on in the Charity Schools, which are under their influence. A tantalizing glimpse of an unknown region is afforded by a letter from Dr Moses Hodges of Warwick (26 January 1712): two boys are taught and clothed out of fines laid upon the members of a Singing Society of young men.

Some schools were made safe by munificent patronage. In 1709 it was reported that the Earl of Ranelagh had built a Charity School in Windsor Forest with a chapel, and rooms for the master and mistress, and had provided furniture for them. Each child is given a Bible, Prayer Book, and *Whole Duty of Man*; also a spelling book. The school is endowed with land yielding £120 a year, the overplus after paying salaries and clothing 20 boys and 20 girls to be invested to form a fund for apprenticing. The Kensington School, founded in 1707, in 1799 received an annual subscription from the King of £80, and every child was given a dinner on Sunday from Michaelmas to Lady Day.

TEACHERS

The recruiting of teachers was effected locally by the trustees of the individual schools. Probably all records of the interviews have been lost, so the exceptional cases in which the Society was asked to procure teachers are of some interest. This work was on a very small scale, for in 1715 it was reported that 22 teachers so far had been sent to the country from London; though there were many unsuccessful attempts to help. London enjoyed considerable prestige and men were sent there from the country to observe the ways of its schools; for example, one from Wolverhampton in March 1712. The Committee took great trouble to help country schools. On 14 March 1721 they interviewed James Richmond of Yeovil, who produced a certificate of honesty and sobriety from the trustees of Yeovil Charity School, where he had been an assistant teacher. It was agreed to recommend him to Wotton-under-Edge (Glos.) after he had taken oaths to the Government administered by the Chairman. On 21 February 1716 three masters were interviewed for the post of master at the school of Eye (Suffolk), to the trustees of which detailed descriptions of two were sent, with specimens of their handwriting. When Thomas Ashton was recommended for Neath on 8 July 1719 it was as "a constant frequenter of the Church and a communicant therein, well affected to His Majesty King George and the present Government, of a sober life and conversation". One instructive episode is preserved. In August 1709 the salary of the Society's messenger was doubled and it was agreed to pay the cost of instructing him to write and cast accounts, to enable him to qualify as a master. The arrangements entailed a good deal of trouble to the Secretary. Thus on 20 March 1719 Henry Newman instructs Mr Good of Ipswich, who is going to teach at Stroud: "Goods must be brought to Billingsgate in a boat. There they will be put in a Gravesend boat, with you and your wife. You will sleep in the boat. Next morning Mr Green, the Rochester carrier, will put you in his wagon; if it is too full, he will get you places in the Stroud coach. The passage to Gravesend will cost 12d. each, the wagon 12d., the coach 1s. 6d."

The qualifications required were concerned primarily with character and orthodoxy. The Rules for Charity Schools laid down that the master must be at least 25 years of age, a communicant, of a meek temper, able to stand an examination in the Christian religion, a keeper of good order in his family, and approved by the minister of the parish, so that he could be presented to the Bishop to receive his licence. He was to consult with other masters to learn their ways. On 17 December 1717 Newman inquired about a schoolmaster. Is he religiously disposed? Well affected to the present Government? "Has he the qualities of meekness and humility in such a measure as to be a fit person for young children to copy after?" On 12 April 1720 the Reverend Mr Raynes of Tiverton wrote to say that the trustees of their school do not think that the "scrophulous swelling in his Adam's neck ... should make him disagreeable or be an objection to his undertaking the charge of the school".

Evidently trustees had to accept practically anyone they could get. There was no training, except by visiting schools where the new methods were in use. A plan referred to by Dr Waterland in his Anniversary Sermon of 1723, to erect "a Superior School, for the training of schoolmasters and schoolmistresses", came to nothing. But everything possible was done to get persons of character and loyalty to be put in charge of the children.

The clergy often taught in the schools without payment or appointed a man as parish clerk on condition of his teaching the children gratis. In 1710 Dr Chetwood, Dean of Gloucester, wrote to say that the local school had 85 boys and girls and that a clergyman was master, being paid £30 p.a. plus a living, "which he finds inconvenient for a schoolmaster". Of the Bishop of Salisbury (Gilbert Burnet) it is reported in 1707 that he "often visits the school, and catechizes the children, and appoints portions of Scripture for them to learn by heart, which he sees them perform, and encourages their so doing, by giving them Common Prayer Books and money, etc.".

The schools were run as cheaply as possible, and what Lady Elizabeth Hastings wrote on 15 June 1734 probably applied elsewhere: "Our Charity Schools here never keep ushers because they can't afford it, but the masters make some of the elder boys assist them in teaching the lesser children in large schools, which answers the end of ushers, for which they have no consideration other than being preferred to service the first opportunity, and by favour of the trustees"—thus anticipating the Bell and Lancaster systems at the beginning of the nineteenth century.

Salaries of teachers were very low. In London a man was paid as a rule £30 a year plus a house and coal (1713). Londoners would not take a post in the country for less, but a lower salary was often made up by the opportunity of teaching children out of school hours. The practice of taking paying pupils in the school was discouraged, lest the master should favour such children, but it could not be entirely prevented. In March 1722 Henry Newman, asked to find a master for Marlborough, replied: Will he be able to teach "the children of fashion out of school hours?" In theory no paying pupils were allowed in London schools, but the last word rested with the trustees, who in 1709 sanctioned the practice at St Anne, Blackfriars. Some examples of salaries are as follows: Barrington (Cambs.) (1719), £20 for a man; Bury St Edmunds (1706), £12 10s. for a woman; Horsted Keynes, Sussex (1707), £20 for a man, with leave to take 20 paying pupils; Ipswich (1710), £30 for a man, with house and coals and exemption from rates; Launceston (1709), £10 for a woman; Ross (1710), £18 for a man, £12 for a woman, with leave to take paying pupils; Wakefield (1707), £21 for a man, with a very good school house. A system of payments by results was suggested in the official Rules (1724), to be made when a child "can name and distinguish all the letters in the alphabet", when he can spell well, and when he can read well and distinctly and repeat the Catechism. The method was tried at Box, in Wiltshire, where the minister obtained a person to teach young men and women, 5s. being paid for each person taught to read and 5s. to each person taught to read when the Bible could be read (1716).

An occasional reference to the Society of Schoolmasters rouses curiosity that cannot be satisfied. In July 1718 a candidate interviewed for a post at Neath brought a recommendation signed by 14 members of this Society. A master at Islington Charity School who was accused of drinking the health of the Pretender under fictitious names was denounced to the Society of Schoolmasters. In 1712 the S.P.C.K. was urged by Sir John Philipps of Picton Castle to give financial support, without which the Society of Schoolmasters would lapse, even at the cost of economizing on other things.

The spirit which animated these ill-paid men and women may be inferred from a teacher's manual, commissioned by the S.P.C.K. and published at its expense in 1707: *The Christian School-Master: or The Duty of those who are Employ'd in the Publick Instruction of Children: Especially in Charity Schools*, which had a vogue throughout the century. Teachers had to be marked by patriotism, virtue, and learning. A newly appointed teacher must not be under 25 and must be free from deformity of person or defect of speech. He will learn by visiting other schools and giving lessons in them under supervision. He is to be diligent in prayer for his better carrying out of his pastoral office.

THE SCHOOL AND ITS LESSONS

By the gift of generous donors an existing house was sometimes obtained and adapted for the new purpose. The S.P.C.K. records give little evidence as to the buildings used. However, Wisbech in 1709 erected a school house 70 feet by 16, to hold 100 girls. At Yarpol (Hereford) a building was being constructed at a cost of £1,200 in 1709. In country places parents were reluctant to send their children, for fear of incurring the resentment of the farmers. Even the tiny earnings of young children in the home or on the fields were with difficulty sacrificed by the very poor. Probably the clothing of the children and the teaching of manual labour (see below) were necessary steps, if the schools were to survive. At Prendergast (Pembs.) parents were paid a maintenance grant of 5s. a quarter per child. There are a number of records of the cost of running a school, but so many factors are uncertain (whether rent was paid, whether clothing was included, etc.) that accurate conclusions are usually impossible. However, a letter of 20 October 1707 states categorically that a Charity School at Shrewsbury costs £60 a year for 120 children, including salaries and rent, towards which £70 is obtained from subscriptions, leaving a yearly balance to be set aside for apprenticing. A note in 1704 says that in a Shrewsbury school 50 boys, including clothes, cost £75; 50 girls, £60.

The Charity Schools were for boys, or girls, or were mixed. What would seem natural to us, could we visit the last, was then a startling innovation—that girls and boys were educated in approximately equal numbers.[1] The offering of elementary education to all girls who cared to come was a forward step for which the pioneers of the S.P.C.K. deserve unstinted praise. Two voices deserve to be heard. R. Smith, of Upton-upon-Severn (Worcs.), wrote on 29 March 1712 to say that he paid for the education of 16 girls, rather than boys, because they will teach their children when they are mothers. In December 1717 Mr Barrington of Shrivenham (Berks.), wrote: "The first regard would be more properly bestowed on the girls because the care of families (in the country especially) falls under the direction of the mother, and the great complaint in the country is that they cannot get maid servants qualified for sense, so easily as men servants, which might be in good measure removed by this care of the families."

Recommended hours for schools were 7–11 a.m., 1–5 p.m. in summer; 8–11 a.m., 1–4 p.m. in winter. Dr Hutchinson wrote from Bury, Suffolk, in 1713, urging later hours in winter. "If they don't learn by candles as most schools do, yet at least he thinks they should stay as long as they can see." Holidays were three weeks at Christmas and one week at Easter and Whitsuntide; another plan was the week before and after the three great festivals. The harvest month was to be avoided, lest the children get into bad company when gleaning.

School began and ended with prayer. An official handbook of prayer for the Charity Schools contained prayer for the Royal Family as well as for the King, for whom in 1716 the Society recommended prayer to be made twice a day in school. Even the private prayers taught to be said at home included one for the Royal Family.

Other manuals put out in the eighteenth century had, let us hope, less vogue. In H. Scougat's *The Duty and Pleasure of Praise and Thanksgiving* (1770) we read: "O what an unspeakable blessing it is, that we are not roaring in some Bedlam." The Society at first took a liberal view of music, but led by Bishop Gibson, of London, recommended that nothing be sung except (metrical) psalms. On 4 September 1716 a resolution was passed declining to interfere in local schools but recommending the practice, almost universal in London, of standing

[1] In some cases the S.P.C.K. returns describe unspecified children as boys, so the proportion of boys to girls, about three to one, means nothing.

for the Psalms. (What is meant by "Psalms" is not clear.) Earlier, in 1708, the Society had set its face against solo-singing by children.

The ideal was to bring the children to church at least on Sundays and Holy days; in some places on Wednesdays and Fridays also, or even every day, as at Sheldon, Dr Bray's parish. We can picture them in an unheated church in the winter months, but perhaps the school room was nearly as cold. Bringing the scholars to church implies that the clergyman was there to take the service. The clergy come out much better so far as the duty of catechizing goes than some might have expected; generally speaking, our records show that it was faithfully performed on a large scale, both before and after the coming of the Charity Schools. But only the zealous clergy wrote to the Society, and there must have been many black spots due to non-residence. A letter from John Hutton, of Standford (Berks.), deserves notice (14 December 1709). Children were backward in coming to church, so he catechizes them every Saturday afternoon and gives them his tithe fruit. The effect is that the children come in good numbers and learn with eagerness and emulation.

Four years seems to have been the period of schooling aimed at, from the age of about 7 to 11, but in some places the leaving age may have been as late as 14. The children were very young and, as they generally came from illiterate homes, the teachers must have done good work if the three Rs were mastered in the time. There were four classes.[1] The first learned elementary reading; the second to read the New Testament and the Psalms; the third to read the whole Bible and to write; the fourth learned arithmetic. There was a prevailing opinion that Latin was essential to education and very humble parents mistrusted a school where it was not taught. A few instances occur where Latin was a subject: e.g., Yelvertoft (Northants., September 1711), and Brentford, where in September, 1709, the school is reported to be declining "because the master has undertaken to teach Latin and thereby discouraged the school"; but it was rightly held that the small amount that could be learned at so early an age would be useless. The Bible was the chief reading book after the primary stage, when exercises were largely based on it. The rule was to introduce writing only when reading was mastered. The Cirencester Blue Coat School, founded in

[1] The chief source of information is James Talbott's *The Christian School-Master*, the Society's text-book from 1707 onwards.

1714, in its first ten years bought 8,200 quills.[1] Arithmetic was necessary for boys if they were to be accepted as apprentices to business, but did not go beyond the first four rules.

As the Rules put out by the Society in 1715 insist, the chief business of the schools was to instruct the young in the principles of the Christian religion as professed by the Church of England. So the Catechism was taught continually. When enough children could say it, notice was given to the minister, who had them to church for a public examination. There were also frequent "open days", when the trustees and benefactors came to the school to hear the children's answers. That generation believed in learning formularies by heart; there seems to be no direct evidence to show that the substance of the Catechism was brought home to the children by means of illustrative matter, but as *The Christian Schoolmaster* devotes one-third of its 144 pages to ethics, based on the "Duty towards my neighbour", this may be safely inferred.

Discipline was presumably severe by modern standards, but was mild judged by the standards of the time. The teacher's manual insisted that the rod be used with great discretion, and expulsion only as a last resort; the child must be shown the justice of the punishment. In 1707 the Society had a faults' book printed, each month occupying one page. The symbols were A(bsent), * for Late, C(ursing), L(ying), P(laying in) C(hurch), S(tealing), T(ruant). The book was to be kept daily and shown to the trustees. At St Andrew's Holborn Workhouse School the worst punishment was to be set on a stool at dinner time with a paper fixed on the breast on which "Infamous Liar" was written. The Society called attention to a Greenwich Girls' School managed by ladies, where each girl had a peg put in the highest of seven holes; at each offence the peg was moved down. By the fifth hole the girl became "high criminal". After this, if she did not amend, a rod was pinned to her dress.

The parents had to accept various conditions when the child entered the school, neglect of which might entail his expulsion and the forfeiture of school clothes. He had to come to school with clean face and hands and hair combed. The trustees and the teachers could enforce good behaviour out of school. Orders issued by the Society in 1716 included "not to suffer their children to go in or to be seen with any

[2] Platts and Hainton, op. cit.

43

mob, in a tumultuous manner, upon any occasion whatsoever, nor to go about begging money for bonfires; nor to use any badges or marks of party distinction on any days of public rejoicing or thanksgiving". Next year attention was called to the great offence caused by Charity Scholars who "join with those that play at dice in wheelbarrows and other unlawful games in the street". A successful master was greatly honoured. Henry Newman on 23 June 1718 wrote in high praise of Mr Dixon, "the celebrated master of the most exemplary Charity School in Bath"; though his school is "generally made up of black guards, not one of them has ever dared to appear upon any occasions of tumult to affront the Government".

"WORKING SCHOOLS"

"Working Schools" was the name given to schools in which manual labour filled a substantial part of the time. By 1723, this had become the normal practice. When the initial enthusiasm died down trustees had great difficulty in carrying on the schools, and the idea of making them largely self-supporting by the sale of the children's work had a strong appeal. It also silenced critics; as Mr Wisdom, Treasurer of the Grey Coat Hospital, Westminster, wrote in 1723: working schools remove the main objection to Charity Schools, that while they care for the minds and morals of the children, they are unfitted for a life of industry which they must lead. We may also suppose that the original curriculum proved tedious and a greater variety of occupation made discipline easier.

Girls' employment was easy to find. Knitting, sewing, lace-making, and spinning were part of traditional housewives' lore. Boys' work was more of a problem: shoe-making and mending and gardening were especially suited to them. But a common practice was for girls in their last year to substitute handwork for arithmetic, which the boys went on to learn because masters required it in their apprentices. A few examples are now given. The school at Wisbech, already mentioned, was built for spinning at the cost of Joseph Taylor, who also maintained it (1709). At Launceston the girls were taught to read, knit, sew, and make lace, and received the net earnings (1709). In the same year Uffington (Lincs.) reports that 160 work two or three days a week in a spinning school, the products of which earn £250 a year.

In 1712 the Society sent a letter to its corresponding members directing that manual labour be on alternate days. At North Boughton (Lancs.) the girls learned to read, but manual work took the place of writing as well as arithmetic. The Eccleshall (Staffs.) girls in 1711 made their own clothes and to a certain extent those of the boys. The Society in 1716 agreed on a circular letter to all Charity Schools, asking questions like: How much do the several age groups earn? Where do you buy your wool, hemp, or flax? How do you dispose of the finished product?

The model school was at Irthlingborough (Northants.), which was so esteemed that teachers were sent there to learn its methods. There were 60 children. "This school", says the Annual Report, "deserves a particular history to be given of it, as an example to other places. By the assistance and direction of two charitable persons, one on the place, and the other in London, and the care of a good mistress, who was able to teach to knit and spin, as well as to read; this school is from a small beginning for 1d. a week teaching each child to read, become a considerable warehouse, where the children clothe themselves by their own industry; and pay the mistress for their learning, out of the earnings of their labour; viz. those that knit 1½d. a week, and the spinners 2d. a week."[1] In other words, a small factory had been set up. Probably the children would have been doing similar work at home, had there been no school, and without the companionship of other children. But we can imagine the difficulties which would arise over the proportion of earnings paid to children. In 1713 Blewbury (Berks.) reported that all the children are clothed by their own manufacture; in the last year they have woven 120 yards of green cloth. When they leave each receives a Bible, Prayer Book, and (spinning) wheel. Clearly this manual education had a utilitarian purpose and was not devised in accordance with any theory about the proper proportion of literary and handwork in school.

By the middle of the century these activities were beginning to die out. Except in a few places it was not possible to make them self-supporting and with the decay of enthusiasm they were the first things to be dropped; also spinning, the most important activity, was affected by the coming of machinery.

[1] This is the only reference I have found in the records to school pence. Certainly the Society's intention was to give free education.

CLOTHING

The children were put into uniform for several reasons: the example of older foundations, the need of making the children from very poor homes respectable, the pleasing of benefactors who would have a visible token of their generosity, and the preserving of discipline out of school. In some places there was the attraction of being able to weave the cloth and make the garments. When clothes were bought, individual friends would often defray the cost for all or some. The Duke of Bedford clothed 30 boys (Woburn, 1710). Mr Colston at Bristol partly clothed the boys of one school. Glasbury (Brecknock) reported in 1713 that they found you must clothe all or none. Norwich in 1709 said that 230 boys were given cap and bands, 80 completely clothed. At Warwick in 1712 the Corporation clothed 20 boys. Colours varied, blue, grey, green, and red being mentioned, and even in one London school orange.

The S.P.C.K. Report for 1718 gives the following table:

The charge of clothing a boy

	s.	d.
A yard and half-quarter and nail of grey Yorkshire Broad-cloth, 6 quarters wide, at 3s. 6d. per yard, makes a coat for a boy nine years old	4	2
Making the coat with pewter buttons, and all other material	1	0
A waistcoat of the same cloth lined	4	4
A pair of breeches of cloth or leather lined	3	0
1 knit cap, with tuft and string, of any colour		10
1 band		2
1 shirt	1	6
1 pair of woollen stockings		10
1 pair of shoes	2	0
1 pair of buckles		1
1 pair of knit or wash-leather gloves		7
	18	6

or blue kersey at the same price instead of broad-cloth.

The charge of clothing a girl

	s.	d.
4 yards of blue long ells, about yard wide, at 18d. p. yard, makes a gown and petticoat for a girl 9 years old	6	0
making thereof, strings, body-lining, and other materials	1	0
A coif and band of fine ghenting	1	0
A shift	1	6
A white, blue, or chequer'd apron	1	0
A pair of leather bodice and stomacher	2	6
1 pair of woollen stockings		10
1 pair of shoes	1	10
A pair of pattens		9
1 pair of buckles		1
1 pair of knit or wash-leather gloves		7
	17	1

The London firm that quoted these prices was recommended by the Society; it probably did a good trade, for country places demanded London fashion. A note was added: "Where the clothing of a boy or girl is to last them for one year, there must be an allowance made of 1 shirt and 1 band more for the boys and of 1 shift, 1 coif, 1 band, and 1 apron more for the girls. And so of stockings, shoes, and gloves, etc., for both boys and girls, where found necessary." In 1774 the Society decreed that bands be not worn in future, but badges were to be universally used.

Two omissions may be noted in the lists. There is no overcoat and no washable underclothing to be worn next the skin. Not till the early nineteenth century did the coming of cotton on a large scale make the latter possible, and with it personal cleanliness.

By 1791 prices had risen and the following price list for Charity Schools was advertised in the Report.

Boy	£	s.	d.
suit		14	0
dowlas shirt		2	6
stockings			10
knit cap			10
band			3
shoes		3	0
	£1	1	5

Girl	£	s.	d.
gown and petticoat		9	6
coif and band		1	6
shift, dowlas		2	6
apron		1	0
leather stays		4	6
stockings			10
shoes		2	6
	£1	2	4

Care had to be taken that children expelled from school did not take their uniform, for some would use it in order to beg the better.

APPRENTICING

Funds for apprenticing children, mainly boys, which was the completion of the Charity School plan, were provided from various sources. The Corporation in some towns, e.g., Shrewsbury and Warwick in 1712, paid for some; Newbury for all. Elsewhere, e.g. Eccleshall in 1713, private benefactors undertook individual children. Mr Blundell, of Liverpool, looking back in 1744 on the 30 years during which he had been Treasurer of the local school, wrote to say he had been responsible for putting out nearly 200 children. "Some of which are now masters of ships, some mates in the Ginny (Guinea) trade, and that trades to other parts, and many that have attained to be masters in other trades on shore." The poor tax had been cut down considerably thanks to the School's training of children, so as not to be a liability to the community. The trustees were expected to take pains to put out children to good Christian homes. In 1743 the Bishop of Oxford (Thomas Secker), preaching at the Anniversary Service, discusses and defends the existing method. With some no money is given. £2 is the usual premium, a few get as much as £5. Girls are now paid 50s. to 60s. a year. True, the cost of living and the rates of wages have gone up in half a century, but not owing to our schools. If girls now have the chance of bettering their condition, surely this "should not be envied them". One difficulty was to get London children to accept work in the country.

Henry Newman's private correspondence shows him taking a personal interest in apprenticeship. In 1720 he writes about getting a girl apprenticed to a laundress, who has a very good character, goes to church on Sunday, and promises to spend the premium on clothing for the girl. We also find him discussing a premium of £40 for a boy named Dickie, at a tobacconist's.

WORKHOUSE SCHOOLS

The Society took a great interest in workhouses, prisons, etc., for in early days the London members felt they had a kind of roving commission to inquire into abuses of every kind. The result of an investigation is found in a book entitled *An Account of Several Workhouses for employing the Poor ... as also of several Charity Schools for Promoting Work and Labour* (second edition, 1732). Their special interest was in the care of the young, in which the parish interest and that of the Church overlapped, for inasmuch as schoolteachers had to be licensed by the Bishop, education came under Church authority. In any case the fashionable method of the day, by which book-learning and manual work went together, would naturally commend itself to the parish authorities as the best way of dealing with the children of the ablebodied unemployed poor. At the end of the book the Rules for Charity Schools, signed by all the Bishops, are printed.

At Bishopsgate, London, the 129 children had two hours a day schooling, at Ware half the day. At Beverley they received 2d. in the 1s. on the money they earned by handwork. The Wisbech children slept three in a bed, and their food is described as "good beef, dumplins, pease-porridge, milk-porridge, bread and cheese; the quantity according to everyone's stomach at noon"—less at the other meals.

How many of the Charity Schools were residential does not appear, nor whether or not in the day schools it was usual to provide dinner. According to the Reports of the Charity Commission some 1,100 Charity Schools received endowments in the eighteenth century. When the income was large enough, in many cases children were received as boarders, and we may suppose that conditions were not unlike those of the Workhouse Schools. *The Christian Schoolmaster* does not draw the dividing line between boarding and day schools but merely says that when dinner is provided great care must be taken over manners; after the meal a story from the Bible is read by an elder boy on Sundays and Holy days, at other times a fable from Aesop. The mention of dinner only suggests that some at least of the day schools provided a midday meal.

BOOKS

The evidence for the books used in Charity Schools is not so full as we could wish. The universal text book was the Bible, generally bound with the Prayer Book and often with the Metrical Psalms too —a cumbrous book for small hands. For the frequent visits to church this book was necessary. A large proportion of those responsible for running the schools were members of the Society and bought Bibles, etc., under cost price. The Society published a number of little books containing passages from the Bible, etc., which would be suitable for the youngest children. The predominance of the Bible is partly accounted for by the practical non-existence of children's books as we know them. The weight of opinion was in favour of treating children as little men and women, to be introduced to adult responsibilities as soon as possible; certainly childhood was not cultivated as an end in itself. Children's books began to appear in the middle of the eighteenth century, but there is nothing to show that they were introduced into schools. However, the Bible alone was a potent educational influence,

Dolls dressed as Gloucester Charity School Children, at Cam

An 18th-century classroom

"Members used their influence . . . in promoting Charity Schools"

Parochial Library cupboard and
list at Llanrhos

S. J. Edwards

*"For the better Preservation of
Parochial Libraries"*

introducing scholars to a remote and yet living culture far more effectively than Latin did the average boy at a Grammar School.

The Christian Schoolmaster recommends profitable and pleasant books, but Aesop's Fables is the only one mentioned by name: *The Whole Duty of Man*, prescribed for the senior children, could hardly have sweetened the children's labours, as the author desired.

The teachers' lists of recommended books, published by the S.P.C.K. in 1715, contains 68 titles, 58 on religious subjects. Of the others we note three English Dictionaries, one Grammar, two Arithmetic books, Vernon's *Compleat Country House*, and Ayres' *Youth's Introduction to Trade*. A note says: "Many of the forementioned list of books have been provided at the charge of the benefactors to the schools and kept in a press for the use of the masters for the time being."

Towards the end of the Charity School period, in 1813, much educational material was published; in Hedingham Deanery, Essex, 30 out of 40 parishes had schools, with 2,300 children in them, and nearly all the books came from the S.P.C.K.

OTHER DEVELOPMENTS

As early as 1701 Mr Justice Hooke saw in the Charity Schools a nursery for seamen, pilots, engineers, etc. In 1711 it was reported that two boys had been moved from an ordinary Charity School to "the Charity School for Teaching Navigation". This subject was at the time taught at St Dunstan-in-the-West (London), Brighton, Exeter, and Southampton. A letter of May in that year describes the Society's methods applied on board ship, the boys being taught reading, writing, navigation, and to say psalms, "a delight to the whole ship's crew". In 1708 a Mr Bromfield of Boston (New England) wrote to say that there were two Charity Schools in his town. A Mr Evans of Philadelphia, who wrote in 1709 to ask for help in setting up a school, was told that "the charity of this Society is confined to this kingdom, excepting sometime for a small parcel of books, and that they leave entirely the care of the plantations to the Corporation Society" (i.e., the S.P.G.).

In February 1740 the Reverend Arthur Holt wrote from Chester, Maryland. There is little inducement to study in this plentiful country, where conveniences are so easily obtained. He asks that trained Charity

School scholars of good principles be sent to Maryland with the passage paid and promising to stay three, five, or seven years. He will build a school and supply necessaries and give him "my clerk's place if he be capable of discharging that office". It is impossible to get teachers here. Anyone "that has a tolerable use of his pen" is quickly tempted away "for some writing office". No examination into the principles of a master is possible, for he takes affront. The writer will send as many children as the Charity School teacher can teach, negroes also at the proper time.

SOME PARTICULAR SCHOOLS

Fuller accounts of particular schools may be of interest.

Bath. In October 1711 the Society was informed that £132 7s. had been collected for a boys' school, £134 5s. 6d. for a girls', and £142 11s. 6d. in annual subscriptions. Robert Nelson and John Leason had been all over Bath to find a suitable place for the girls and had chosen a room 60 feet by 14, with the approval of the Corporation. In December the girls' school was opened with "great solemnity, the Mayor, Justices, and Corporation attending them to Church in their formalities". In March 1712 both boys and girls were examined in the Town Hall "before people of the best note, who expressed wonder at their progress". In March 1713 a letter describes the ceremony of the Queen's Accession. The children waited on the Mayor and Corporation, who treated them to refreshments and went with them to Church. Three boys and three girls sang an anthem, and the children's answers to questions gave great satisfaction. "Some of the best in the town . . . have sent some of their children to sit among the Charity children." The Corporation are rebuilding the decayed school premises at their own costs. Mr Leason reports in May that the girls have spun 60 yards of broadcloth for the boys' coats. They work out more expensively than London prices, but the quality is much better. Suitable occupation for boys is hard to find. It is proposed to have a school garden. The Archdeacon (Parnel, Vicar of Bath) has announced that he will baptize no children at home and that he will catechize every Wednesday and Friday. The same correspondent in June says that the children are to go in procession for the Peace celebration, singing a hymn, and carrying garlands of laurel and flowers, the leaders wearing ribbons with a motto relating to peace. A little later a wash-house was completed, next door to the girls' school, for teaching them laundry, starching, etc. The problem of manual labour for the girls was simple, for a letter dated 28 October describes the funeral of Mrs Burkett, "at which the children of the Charity Schools attended and had each a pair of gloves with a wax taper given them, which added much to the solemnity", and goes on to say that "the washhouse and brewhouse being finished the girls were that day brewing for Mrs Bell as they would next week for Mr Dixon". In these early days a church door collection was taken for the schools on the last Sunday of every month.

Bristol. A curious letter from William Carey, of Bristol, dated 20 July 1715 says that the Temple School is "sinking". Mr Colston has told the trustees not to clothe the boys whose parents voted against his kinsmen (Mr Edwards and Captain Freetinge) at the last election. Subscriptions have been withdrawn. Will the Society interpose its good offices?

Chichester. William Hayley (Dean of Chichester, 1699–1715) joined the Society in April 1699. He was also Rector of St Giles-in-the-Fields, London, and except for his three months' residence in the summer attended almost every meeting, often taking the chair. In 1711 he reported that two Charity Schools were in existence at Chichester; the children who attended Church both morning and afternoon each received a twopenny loaf. The boys' school was actually opened on 25 March 1710 for 28 boys. The boys were dressed in grey, the girls in blue. The master of the boys was paid £20 a year and the rest of the income was spent on clothes. Things went on without much change for 100 years. The money came mainly from the Cathedral clergy and the Duke of Richmond, and the whole of the "Sacrament money" (alms at Holy Communion once a month and at the great festivals) and proceeds of "Charity Sermons" was divided equally between the two schools, each of which had about 25 children. In 1761 these schools actually published their own hymn book with music, printed in the city and put on the London market. In this case we are able to trace a continuous history from the minutes of the Charity Schools and the National Schools with which they were merged after 1811. The income, now derived in part from small endowments, was spent partly on clothes, the balance going to the funds of the National Schools. Up to 1821 each girl received every

Christmas a pair of shoes, pattens, shift, cap, tippet, and checked apron; every other year, stays. At Whitsuntide they had bonnets, shoes, stockings, shifts, caps, tippets, checked aprons, gowns, and coats; every other year gloves and white aprons. New cloaks were issued every four years.

The Charity children, then, went to school with others but were distinctively clothed. After 1861 the trustees had a new scheme, by which boys and girls both received boots.

The surplus income was used to pay a bonus of 10s. to girls who stayed a year in their first place, £1 if they stayed two years. By the end of the century the income had dried up except for a few pounds from ancient endowments, which were paid by the Cathedral direct to the managers of the schools, as they are still.

Westbury-on-Severn. Here lived Colonel Colchester, one of the founders of the S.P.C.K. Records have been preserved of seven schools maintained by him on his estates, some of them dating from before the founding of the S.P.C.K. For example, at Westbury, in 1697, 80 children were educated, nearly all receiving bread and some of them being clothed. The school was equipped with hornbooks, primers, writing books, New Testaments, and copies of *The Whole Duty of Man*. In 1714 a stocktaking of four schools in outlying hamlets shows 40 children, aged 5 to 13, with notes on their progress. The teachers were paid £8 a year. Girls made their own shifts and stockings. On 1 April each year the schools came to Colchester's house and were paid 2s. if a teacher, 3d. if a child.[1]

Worcester. William Lloyd, Bishop of Worcester, as lord of the manor had an estate escheated to him, the owner being hanged for murder. With the income, £75 a year gross, he founded in 1713 two Charity Schools in Worcester. A body of trustees was appointed with the assistance of the incumbents of the city and the trustees of the workhouses, who were to inform them of the children in need. Master and Dame were to be communicants of the Church of England; the Master to write a good hand and teach arithmetic. No other children to be taken (this rule was relaxed later). None to be admitted before the age of 6 and schooling to last six years. Holidays were the week before and after the three great festivals. Hours of attendance were 7 to 11 a.m. from 2 February to 1 November, 1–6 p.m. from

[1] See A. Platts and G. H. Hainton, *Education in Gloucestershire*.

Lady Day to Michaelmas; shorter hours in the winter. All children had to learn the Catechism and, when perfect, to make an exposition of it; and to go to church with their teachers twice on Sundays and Holy days, also on Wednesday and Friday. The schools were very successful at first.[1]

WELSH SCHOOLS

There are good reasons for devoting a separate section to Wales, where conditions differed greatly from those in England. The extreme poverty of the country, the virtual absence of a middle class in the sense that the term would apply in England, the complication of two languages, and the fact that no political trouble arose from outwardly expressed Jacobite sympathies—all conspired to make the problem very serious, but in some ways easier to solve. Besides, nothing so heroic as the Circulating Schools was attempted in England.[2]

The poverty of Wales is illustrated by the difficulty experienced in the seventeenth century of finding men with an income of £4 a year to serve on Anglesey juries.[3] The people were mostly small farmers, producing for their own consumption, and very little money was in circulation. Houses were often only a loft over a cow-house, approached by a ladder. Peat was the chief fuel. The absence of a middle class meant that below the chief landowners there was a homogeneous body of land-workers, among whom a real democracy prevailed. The Church was miserably poor, and the clergy could do little out of their own resources to help education. The Bishops were nearly always Englishmen, who were frequently translated to English dioceses. Wales was Royalist in the Civil War and probably in the eighteenth century many of the squires had Jacobite sympathies, but there is nothing to show that this interfered with the development of the schools. Further, there was no need felt to "condition" the poor or to

[1] Abridged from A. Tindal Hart, *William Lloyd*.

[2] The work of research has been excellently done by Dr Mary Clement in two monographs, *Correspondence and Minutes of the S.P.C.K. relating to Wales, 1699–1740* (University of Wales Press, 1952) and *The S.P.C.K. and Wales* (S.P.C.K., 1954). See also Dr M. G. Jones, *The Charity School Movement*.

[3] A. H. Dodd, "Anglesey in the Civil War", *Anglesey Antiquarian Society and Field Club Translations*, 1952.

combine manual labour with book-learning; the clergy were as poor as their flocks, and children were normally brought up to work with their hands. We must not exaggerate the plight of the people. As Dr Jones says, they were a people of dance, song, and poetry. The religious reformers, whether Anglicans or Dissenters, agreed in deploring this; indeed, by our standards, the Church of England, so far as it was active, was Puritan. It, to begin with, and then the Nonconformist Churches, succeeded in turning Wales into a country for which religion was the primary concern.

The Commonwealth saw the first attempt at popular education.[1] The Act for the better Propagation of the Gospel, 1650–53, and the work of the Trustees for the Maintenance of Ministers, 1653–60, provided schools in all the counties. The beginnings of State aid are seen in the allocation of one-sixth of the tithes for their upkeep. The schools collapsed at the Restoration, when the Church's money was restored. The next landmark was the work of Thomas Gouge. Ejected from his living in 1662, he devoted himself to Wales, and about 1672 founded the Welsh Trust, which was largely concerned with the provision of Welsh literature and the erection of schools. By 1681, when he died, from 1,600 to 2,000 children were said to be under his care.[2] The funds were raised largely in the City of London. After his death the movement came to an end so far as Wales was concerned, owing to controversy about the language in which teaching was to be given. The Trust, while circulating Welsh literature, insisted on the use of English in schools. Its operations were then removed to London. Strype, describing the Charity Schools' gathering of 1720, said that "this favour of the Londoners towards poor children began divers years ago in North and South Wales, and when it lessened in Wales, it began nearer home."[3] Here we have one of the influences that led to the work of the S.P.C.K.

Four of the five founders of the S.P.C.K. had Welsh connections. Dr Bray was of Welsh extraction and born on the borders of Wales; Sir Humphrey Mackworth lived at Neath, in Glamorgan; Hooke

---

[1] See Sir Leonard Davies and A. Edwards, *Welsh Life in the Eighteenth Century.*

[2] Dr Clement (*The S.P.C.K and Wales*, p. 1) gives at least 59 (one authority says 80) for the schools founded under the Commonwealth and 300 for the Gouge Schools.

[3] In his edition of Stowe's *Survey of London.*

lived at Caernarvon for part of his life; and Colchester, a native of Gloucestershire, supported Welsh Schools as well as those on his estate. This accounts for the relatively large number of Welshmen among the early correspondents of the Society. Two may be singled out for special mention, John Jones,[1] and Sir John Philipps.

Jones, an Anglesey man, who graduated at Trinity College, Cambridge, in 1689 became Dean of Bangor. In December 1699 he wrote to the Society to say he had already set up schools at his own expense, but "of late their poverty is so great that they cannot allow themselves time to learn". Next year he agreed to act as correspondent for Anglesey. Apparently the Gouge schools had collapsed and education had to make a new start. But there was much self-help, private persons helping their neighbours to learn to read, and promising boys could find teachers to prepare them for entering the Grammar Schools. In 1716 Jones reported to the S.P.C.K. on the state of the Charity Schools. Numbers were very small, for it was impossible to keep children at school regularly—they had to beg for victuals from door to door. In his will he left £100 each for six parishes and £50 each for four others. The money was to be invested and the interest to be "a fund for instructing poor children to read Welsh perfectly". The Bible, Prayer Book, and Catechism were to be taught, in Welsh, and writing and arithmetic, if possible. At Bangor and Beaumaris Welsh was not to be obligatory. The favourable view of the Welsh language, unexpected in Englishmen of that day, which was taken by the S.P.C.K. was doubtless due to the pastoral-hearted leaders, who knew that teaching could be given only in the mother-tongue.

Sir John Philipps, of Picton Castle, Pembrokeshire, was a great benefactor. He "set up" twenty-two Charity Schools in his own county besides several elsewhere; this meant being wholly responsible for them, even for food and clothes for the poorer children. He was a frequent correspondent with the Society and his letters are full of constructive ideas.

The Welsh schools, like the English, declined after 1715. The Dissenters, who had hitherto co-operated, established schools of their own, and probably the gentry did not wish to be involved in the disputes which beset the movement.

[1] See "Dean John Jones (1650–1727)" in *Anglesey Antiquarian and Field Club Transactions*, 1952, by E. G. Wright.

The Welsh Circulating Schools[1] were started by Griffith Jones, minister of Llandowror in Carmarthenshire, who regarded them as an extension of the work of the S.P.C.K. No money help was received from the Society, which, however, supplied large quantities of books. Jones had weak health and spent much of his later years in Bath, where he got to know influential people and enlisted support. Sympathizers were enrolled in a Corresponding Society, the members of which joined in intercession, particularly for his work, gave to it, prepared for the setting up of schools, and inspected them when established. Griffith Jones drew up an annual report, which he sent to members, its form being suggested by Professor Francke's *Pietas Hallensis*; it consisted of: (a) a preface; (b) a letter from the founder; (c) a list of schools with particulars of numbers; (d) letters in praise of the schools. The first letter was dated 1738; from 1746 onwards the Report was printed in London by J. Oliver, printer to the S.P.C.K. The 1739 Report says that sermons as commonly understood are useless as a means of dissipating ignorance. The money received is spent on agents, hardly at all on buildings or clerical expenses.

"Circulating Schools" was a literal description. The school, that is, the teachers, came to a place for four or five months between September and May and gave an intensive course in the Welsh language, the lessons lasting four hours at least in a day. It returned in the following year. By the end of this time the parish had been thoroughly grounded in Welsh. The books were provided by the S.P.C.K., which in the first year, 1737–8, sent 740 Bibles, many Psalters and Catechisms, and 13,000 other books, all in Welsh. Private houses were used, or sometimes the church building. Jones claimed that this method produced in three or four months results which took the same number of years in the English Charity Schools. In some places two-thirds of the scholars were adults. The movement was on Church lines and led up to Holy Communion; churches were filled with eager congregations, now that the clergy had adopted a "familiar and explanatory way of catechizing". In the first twenty-four years of their existence the schools taught 158,000 persons to read, largely adults. When Griffith Jones died he bequeathed the work to his friend Madam Bevan, who continued it on similar lines. On her death in 1777 the movement died out for lack of funds, since her will was in Chancery until 1804.

[1] See W. M. Williams, *Selections from the Welsh Piety*, Cardiff, 1938.

5

East India Mission

THE STORY now to be told is unique in the annals of the Church of England. It describes how a foreign mission began in a land more than six months distant by sailing ship, conducted by Danish and German missionaries under the fatherly eye of the S.P.C.K., a staunchly Anglican Society, which co-operated with Lutherans and yet tried to be loyal to its own principles; and how the original provisional arrangements lasted for more than a century.

Why were the Reformed Churches so slow in beginning missionary work? The main reason was the strong link between Church and State, which rendered independent action on the part of the former very difficult. The Church, anyhow in England, had to discover an agency with which to conduct operations overseas, and not until the device of a voluntary society had been discovered could it make a start. Dr Bray's plans resulted in the formation of a special society for missionary work, the S.P.G., which by its constitution was confined to the American colonies and the West Indies, and work outside the King's dominions was undertaken by the S.P.C.K. almost in a fit of absent-mindedness. Further, the passions aroused by the wars of religion and the resulting political convulsions had to die down in a measure before such enterprises were possible. The Roman Catholic Church, thanks to its religious orders, was free to move long before the Reformed Churches; the *Congregatio de propaganda fide*, founded in 1622, was supervised by the Pope. Given the background of the period, the initiative of the S.P.C.K. was surprising and reflected the greatest credit on the far-sighted men who guided its counsels.

BEGINNINGS

The story begins with the accession of Frederick IV to the throne of Denmark in 1699. Inspired by his German chaplain Lütkens, he showed a great zeal for missions, but no Dane could be found to volunteer for service overseas. Lütkens enlisted the help of his friends in Berlin, Pastors Lysius and Campe, who were able to recommend two men, Bartholomew Ziegenbalg and Heinrich Plutschau. Both Ziegenbalg and Plutschau had studied at the Friedrich Werber Gymnasium in Berlin, and at the University of Halle, where they had come under the influence of A. H. Francke. Though Francke was not consulted in the selection of the two men, the East India Mission owed much to him thereafter. Francke in a remarkable manner combined pietism, scholarship, and administrative ability. At Leipzig he gave popular lectures on theology to working-men, which made him unpopular in University circles. In 1698 he moved to Halle, where he became Professor of Oriental Languages in the newly founded University. He was a noted pastor at the Ulrichskirche in that city and founded educational institutions, a book store, and a Bible society. He originated the first monthly journal dealing with the interpretation of the Bible, *Observationes Biblicae*. His methods were strictly Puritan, games and fairy stories being forbidden in his schools. He had an influence on Frederick William I of Prussia as well as on the King of Denmark, and was highly esteemed by the leaders of the S.P.C.K., whose correspondence with him was marked by unfailing friendliness and understanding on both sides.

The two Germans sailed for India in 1705, their voyage lasting eight months. The Danish King had promised to pay their salaries, which amounted to something less than £40 each, and the Bishop of Zealand had ordained them for their mission. Their field of work was Tranquebar, on the east coast of South India, which at that time was a Danish trading settlement, south of Pondicherry. It would not have occurred to the King to send them to a place that had no links with Denmark, though the missionaries at first believed that they would be sent to Africa.

In 1714 the King issued Orders and Rules for the College of Missionaries at Copenhagen. The Director was to be a member of the Privy Council nominated by him. The College was to care especially for the existing missionaries, to draw up for the King's approval rules for the conduct of the Governor and Council at Tranquebar in regard to the missionaries, to report to him, and to ask for more support if necessary. The Danes relied almost entirely on Francke for men, the S.P.C.K. and the Germans provided funds, and the tripartite responsibility continued for many years without any apparent friction.

Ziegenbalg and Plutschau were received by the Danes in Tranquebar in an unfriendly manner and at first had no way of getting into touch with the Indians. They had learned Portuguese on board ship and found it useful in dealing with certain people who had come across from Goa to Tranquebar and its neighbourhood. To learn Tamil they went to school with native children, writing letters on the sand with their fingers. Ziegenbalg was able to preach an extempore sermon in Tamil after eight months. By August 1707 a church was opened, called New Jerusalem, the Consecration Service being in Tamil and Portuguese. In 1711 Ziegenbalg wrote to say that the whole of the New Testament had been translated by him into Tamil.[1]

THE APPEAL TO THE S.P.C.K.

In 1709 A. W. Böhme, Chaplain to Prince George of Denmark (consort of Queen Anne), published an English translation of the missionaries' letters, in which they described their early struggles, and dedicated it to the S.P.G., which Society he invited to help. As the S.P.G. was judged to be bound by its charter not to go beyond the English plantations and colonies, the S.P.C.K., which was free to experiment, was appealed to next. Members of the Society were interested and in September 1710 a subscription was opened, to be formally adopted by the Society on 12 December. A special Malabar (as it was termed) Committee was appointed, the personnel of which must have been practically identical with that of the ordinary Committee, for several times in 1713 the latter resolved itself into the Malabar Committee. The East India Mission from the first had a separate fund with its own treasurer, an arrangement which lasted all the time during which the Society was connected with it and even

[1] The Rev. G E. Marrison, who had spent a year in Germany studying the Halle Mission and similar problems, wrote to the S.P.C.K. in 1951 enclosing notes, in which he said that the international contacts of Ziegenbalg reflect the influence of the seventeenth-century reunion movement (Archbishop Wake, Leibniz, Bossuet, etc.) and that Ziegenbalg made a close study of the Jesuit Mission in Madura, some of whose methods, such as the toleration of caste, he followed.

afterwards. The Annual Report of 1737 explains the procedure. In 1710 the Society undertook the management of such charities as were, or should be, put into their hands, for the support and enlargement of the Protestant Mission, then maintained by the King of Denmark at Tranquebar. The average income for the purpose was £140, to meet disbursements amounting to £360. The balance was met by the sale of an estate left for the purpose, by remittances from Halle, and by an anonymous donation. This being insufficient, the Society had been obliged to apply £713 to the purpose out of the interest (the capital being left intact) on Mrs Palmer's legacy of £4,000 to the general purposes of the Society. (Among special gifts may be noted £40 in October 1711 as a first contribution from the University of Cambridge.) Again, in 1769 the preacher, the Bishop of Norwich, defined the S.P.C.K. work as "aiding the pious endeavours of others for the conversion of the pagan world". Earmarked legacies were invited, and in 1760, £1,000 left by Samuel Percivall for foreign missions was devoted to India because the Society had no other field of work overseas.

What line would have been followed if English missionaries had been employed cannot be known, for all attempts to find them failed. It is worth recalling some of the early efforts to find candidates. Griffith Jones, the founder of the Welsh Circulating Schools, who at one time thought of volunteering, wrote on 29 May 1713 to say that he longed to come to London to meet the Committee, but did not feel able to leave his flock. He was unable to go to India owing to his "unmeekness and insufficiency" as well as "the extremely miserable blindness of his native country". In December "he thinks himself obliged to decline it upon the prospect of doing more service in his native country that he can propose to do abroad". The minutes of the same month report other efforts to find Englishmen. In 1714 Mr Salmon of Oriel College, Oxford, met two men who might be willing to go. The next year a Mr Martin of Maidstone declined a proposal to go to India, having "neither the qualifications nor the constitution of body". A prospective missionary from Dublin had to be refused in January 1718 because there were no funds to support him, and other men in November 1719 for the same reason. In 1719 Henry Newman wrote to Bishop Wilson of Sodor and Man on the subject, stating that the funds were barely sufficient to maintain one missionary, in addition to assisting those who were already there. The three missionaries now in India (Gründler had gone out in 1709) "are content with plain living and seem to have all things in common among them, one chest sufficing for their common store, and one room to lodge in, and an Arabick or Syriack book is of more value to them than a suit of clothes would be above what they at present want. I am afraid we shall never find these qualities in the education of Great Britain, but I don't despair of them in the Isle of Man, if there were a fund to train up missionaries under your lordship's example and direction."

THE SOCIETY AND EPISCOPACY

The relations of the Society to Lutheran missionaries are a subject of interest to Anglicans, for they are apparently an exception to the generally consistent witness of the Church of England to the necessity of episcopal ordination. At home the Society was a zealous upholder of episcopacy and had no desire to act independently. What follows is drawn from the careful investigations of a Swedish scholar[1] into both English and Continental records, except for the extracts from the S.P.C.K. letters.

Dr Bray's drafts of a plan that eventuated in the S.P.C.K. and the S.P.G. provided for the Bishop of London as *ex officio* president. At meetings of the Society a diocesan Bishop, if present, automatically took the chair, and the Secretary referred all important matters to the Archbishop of Canterbury, or the Bishop of London, or both. As we have seen, the East India Mission was regarded at the outset as a praiseworthy enterprise which the Society assisted, rather than as its own child. The Lutheran Church naturally stood well in its eyes in view of the Lutheran antecedents of the Royal Family, first Prince George of Denmark, then the Hanoverian kings. Probably co-operation with the Reformed (Calvinist) Churches of the Continent would have been viewed differently. Had the attempts to secure English missionaries been successful, difficulties must have arisen, for they would have been ordained by the Bishop of London for service overseas and would have worked side by side with Lutherans; two classes of missionaries, following different traditions in a small mission, would have caused friction.

[1] H. Cnattingius, *Bishops and Societies*, 1952.

Close supervision from England was impossible. In 1735 the Society issued "Instructions for the Protestant Missions in the English colonies at Madras, Cuddalore, etc." There is no chief direction of the Mission. Its members are urged to consult together in a "weekly general conference", attended also by catechists and teachers. A book of minutes is to be kept, and submitted yearly to the S.P.C.K. The senior missionary at Madras is the organ of communication with London.

There is no evidence that re-ordination of Lutherans ever took place. Bishop Heber in a paper of 1812 says that the S.P.C.K. recognized their ordination, and no one will blame the Society.

Archbishop Wake's letter to Ziegenbalg in 1719 shows that the official Church of England was behind the Society. Addressed to Ziegenbalg and Gründler, it arrived after the former's death. The Archbishop says that their lot is higher than that of prelates, patriarchs, and popes, and their recompense will be more magnificent. Later in the century the German records show that the Society was criticized in some quarters. A letter written by Pasche in 1779 (German Court chaplain in London and a member of the East India Mission Committee) says that some people demur at the new missionaries not being properly ordained. This was only to be expected, for it was generally agreed that Lutheran orders were at the least irregular. In 1784 Schwartz obtained leave from the Society to ordain the son of the missionary Kohlhoff. In 1793 the Society asked Halle to provide two candidates to be trained in England as missionaries to Bengal and to receive English orders, a proposal not accepted by Halle. The S.P.C.K. letters are as follows.

1735. 6 June. Newman to Francke, at Halle.

A missionary has sent Francke's letter in reply to "the enquiry he was desir'd to make of the power vested in the missionaries at Tranquebar to confer Orders on such persons among the Malabar converts to Christianity as shall be found fitly qualify'd for Divine Offices, particularly the administration of the Holy Sacraments". A full meeting of the Society expressed its entire satisfaction at your account and ordered Newman to remind them to give directions "for preventing any difficulties or misunderstandings that may hereafter grow in those parts upon a supposition of the Holy Orders conferr'd in India not being valid".

1736. 4 *February. Newman to the Reverend Mr Wynch, Chaplain at Fort St George*, about the ordination of Pastor Aaron at Tranquebar.

"They (the Society) declined giving me any instructions, it being a tender point for the Society to engage themselves in, to make a comparison of the validity of episcopal with foreign Ordinations, which could yield no service to this mission but might do abundance of mischief. The sending over of candidates for orders to Europe would be attended with insuperable difficulties. You have seen the Archbishop of Canterbury's opinion in favour of ordination in India, and according to your desire I herewith send you copies of what the Society have received from Professor Francke in Germany to warrant the regularity of what the missionaries at Tranquebar have done."

1739. 31 *January. Henry Newman to Archdeacon Denne.*

"Mr Howard is a rigid warm man and will allow of no Pastor Aarons[1] to preach the gospel without they come over to England for episcopal ordination, or some bishop goes over to India to ordain them. Mr Wynch I know is of more catholic principles suited to the case of the Protestant Churches abroad."

It is not clearly stated whether by episcopal ordination, and "a visit to Europe", England or Denmark is meant, but as the original missionaries were ordained by Danish bishops the latter seems probable. What did "valid" mean to the writer of these letters? Surely that the Sacraments were legitimately administered according to the Lutheran rite, although the Germans and Danes were far from their Home Churches. The question of recognizing those thus ordained as authorized to minister in the Church of England would not have occurred to anybody.

PROGRESS OF THE MISSION

The first help given by the Society was the provision of a large edition of the Portuguese New Testament, which was printed at Amsterdam and sent to India. Hearing that the missionaries were spending much time in making hand-copies of Tamil books, it next sent a printing press with a trained printer. The frigate that carried it

[1] Aaron was the first Indian to be ordained by the mission.

was captured by the French and taken to Rio de Janeiro, where it was ransomed, the Society's share being £150. Unfortunately the printer died before the ship reached India, but an English soldier was found who could work the press and operations began at once. In 1713 the Society heard that the Portuguese Testaments had arrived and the press had produced five books in Portuguese and one tract in Tamil. The translation of the Old Testament into Portuguese had begun. New machinery and three printers arrived in 1715.

If we may judge by the books sent to the missionaries, they were indeed remarkable men. In 1719 a large consignment was shipped, mostly in Latin, including folios on the Bible, the works of Grotius, Suidas' Greek Lexicon, and Tillotson's Sermons. Abundant stores were purchased, including linen, clothes, beer, wine, cheese, spectacles, sealing-wax, pen-knives, and all kinds of supplies for the press, even on one occasion, "patterns of flowers for the charity children to imitate on calico". The East India Company gave free passages to missionaries and conveyed money and goods without charge except for insurance, which on one occasion was said to be £3 3s. per cent. In 1712 the Archbishop of Canterbury supplemented the stores liberally. The difficulties of the age are illustrated by the fate of a gift from the King of Denmark in 1714, who sent 2,000 rixdollars (= £400) to the Danish missionaries, plus 500 from Prince Charles and 55 ducats from Princess Sophia Hedwig. The ship was lost off Jutland and only the Princess's contribution had been insured.

Much was expected of the missionaries. In 1729 Mr Stevenson, chaplain at Fort St George, Madras, wrote to describe the qualifications needed: "Besides his learning, which includes a knowledge of the Latin, Greek, and Hebrew languages, it is wished that he might have a genius for acquiring any language because he must be able offhand to address himself to the heathen in their own tongue ... that he be well read in the best commentaries on the Holy Scriptures, have a good knowledge in Theology, Natural Philosophy, particularly in medicine, and understand at least the rudiments of Arithmetic and Geometry, Astronomy, Music, and other parts of the mathematics." He goes on to speak of spiritual qualifications. In 1729 the Society agreed to tell new missionaries to insist that Christianity is not a new religion but goes back to St Thomas. In 1712 Plutschau returned and on his way home came to London, where he was addressed by the Society in a Latin speech, to which he replied suitably; he went to other work in Germany. Ziegenbalg followed him in 1715. During his stay in England Newman was ordered to show him "the remarkables" of London.

Relations between the S.P.C.K. and the East India Company were uniformly friendly. Thus in 1720 letters were sent to the Governors of Fort St George and Fort St David in identical terms, stating that a bag of silver was being sent to each, weighing 252 oz. 13 dr. (value £70), to be disposed of at their discretion, though with a suggestion that it be spent on a school for Indians. A letter written in 1714 by John Martin, of Sandwich, thanks the Society for "designing" him to be chaplain to the East India Company at Bombay. The Company must have asked the Society to recommend a suitable man. With the death of Ziegenbalg in 1719 the first phase of the mission ended.

SCHULTZE

Schultze arrived in Tranquebar in 1719, just after Ziegenbalg's death, and was ordained by Gründler. He was a man of outstanding gifts and completed the translation of the Old Testament into Tamil. In 1724 Newman wrote to Dr Bray to say that three new missionaries, chosen by Francke, had been sent to Copenhagen to be approved by the King and the College, and would proceed to Halle for instructions and then to London to meet the S.P.C.K. The arrival of these men at Tranquebar strengthened the mission, and in 1726 Schultze felt able to break new ground. He visited several places and finally decided to settle at Madras. This was a new departure, involving work at a place under British control. The Society therefore consulted the East India Company, which in 1727 sent a direction to the Governors and officers under its jurisdiction as follows: "At the desire of the Society for Promoting Christian Knowledge, That if any Danish missionaries shall visit or reside at places under the Company's jurisdiction, our Governors and officers may give them their protection, we hereby consent thereunto upon supposition that they behaved themselves respectfully and suitably to the needs of the place."

This was an innovation, since for the first time the Society took responsibility for a mission. Schultze became a missionary of the S.P.C.K., his salary being fixed at £60, that of his assistant Sartorius at £45; there were also salaries to be paid to a schoolmaster and a catechist, with other expenses. The special contributions to the mission were insufficient to bear the new burden and had frequently to be supplemented by grants from the General Fund. Schultze learned Telegu (then called Gentoo) and translated the whole Bible into that language. He also learned Hindustani (called Moorish, as it was spoken by the Muslims) and translated the New Testament and part of the Old into it, besides writing a Hindustani Grammar. Unfortunately he was too dictatorial to get on well with his colleagues, and in 1736 the Society urged him to leave Madras and open a new Mission at Cuddalore. The Secretary wrote: "You have, good Sir, we believe, as few failings as any missionary in India, and as warm a zeal to promote the Glory of God. Do what you can to sacrifice your chiefest failing to this zeal, and to mortify the least degree of pride that can tempt you to assume a superiority or rule over your fellow labourers, altho' your merit may make you worthy of it, and would probably command it from them, if you did not assume it." Similarly, Sartorius and Geister were urged to put away the "unhappy animosities" between themselves and Schultze and to restore Christian love and harmony.[1]

However, the colleagues left Madras to open a mission at Cuddalore and Schultze stayed behind until his breakdown in health in 1743, when he returned to Europe, having built up a Christian community in Madras as a result of 700 baptisms. Apparently a special gift from Halle had eased the situation. In 1738 the missionaries at Tranquebar numbered six, the congregation had increased by 484 in a year, and the total Christian community in Tranquebar and its neighbourhood was 2,736. In the Society's report for 1747 we read that the missionaries preach alternately in Tamil and Portuguese, and have a *colloquium biblicum* with their schoolmasters and catechists every evening in Tamil. Schultze lived at Halle for several years after his return, instructing missionary students, among them Christian Frederick Schwartz.[2]

---

[1] As early as 3 February 1731 Newman had written to the missionaries at Tranquebar, urging peaceful relations with Madras. The Archbishop (Wake) had not written, owing to "his great age and infirmities, which have in a measure deprived him of any more taking a pen into his hand".

[2] In 1741 Newman wrote to Archdeacon Denne to say that Schultze had drawn freely upon "the Church stock" at Madras, without authorization. This was

FROM SCHULTZE TO SCHWARTZ

The period between Schultze's leaving Tranquebar in 1726 and the arrival of Schwartz in 1750 was marked by steady progress in spite of war. The ordination of Aaron in 1733 and of Diego in 1741, after consultation with the S.P.C.K. and Copenhagen, marked the beginning of a native ministry; both laboured with marked success. Sartorius died at Cuddalore in 1738 and Kiernander, afterwards the pioneer missionary in Bengal, came to join Geister. A new mission was opened at Tanjore by a poor outcaste named Rajanaiken, who was led by his study of the Bible to leave the Roman Catholic Church and become a catechist in the Danish Mission.

All this work was pursued on a background of war. The East India Company had three chief centres: Fort William (Calcutta), Bombay, and Fort St George (Madras) with Fort St David (fifteen miles south of Pondicherry, and north of Cuddalore and Tranquebar). These were intended as trading settlements, and the Company was obliged to maintain military forces by the rivalries of European powers. As early as 1726 the Society's report states that owing to war conditions the refugees in the Company's settlements had eaten the food intended for the missionaries; these had been taken prisoners by the French but were subsequently released. In 1744 Labourdonnais decided to fight the British in India. He arrived at Pondicherry in 1746 but quarrelled with the Governor, Dupleix. However, the French made headway, but by the peace of Aix-la-Chapelle had to restore their conquests. Dupleix, by his clever diplomacy, was able to enlist the support of powerful Indian rulers and by 1751 controlled much of South India. The skill and valour of Clive turned the scale. In 1754 a French envoy arrived and ordered Dupleix to make peace. War between French and English broke out again in 1759 and further hostilities took place later in the century.

Our admiration of the missionaries increases when we realize the conditions under which they worked. At least six months distant from the home base, they were liable to have their supplies of money and

apparently the Church fund referred to in another letter of that year as being held by the two chaplains and the churchwardens of the English Church at Madras. Remittances were irregular, especially in time of war, and probably Schultze was compelled to borrow money.

other requisites cut off at any time, their converts were slain and pillaged, and the country was devastated by invading armies; those of the French and English were small in number, but the rivalries of the native rulers, exploited by the European combatants, inflicted great sufferings on the Indian population.

SCHWARTZ 1749–98

Schwartz, who was born in 1726, was led to his Indian work by the influence of Schultze. With two others he came to London in 1749 and, having been received by the S.P.C.K., sailed for India, reaching Tranquebar in 1750. He travelled widely, visiting Ceylon in 1760, besides other places. In 1762 he went to Tanjore, where he preached in the King's palace, and then to Trichinopoly. The Society was informed in 1767 that the college at Copenhagen had agreed to release him from Tranquebar, and he now became a regular missionary of the S.P.C.K. The King of Tanjore became his friend and on his death-bed wished to make him guardian of his nine-year-old son Serfogee. Schwartz refused but was able to help the young man in many ways. He played a great part in political negotiations between the East India Company and native rulers, being trusted by both sides, and was assiduous in his care for English and German soldiers in the employ of the Company, in return for which service the Governor of Madras granted him £100 a year; Schwartz paid this into the mission funds for some time but then asked the Society's permission to take half for his personal needs.

In his younger days Schwartz was described by a visitor to India as "a stout, well made man, somewhat above the middle size, erect in his carriage and address, with a complexion rather dark, though healthy, black curled hair, and a manly engaging countenance expressive of unaffected candour, ingenuousness, and benevolence". Some original letters written by Schwartz to John Kohlhoff, a fellow-missionary, add details to the portrait.[1] They overflow with affection and piety, and the writer was evidently a man of personal charm. On 28 January 1779 he wrote: "I have no snuff. Could you send me 4 or 6 bottles—it[em] some sugar candy—some small portion of barley—some soup-plates. N.B. if you can spare them." In another letter he asks for his "pair of

[1] Recently given to the S.P.C.K. by Mrs Nare.

spectacles inclosed in white ivory" and in a third gives instructions about the planting of beans. When he died in 1798 the Society erected a monument to him in Madras and the Rajah Serfogee another in the church at Tanjore. This was executed by Flaxman under the supervision of the S.P.C.K. and represents the last visit of Serfogee to Schwartz.

Some details of the work during this period may be added here.

1762. The missionaries explained to the Indians that the drought that year was due to idolatry; they distributed copies of the first and second commandments and explained them. One man answered that "God must be worshipped by images, until he should represent himself to their eyes". He was told to look at the sun; he could not, therefore "he could not look at God if he did reveal himself".

1769. At Cuddalore lectures are given every evening from 7 to 8 on the Psalms and the Epistle to the Romans.

1776. The mission property at Madras consisted of the church at Vepery, a house and garden, a cemetery, two rooms for the Portuguese schoolmaster, another cemetery in Madras, a small house, a paddy field, and buildings for the care of English orphans.

1789. Schwartz writes to say that the English liturgy has been translated and is used regularly before the sermon. In 1744, the Society's minutes record: "Recommended to the missionaries to continue the use of the Church of England Catechism and to baptize in the form of Common Prayer."

As regards finance, three typical years illustrate the scanty support received by the special fund. In 1766, £1,494 was spent, towards which £1,085 was received, £900 of it from Germany. In 1782 there was only one donation apart from a large German one. In 1797 the cost of the mission was £2,555, towards which special gifts provided £164, £132 came from the German congregation in London (covering two years), and £30 from a legacy. A large part of the free income of the Society was devoted to making up the deficits, though theoretically the India fund was not in the main line of its work; indeed the affairs of the mission were rarely brought before either the Standing Committee or the General Meeting.

A further development during this period was the opening of new work in Bengal. Kiernander, one of the missionaries at Cuddalore, driven out by the French occupation of the town in 1758, went to

Calcutta. By 1760 he had a school of 135 children and had baptized fifteen adults. The chaplains of the East India Company were very helpful to him. Later, as a result of unfortunate business speculations, he was ruined financially and had to retire, at the age of 79. David Brown, a chaplain at Calcutta, took over the work, and with the help of two civilians, cleared off the debts with which the mission was saddled, and then resigned his post in order to be a missionary, continuing the work for twenty years. At last in 1789 the Society found a priest, A. T. Clarke, to go to Calcutta. This was an occasion of great joy, that there was now a prospect of English missions; but in 1791 he resigned, to become a chaplain under the Company.

HANDING OVER TO THE S.P.G.

It remains to trace the steps by which the S.P.C.K. was led to transfer the East India mission to other hands. In 1802 Professor Knapp of Halle wrote a letter[1] saying that the Society had been for some time considering the possibility of ridding itself entirely of the Germans. There is nothing resembling this in the archives, but the Report of 1791 speaks of giving the natives a Church of their own, with bishops "who might ordain deacons and priests, and secure a regular succession of truly apostolical pastors, even if all communications with their parent Church should be annihilated". George Gaskin (secretary of the S.P.C.K. 1785–1823) in a printed sermon spoke of "a lineal and regular succession . . . perpetuated by the imposition of episcopal hands". These opinions in favour of insisting on episcopacy were crystallized by the appointment of the first Anglican Bishop in India. The mission was in low water. Owing to the long continued European wars and the prevalence of nationalism on the Continent, the scanty supply of missionaries from Germany and Denmark had almost dried up. It had long been impossible to recruit English clergy, for who would go to a mission worked on Lutheran lines? In 1811 the mission replied to an S.P.C.K. suggestion that Syrian priests be employed: this was impossible for they held doctrines that militated against the Thirty-nine Articles, the Augustana (Augsburg) Confession, and the Nicene Creed. In 1805 Horst, a Dane, ordained in India by the missionaries, was accepted by the Society owing to the impossibility of finding

[1] Quoted by Cnattingius, *Bishops and Societies*, p. 52.

Germans (evidently the personal recommendation of Halle was considered almost indispensable). When he died in 1810 the problem of staffing the mission became acute. So next year four Indians were ordained. A letter from Pohle is sufficiently interesting to be printed in part.

Trinchinopoly, 29 April 1811

The death of Mr Horst makes it necessary to provide country priests. "With the consent of the Society and the Danish Royal missionaries, assisted by the Rev. John Kohlhoff and the country priest Sattianden, I have ordained at Tanjore four of our fittest catechists country priests according to the Lutheran Ritual, when they previously had been duly examined, and preached their probationary sermons on prescribed texts before us, and acquitted themselves to our satisfaction."

There follows a "Report on Njanapiragasam, catechist".

"By the Name of God, to discharge the duty attached to the priesthood, to preach the Holy Word of God, and to administer the Holy Baptism and Lord's Supper, we called him by the Name of God in presence of the congregation and gave him a sufficient power required to this office.

Signed CHRISTIAN POHLE Ordinator

JOHN CASPER KOHLHOFF Co-ordinator

SATTEYANADEN (*sic*) Country priest."

"Country priest" implies that his ministry was limited to villages. The examination papers are attached to the letter. They are four in number: (a) Moralia, (b) Historia-Ecclesiastica; (c) Dogmatica; (d) Exegetica, and contain 12, 12, 13, 13 questions respectively. The answers are very short, mostly in one sentence, but quite sound. These are specimen questions.

(a) Have we also to esteem other men and nations as our neighbours; for instance, with whom we are at war? Or ought we to esteem them as enemies and to hate them? If not, how ought we to love them? (b) What was the great sin (soon) after the flood? Who is properly and shortly the Antichrist? What was the cause of the corruption of the first Christian Church? (c) Is man's body the prison of the soul? (d) For what reason spoke Jesus in parables? What is the meaning of John 1.17 (compared with Chapter 5.46)?

In the Society's Report for 1812 a prospectus of a scheme for an Ecclesiastical Establishment in British India is printed. The author seems to have been William Wilberforce. That the Society should think in terms of Establishment was inevitable. The East India Company, originally a trading body, had now become the governor of extensive territories. There were signs that, reversing the original policy of friendliness towards missions, it was becoming neutral, and even hostile to missions, for fear of making the task of ruling non-Christians more difficult. Only if the Government was bound by law to protect Christianity could converts escape persecution.

The scheme points to the example of Holland, where the Dutch East Indies Company maintains 30 to 40 missionaries at a cost of £10,000 a year; converts number hundreds of thousands. There is need for a seminary in England, to which Indian students can come; so soon as a bishopric is established it can be transferred to Madras or elsewhere.

Protestant subjects number 63,299 in Bengal (50,000 half-castes), 52,410 in Madras (40,000 half-castes), 13,000 in Tanjore, and 27,348 in Bombay (20,000 half-castes). The half-castes, children of English fathers and Indian women, often three or four generations ago, are in a deplorable state. One-tenth of all European residents make their permanent home in India, at present they cannot be confirmed. The purpose of an Establishment and of the Bishop's being a Government servant is to prevent the persecution of converts. It is suggested that there be an Archbishop of Calcutta, Bishops at Bombay, Madras, and in Ceylon, four Archdeacons, fifty European chaplains, 100 country chaplains, and 200 schoolmasters. A grant of £100,000 a year from the Imperial Parliament is needed. The Society is considering the scheme, which is practically what Archbishop Tenison desired more than 100 years ago.

An Act setting up a Bishop of Calcutta and three Archdeacons, to be paid by the East India Company, was passed in 1813 and next year T. F. Middleton was consecrated Bishop. The task that confronted the new Bishop was colossal, and that he lived eight years longer is surprising. His Letters Patent seemed to exclude missionary work among the Indians, and he contented himself with encouragement and advice, leaving supervision to be exercised by the local Committee of the Societies. In 1816 he visited Madras, Tranquebar, and other parts of South India, where he was deeply impressed by the Society's missions, which were however in great difficulties in regard to both men and money; the latter need was partly met by first-aid relief out of funds entrusted to him by the S.P.C.K. Necessary disciplinary action was taken in some places. The Tranquebar mission was in especial need, since the settlement had been ceded to England and help from Denmark had ceased. The Bishop suggested that the S.P.C.K. should take it over; we note the distinction between Lutheran missions aided by the S.P.C.K. and S.P.C.K. missions staffed by Lutherans in the absence of English missionaries. The former had apparently not adopted the Book of Common Prayer, as the latter had from the time of Schwartz. In 1818 Pohle of Trichinopoly died and responsibility for the mission was transferred to the Madras Committee of the S.P.C.K. Middleton, an enthusiastic supporter of the S.P.C.K., formed Committees of the Society at Calcutta, Bombay, and Madras, which, mainly concerned with books and libraries, were a means of self-expression for the clergy and laity at a time when modern diocesan organization had not been invented. At this point the S.P.G. comes into the story. In 1817 Middleton asked the Archbishop to recommend the S.P.G. to start work in India, and Joshua Watson began to discuss with Dr Christopher Wordsworth and H. H. Norris a forward policy for the S.P.G. Then, as always. leading Churchmen belonged to both Societies and the question was how best the common task could be shared. The transfer of Indian Missions from the S.P.C.K. to the S.P.G. was part of their plan, and so in December Watson wrote to the Archbishop urging that the Church of England should go forward with its three Societies, "each with undivided energy pursuing its own single and simple object"—Education Society (National Society) Bible and Religious Tract Society, and Missionary Society. Watson as Treasurer of the S.P.C.K. must have been able to count on its willingness to take part in the scheme. A general collection for the S.P.G. in 1819 with the support of a Royal Letter brought in £45,747 and the way was prepared for a change so far as finance was concerned.

Bishop Heber, who succeeded Middleton in 1823, was free from some of his predecessor's difficulties and not debarred from ordaining Indians. He felt strongly the objections to an Anglican Society's employing Lutheran clergy, about which Middleton had been uneasy, and not only ordained two Indians but also gave Anglican orders to three Lutherans working for the Church Missionary Society in Bengal.

Finally, in 1825 the General Meeting received a report from the Standing Committee. The mission was on a small scale and in rather a feeble state, but could not be abandoned. The opening of Bishop's College, Calcutta, consequent on the founding of the bishopric, provided an opportunity for a change. "A Chartered Society with a perpetual succession of *ex officio* members gives a pledge for continuous good management which no voluntary association can offer." The report was accepted and on 7 June it was "Resolved that this Society do continue to maintain the missionaries now employed by it in the South of India during the remainder of their lives and that the management and superintendence of the missions be transferred to the Society for the Propagation of the Gospel". The Society then voted £5,000 for this object, supplementing various trust funds which had been accumulated during a century. Further grants were made later to keep the trust in funds. Looking ahead thirty-five years, to 1860, we find that special grants were made to the East India Mission account at Hoare's Bank, which was kept separately from the rest of the Society's money at Gosling's Bank, and that from it payments were made to three seminaries, seven female boarding schools, and the support of catechists at Tanjore.

The Christian community handed over to the S.P.G. numbered about 8,000.

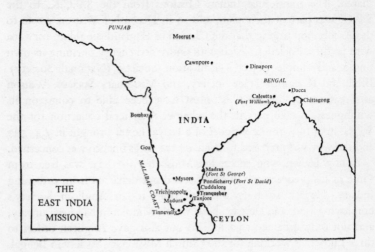

6

Literature

(a) LIBRARIES

DR BRAY'S efforts to circulate books were so great that they deserve separate treatment.

The Sion College manuscripts contain a good deal of information. In preparation for his visit to America he drew up a list of books under four heads, called *Bibliotheca Americana quadripartita*. The first was for the central library at Annapolis. The others covered Provincial, Deanery, and Parochial Libraries. Divine and Human knowledge were both represented; the latter included Anatomy, Arithmetic, Astronomy, Chemistry, Chirurgery, Commerce, Geometry, Grammar, Heathen Moralists, Logic, Mathematics, Pharmocopy, Philosophy, Physiology, Poetry, Rhetoric, Trade, Travels, and Voyages. A Catalogue of books sent to Pamlico, North Carolina, on 2 December 1700, includes Buxtorf's Hebrew Lexicon and the works of Grotius; the same place also had a Layman's Library sent to it.

Another document is called "Design for a Lending Library in every Deanery". It was based on Bray's own experiences as a newly-ordained priest in need of books and was his reply to the objection raised to sending books to America when the need of the Home Church was so great. "I thought it not amiss to strike the nail that would drive." The libraries for the poor clergy should be kept in a separate meeting place "rather than in their own private houses which will cause expense, or in Public Houses which will, beside the expense, give scandal". The clergy were to meet for study and edification; "at every meeting they should read over some part of their Ordination Vows, of the Articles, Rubrics, and Canons of the Church, and debate upon the same in order the better to know their duty, to take the best measures about it, and to excite and invigorate one another in it."

An example of Bray's care for details may be seen in his "Directions for the use and preservation of the Library sent with his Excellency the Earl of Bellamont to New York in America". The Library is designed for Church of England Ministers and Chaplains of H.M.'s ships. It is to be kept in a public place, such as the vestry of the church. There are to be three registers, in the custody of the Bishop of London, the Governor, and the Librarian. The gentlemen of the vestry are desired to inspect the books annually and inform the Bishop and Governor of their safety. The good doctor thought of everything except the difficulty of getting people to read to good purpose the books provided, and of keeping a library up to date. His ruling passion is illustrated by his letters to the S.P.C.K. on his voyage out to Maryland. He started a Lending Library at Gravesend for the Deanery of Rochester, specially intended for the clergy and laity detained at Gravesend on their outward journey (16 December 1699). On 20 December he wrote to say that he had founded a library at Deal. On the 24th he arrived at Plymouth, where he found a library with good books in it but "overwhelmed with filth and rubbish".

After 1704 the library project was carried on mainly by an *ad hoc* Committee, whose minute book is preserved in the S.P.C.K. archives. It is called "The Proceedings of the Trustees for erecting Parochial Libraries and promoting other Charitable Designs". Twelve Trustees were present at the inaugural meeting, including Bray, Mackworth, and Nelson, and made this declaration: "We whose names are hereunto subscribed do agree to meet and consult together, for advancing religion and learning, by erecting Parochial Libraries in the meanly endowed cures throughout this kingdom and for promoting other charitable designs. 30th July 1705." Bray engaged to provide a list of parishes with an income of less than £20 a year, which he did with the help of the Bishops. In March 1706 Henry Newman was appointed Secretary, two years before he became Secretary of the S.P.C.K. Liberal contributions of books were made, authors giving large numbers of their books. Thus Bray gave 500 copies of his Lectures on the Catechism, valued at £150. Donations in money were used to buy books, often from the authors, who at that time were frequently proprietors of their own books. On 13 March 1706 it was agreed to buy 500 copies of Kettlewell's *Christian Believer* at £125 and 500 each of Allen's *On the Covenant* and *Fasts*. It was generally possible to get books at two-thirds of the published price. Two rooms were hired from Mrs Kettlewell in her house at the corner of Southampton Street, at a rent of £5. In one of them, called the Repository, a model library was stored. All the Trustees had to approve each book and a latecomer to a meeting was fined 1s. Later, the Archbishop of York gave the Committee the use of a closet in the Almoner's lodgings in which to store books. In 1715, Mrs Kettlewell having left her house, the Bishop of London gave the Trustees permission to store books in London House free of charge.

Apparently the work had grown to such proportions that it was considered necessary to get the sanction of a Parliamentary measure, which after amendments proposed by the Archbishop received Royal Assent on 21 April 1709. It was called "Act for the Better Preservation of Parochial Libraries" and involved the Trustees in no expense. They were tied by their own rules and in 1711 had to refuse a request to move a library to a more convenient place as being contrary to the Act of Parliament. The extent of their operations is illustrated by their buying in 1707 250 copies of Eusebius' *Ecclesiastical History* in quires at 12s. a copy.

Dr Smalridge on 15 December 1708 produced a device and motto with which to stamp the books. It represented a clergyman on his knees with a ray of light coming down to his eye, with the words *tolle, lege* in the ray, and one of the parochial bookcases open behind him; at the foot was the reference to St Augustine's Confessions. Mr Nelson was asked to get a block made of the drawing.

The Committee were hampered by their own rules. A plan submitted by the Bishop of Carlisle was turned down because the living in question was worth £30. Many must have been scared by the rule that an Incumbent of a parish where a library was placed had to sign a bond for £30 for the safe keeping of the books and to promise to keep them clean. Sometimes special places were fitted up in which to store books; a part of the church was set aside or, as at Oundle, the room over the church porch.

By 1729 the original trustees were for the most part dead or else they lived at a distance from one another, so that it was impracticable to continue the trust. Dr Bray proposed that the funds be transferred to Dr Horneck's Charity for instructing Negroes in the

Plantations.[1] Final arrangements for handing over were made on 3 March 1730. The work, which had been done by the Secretary of the S.P.C.K., with certain members of the Society, went on without a break as part of its normal work.

The S.P.C.K. was specially interested in Wales, and the arrangements for the Bangor Library will serve as an illustration of the work. The Bishop of Bangor recommended twelve Trustees or Feoffees to the Society. At least three of their number had to report to the Bishop once in three years, if not oftener. The library was to be open on market days between 10 a.m. and noon. All books could be lent, to persons living within a radius of ten miles, provided they were clergymen, schoolmasters, trustees, or subscribers of at least 10s. The borrower had to deposit the value of the book. The library included the works of Calvin, Grotius, Josephus, Justin Martyr, Tertullian, Thomas Aquinas, Vincent of Lerins; also a Hebrew Bible and a Septuagint. The end of the S.P.C.K. library at Carmarthen is probably typical of many others: in 1765 the Society was informed that it was dormant, for all the trustees were dead and no one was authorized to take any action. It was decided to hand the books over to the informant. Newman, writing to Nelson in 1710, said that the lending libraries had given him more trouble than all the other literature put together. This we can well understand. The Society had bound itself by strict rules and to act through the Bishops. Delays must have been exasperating. On one occasion after a meeting of the trustees Newman was instructed to wait upon all the Bishops, then in town, in turn.

(b) PUBLISHING

The publications of the S.P.C.K. give a valuable picture of the normal currents of English Church life during the eighteenth century.[2] The Society worked under episcopal supervision and through its correspondents was in close touch with the clergy throughout the country. Books and tracts were chosen with great care, mainly from

[1] A casual reference to the Religious Societies on 26 June 1709 is worth recording. It was reported that at their last quarterly meeting they had highly approved the libraries scheme.

[2] This chapter is based mainly on the essay "Pastoralia" in my book *Eighteenth Century Piety*.

what was already printed, and when once approved were regarded as the voice of the Society, not to be lightly changed; they continued on the list for a century or more, perhaps slightly revised but more often not. Thus Bishop Beveridge's *Sermon on the Common Prayer*, first published in 1681, reached its thirty-eighth edition in 1799. A sermon preached at the death of the Earl of Rochester in 1680 was still being reprinted in 1798, to be given away at funerals. Society was static, judged by modern standards, and there was no obvious need to bring out new books. Naturally a publisher who could give large repeated orders found no difficulty in getting people to do his work, and the privilege of being the printer or bookseller to the S.P.C.K. was highly prized. Both posts were filled by election at the General Meeting. In 1703 the Society objected to the printing of Madame Guyon's works by its printer Downing, who agreed to call in all copies, so far as he could, the Society promising to make some allowance for his losses. Dr Sykes says[1] that the publishing of educative religious literature was "controlled almost to monopoly" by the S.P.C.K. in the early eighteenth century. This is clearly correct: no one could compete against a publisher who sold pamphlets to its members at half the cost of production. Towards the end of the century Hannah More produced her Cheap Repository Tracts on more popular lines, and out of them arose the Religious Tract Society, but until then the S.P.C.K. provides the evidence for popular Anglicanism.

The literature is uniformly High Church in the sense defined by Bishop Horsley, of St David's, in a charge of 1790[2]: "To be a High-Church-Man, in the only sense which the word can be allowed to bear, as applicable to any in the present day; God forbid, that this should ever cease to be my public pretension, my pride, my glory! To be a High-Church-Man in the true import of the word in the English language, God forbid, that I should ever deserve the imputation!" Traditionally the word means one who claims the advantages of the Establishment; it has come to mean one who recognizes the spiritual authority of the Church and its ministry. "My reverend brethren, we must be content to be High-Church-Men according to this usage of the word, or we cannot at all be Churchmen." A noteworthy protest was addressed to the Society in 1837 by five Essex incumbents, against

[1] *Edmund Gibson*, p. 197.
[2] This and all the other books mentioned were published by the S.P.C.K.

the unevangelical character of its publications from the first. This is attributed to the circumstances of the time when it was founded. Tillotson, in particular, was responsible for the loss of the true Reformation doctrines. Nelson's books were particularly pernicious; so was *The Whole Duty of Man* in a different way. On the showing of the memorialists, the whole doctrinal position of official Anglicanism since 1699 had been non-Evangelical, and the S.P.C.K. had faithfully represented it.[1]

Similar sentiments are expressed by Thomas Burgess in a tract. Bishop of St David's 1803–25, he falls just outside our period, but he had learned his Churchmanship in the eighteenth century: "As there is one holy Catholic Church, for which Christ died, we have no hope of salvation, but as being faithful members of it. . . . Sects, which are so divided from any true Church, as to have no communion with it, it is to be feared, cannot be parts of the one Catholic Church for which Christ died." In fact the tone of S.P.C.K. Churchmanship had from the first been set by Ken and Nelson, the Non-jurors. Archbishop Wake's book on the Catechism (*The Principles of the Christian Religion Explained*) had immense influence. Of the Catholic Church he says there: "We profess not our faith of any one particular Church; which may cease; and fail (such as the Church of England, or Church of Rome). . . ." A particular Church may not be called "The Catholic Church". "But a Catholic Church, a particular Church may be called; and such ours is." The Church of England is a true part of the Catholic Church, "inasmuch as it professes the true Catholic faith, delivered in the Holy Scriptures, and drawn up in the Creeds of the Church". We have Communion with all the Saints and with the departed, who probably pray for us.

The Bible was the universal text-book for schools and provided many conundrums in spelling, such as "Ke-ren hap-puch". It was accepted by all as the universally recognized authority, and the fundamental difficulties which we feel acutely did not require to be argued. At the end of the period Porteous, Bishop of London 1787–1809, put out a manual of Evidences for the use of those confirmed in his diocese, which showed appreciation of the fact that the authority of the Bible was no longer unchallenged.

The Book of Common Prayer needed no justification. It was the

[1] See "An Evangelical Protest" in *Eighteenth Century Piety*.

indispensable companion to the Bible and was treated as virtually inspired. Commentaries and explanations abounded, graded for different classes of readers. Manuals explaining the services taught preparation for Mattins, beginning at home and continued as the family walked to church and entered the sacred building. It was customary to say the prayers with the minister if you could read; people are taught not to do this audibly and to refrain from joining in the Absolution. The evidence for the Daily Office is conflicting, but seems to show that the attendance was better than it is today, especially on Wednesdays and Fridays. The Catechism, especially, was above criticism, and the Society founded by Dr Bray with the primary purpose of establishing Catechetical Schools never faltered in its zealous affection.

This leads us to Confirmation, the methods of preparation for which have been greatly misunderstood. The best of the clergy faithfully followed the directions of the Prayer Book, which says in the rubrics before the Service that the Minister, if he finds baptized persons whom he thinks meet to be confirmed, "shall earnestly move them to prepare themselves to seek God's grace in Confirmation". The responsibility of preparation is put on the candidates, who according to the Prayer Book plan have been carefully catechized. An instructed body of young people is presupposed. How far it was actually found in practice must have varied greatly in different parishes. But the general idea, that the candidates had learned the Catechism by heart and received many instructions as to its implications and that the special preparation must be devotional, was sound enough. The S.P.C.K. manuals give careful instructions on self-examination and repentance, with devotions for use on the actual day. It was the general practice to postpone teaching on Holy Communion until after Confirmation and to give a further manual for that purpose. Baptism, of course, was practically universal and did not require to be defended.

Holy Communion was celebrated fairly frequently in London, where a number of churches had weekly Communions, but was often very rare in country parishes. A number of books called attention to the weekly Communion implied by the Prayer Book. Probably, as one manual suggests, the first Sunday in the month was Sacrament Sunday in many town parishes. There was no objection to the title "Holy Eucharist" or to the word "Altar"; note the S.P.C.K. manual

A Companion to the Altar. Communion was generally inculcated as part of the Christian's duty. During the Service, for which full devotional helps were provided, the chief thoughts which it was urged should fill the mind were renewal of the baptismal covenant and identification with the Crucified Saviour. The Real Presence would presumably not have been denied, but the emphasis lay on the reality of the Gift. Bishop Fleetwood in *The Reasonable Communicant* writes: "After the Consecration, such a divine power and efficacy doth accompany the Holy Sacrament, as makes the bread and wine become the spiritual and mystical Body of Christ." A tract by Isaac Barrow, reissued as late as 1820, says: "We, in the spiritual intention, communicate of his Very Person, being according to the manner insinuated, intimately united to him." The general idea is the application to the soul of the merits of Calvary and the infusion of new life.

As regards Confession and Absolution, the Society circulated the works of Kettlewell (*A Companion for the Penitent* and *The Trial and Judgement of the Soul*), in which they are taught, for generations. In the questions used by the penitent there is an asterisk prefixed to one which is applicable only to a sick man; so an occasional use of Sacramental Confession by the whole is implied as an ideal in the S.P.C.K. books.

Private devotion was taught in many excellent manuals, especially those of Ken, Nelson, and Thomas Wilson. The pious layman was set a very high standard to live up to. The day began with private prayer, Bible study, family prayers, and devotional reading, followed by service in Church if possible. Ejaculatory prayers were taught. At night came family prayers again and private devotion. Intellectual meditation is recommended and there seems to be nothing in the nature of contemplative prayer. Fast days are to be kept, even to the extent of having no food until the evening. Fasting Communion did not present difficulties, when the ordinary morning meal was so sparse. Bishop Fleetwood (died 1723) concludes that light refreshment may be counted as fasting. "I do not suppose that any one makes a full meal in the morning, that is not going to strong labour, much less upon Sunday morning."

A curious feature of the literature to modern eyes is the extent to which it is designed for special classes—sailors, soldiers, farmers, public-house keepers, and, above all, servants, who were very numerous. The different sections of the nation must have been more sharply differentiated by their callings than they are today, in the absence of standardizing factors. But even then a pamphlet addressed "to all seafaring persons against mutiny and piracy" must have been an ineffective weapon for righteousness.

Two sections of the Society's Catalogue during many years were headed "Against Popery" and "Against Enthusiasm". After the collapse of the rebellion of 1745 there was no longer any fear for the Protestant Succession and the demand for anti-Roman literature died down. However, in the last decade of the century there was a considerable influx of French émigrés, including priests and religious, so that the question came to life again. The point mostly made then was the disloyalty of Roman Catholics to civil laws, due to their obeying a higher authority, the Pope. This was particularly reprehensible in view of the "mildness" of our laws and the fact that the severe ones were not enforced. The picture is different from that which we get in our history books of a severe penal code in the pre-police days, but standards are comparative and English law as actually enforced by magistrates was more lenient than that found on the Continent. "Enthusiasm" in its contemporary sense of claiming special gifts of the Holy Ghost, and as exemplified in Whitefield's Journal, could not be expected to appeal to the heirs of the Restoration Settlement, itself a reaction from the woes inflicted by the excessive enthusiasm of the earlier seventeenth century.

7

The Activities of the Society
1704–1800

IN THIS chapter a number of topics are brought together, which illustrate the daily life of the century so far as it affected the working members who formed the inner group of the Society. The main activities are described in separate chapters.

THE SOCIETY'S NAME

For a long time the Society's name alternated between "Promoting" and "Propagating" (Christian Knowledge). Probably the memory of Dr Bray's original scheme to form a congregation *pro propaganda fide* persisted; men familiar with Latin, as all educated men were then, would think in Latin and translate *propaganda* by either word indifferently. The question was not settled definitely until 1709, when on 4 March a form for making a legacy in favour of the Society was discussed. It was approved in the following form: "I A.B. do hereby give and bequeath unto C.D. the sum of — pounds to the interest and on trust, that he do pay the same to the Treasurer for the time being of a Voluntary Society of diverse worthy persons for the Propagation of Christian Knowledge among the Poor for the carrying on of the charitable designs of the said Society." Next month the form was amended by the omission of "worthy" and "among the poor" and the addition of "which first met about the beginning of the year 1699 and now do or lately did hold their weekly meetings on Thursday in Bartlett's Buildings in the parish of St Andrew in Holborne London". However, in May this was altered to "commonly called or known by the name of the Society for Promoting Christian Knowledge", and instructions were given that "Promoting" was always to be used.

86

Henry Newman in 1708 had written to complain that the Society was confused with the Societies for the Reformation of Manners; its designs were to promote Charity Schools and distribute religious literature. Even in 1719 confusion existed in the public mind and an advertisement was therefore inserted in the newspapers, stating that the Incorporated Society for the Propagation of the Gospel in Foreign Parts is concerned only with His Majesty's Dominions in the West Indies and parts adjoining; "the voluntary Society for Promoting Christian Knowledge have for several years past made it one branch of their designs to assist as much as in them lies the Protestant Mission to the East Indies."

The Latin version of the title has varied. The neatest one seems to be that reported on 9 February 1796 as having been engraved on a presentation piece of plate: *Societias ad doctrinam Christianam promovendam constituta.*

CONSTITUTION

In the seventeenth century the State Church had to move cautiously where voluntary action was concerned. There were legal difficulties connected with the collection of funds, the reception of legacies, etc., and some felt that the way out of the difficulty was to procure a Royal Charter for the S.P.C.K. Proposals to this effect were submitted on 18 April 1700, but when the S.P.G. received a Charter, after the pattern of that of the Sons of the Clergy, the matter was dropped.[1] It was brought up again on 21 March 1709, when the example of the Scottish S.P.C.K. led some members to desire Incorporation. The debate is instructive. The points made were these:

1. Legacies may be obtained at present if benefactors will observe the instructions given.

2. The cost would be considerable.

3. "The Society has hitherto remarkably flourished under the conduct and blessing of Divine Providence in their present capacity, and it would look like mistrusting of that good Providence, by which they have subsisted hitherto, to take sanctuary in human supports."

4. "Many humoursome people that now vigorously encourage

[1] See E. McClure, *A Chapter*, pp. 60–2 for the text of the proposals.

Charity Schools in their respective parishes would withdraw their subscriptions if they knew they were secretly animated by any body of men without themselves."

5. There would be many applications for financial help which would have to be refused and the Society would be in danger of seeming a useless body.

6. The work is already being done under the authority of the Church of England; nothing can be added to this.

7. An incorporated body would have to admit notable persons who might be of little use to the Society.

Further, the Society would be hampered in its task of promoting Christian knowledge in any part of the world; "whilst they are not incorporated they are the more obliged to conduct their proceedings by prudence and a circumspect caution to avoid being liable to any complaint." The Inns of Court are great institutions established neither by Acts of Parliament nor by Charters. "The laws of discretion and common sense answer all purposes."

There is an allusion in these reasons to Briefs, Royal Letters Patent authorizing collections in churches for special objects, which the Society at that time thought it was better without. Writing to Sir Thomas Lowther on 27 September 1720, the Secretary said that the Lord Chancellor had given his opinion that there was nothing in point of law to be objected to in the S.P.C.K.'s method of collecting benefactions.

MEMBERSHIP

The Society began as a company of friends, known to one another; it grew by personal recommendation. A new member was proposed at one meeting and elected at the next, provided no objection was raised. This applied even to Bishops. A distinction was drawn between residing members, who living in or near London could be expected to attend meetings (Bishops with their town houses counted as such), and corresponding members who lived in the country. In 1727 "residing" members became known as "subscribing" members; only they could vote for new members by ballot. Loyalty to the reigning monarch and his Government was insisted on. Corresponding members were chosen only after careful inquiry into their personal life and religion, the Bishop concerned being consulted if necessary. Among them may be mentioned John Wesley (1732), George Whitefield, Gilbert White of Selborne (1710), and the Principal of Edinburgh College, with other prominent Church of Scotland men (1708). The Archbishop of Canterbury not having answered, a letter on the subject was sent to the Scotsmen, inviting the honour of having them as members, on the advice of the Bishop of Chichester. Corresponding members, if they found themselves in London, were allowed to attend meetings but not to vote.

The Annual Report for 1789 recounts the expulsion from the Society of the Reverend Walter Frend, Fellow of Jesus College, Cambridge, who at the previous meeting had put into the hands of those present copies of his pamphlet, *First and Second Address to the Inhabitants of Cambridge and its neighbourhood, exhorting them to turn from the false worship of three Persons, to the worship of the one true God.* Frend was Tutor of Jesus College and Vicar of Madingley. In 1787 he became a Unitarian and resigned his living. He was a friend of Malthus, Coleridge, Joseph Priestley, and other well known persons. He was expelled by the College but not deprived of the emoluments of his fellowship. The Vice-Chancellor's Court banished him from the University, a step which was confirmed by the Court of King's Bench. The undergraduates, we are told, were unanimous in his favour.[1]

In 1712 there were 80 residing members, subscribing £2 to £10, 370 corresponding ones, subscribing £1 to £3 3s. The total number of members never increased to much more than double this figure during the remainder of the century.

Meetings of the Society were held in various places: first at Mr Hooke's house, in 1703 at Sion College, from 1704 to 1714 at Mr Shute's house in Bartlett's Buildings; then a room was found for the Secretary in the Middle Temple, where papers were kept, meetings being held at Lincoln's Inn, St Paul's Chapter House, and elsewhere. In 1728 the Society acquired a house in Bartlett's Buildings, where it stayed till 1758, moving across the road to Hatton Garden from that year till 1777, when it returned to Bartlett's Buildings, No.5. Committee meetings were held in various places, often at St Dunstan's Coffee House.

[1] A. Gray, *Jesus College, Cambridge*, pp. 169-80.

A little book, *The Standing Rules and Orders of the S.P.C.K.*, published in 1732 gives a picture of the Society's routine. It met on the first Tuesday of the month at 10 a.m., notice having been sent to all subscribing members, and to corresponding members in or about London. Four made a quorum; if fewer than four they could act as a Committee. (Henry Newman as Secretary was allowed to count as a member of the Governing Body, if required to make a quorum.) No sum exceeding £20 could be voted unless notice of it appeared in the printed summons. A Sub-Committee (or Standing Committee) could be appointed and a Committee for Receipts and Payments, consisting of Archdeacon Denne and two laymen, kept an account of all money transactions.

The Secretary had to make a fair copy of the proceedings and an abstract of all letters received. In another book he kept copies of letters sent to members, etc. All letters were reported to the Society, which gave instructions how they should be answered. The work varied. Occasionally there is a note that no letters have been received; naturally the interest lessened and frequently "no quorum" is reported.

In 1706 it was agreed to hang up a poor box at meetings, to be opened by the Treasurer once a quarter, the first object being the release from prison of poor debtors. In April 1734 the charity money came to £28 16s. 7d., which liberated from the Fleet prison eight persons, including Mary Lucas, who had been there four years for a debt which cost £3 14s. 3d. to discharge. In 1707 it was stated that 7s. to 10s. would usually pay for the discharge of a prisoner after six months' detention. In such cases the original debt had been settled long ago but prison fees kept mounting up and the unfortunate persons could never get straight. In 1756 the Dean and Chapter of St Paul's contributed £10 to the Society for this purpose; it released twenty-two people, including wives and children.

An annual dinner took place at the beginning of the year. Tickets cost 2s. 6d. each and the messenger read 1 Corinthians 13. This was altered in 1720, when his voice was considered too rough and a Charity School boy from St Dunstan's took his place, reading Matthew 25. A century later the dinner had become a much grander affair. Tickets at 15s. 6d. produced £81 15s., ten stewards at five guineas each contributed £52 10s.—and a collection for the poor realized £30 13s. 6d.

FINANCE

Mr Justice Hooke was appointed Treasurer on 16 March 1699, to be succeeded next year by the Reverend Henry Shute, Lecturer of Whitechapel. On his death in 1722 the work was divided between four men: the Reverend R. Mayo took the general designs of the Society and the Arabic Bible; Mr Witham to receive subscriptions; Mr Tillard to receive for packets of literature; and Mr Henry Hoare for the East India Mission. The work was no sinecure, for each Treasurer had physical charge of the money, which had to be accounted for at an annual audit by members of the Society. In 1715 it was agreed that the Treasurer should give a bond for the money he handled. In 1710 £107 15s. was due to the Treasurer and it was ordered that no expenses be incurred until the debt was paid. However, in 1774 Dr Owen resigned the office of Treasurer, the auditors having pointed out that he owed the Society £70. It was decided that he should pay the debt gradually—it had been as large as £217 13s. in April 1773. In February 1775, it was agreed that there was "right intention and integrity on all sides" and "to investigate the matter no further".

Everything was on a small scale. By 1760 investments had reached £9,830, producing an income of £311 8s. In order to get legacies the Clerk to the Prerogative Office was paid 3d. in the £ for legacies up to £40, after that a fee of 10s. 6d. Taking a typical year, 1760–1, we find that general benefactions (not earmarked) amounted to £486, subscriptions to £657; practically all the income went back to members in the form of books at reduced prices.

PUBLISHING POLICY

The close attention given to the Society's publications, which to our eyes seems excessive, must at least have kept up the interest of the meetings. *The Standing Rules and Orders of the Society* . . . gives these regulations. No manuscript may be printed, or book or paper re-printed, unless (1) the general principle is approved; (2) it has been referred to four members, nominated at four successive meetings; (3) it has been passed by ballot at the monthly meeting of the Society. The same procedure applies to any alteration in a printed publication.

The only exception to the rule is Anniversary Sermons preached for the Charity children, or before the S.P.G. or the Societies for the Reformation of Manners.

Rule XII of the Standing Orders ran thus: "That the Society will always decline the intermeddling with such matters as are foreign to their design of Promoting Christian Knowledge." This seems to go back to very early days, when the Society was asked to recommend an officer for a commission in the Guards. It could be interpreted in different ways. In view of the strong prejudice against Roman Catholicism, which was associated in the public mind with the claims of the Stuarts, we are not surprised to find that the meetings were largely concerned before and after 1715 with the growth of Popery and measures to stop it. But the record is contained in the Secretary's rough minute book, not in the final form of the minutes, and little sign of the discussions is seen in the official acts of the Society. All kinds of rumours were reported at the meetings. Members sometimes would buy up the stock of books from two London popish booksellers, presumably to destroy them.

In 1713 the Standing Committee considered that they were debarred from circulating the Gaelic Book of Common Prayer in the Highlands by the late Standing Order "that they will not meddle with controversial books" (the same rule applied to Popery) and asked for a directive from the Society. No doubt, the difficulty, which was overcome, was the supposed affront to the Church of Scotland. In August 1729 the Secretary wrote to the Reverend Mr Paley, of Leeds: "The Society have purposely declined (as foreign to promoting Christian Knowledge) to concern themselves with the controversies between the Established Church and Dissenters except in the instance you mentioned of defending Infant Baptism; the common result of disputes among Protestants being rather a lessening of charity than a conviction of faith."

In two matters the Society took a definite stand. It denounced to the Bishop of London a number of churches in which light airs were played as voluntaries; and, because it affected Charity Schools, felt able to express its view on the posture adopted for the Psalms. Without using "a dictating manner" the Committee expressed its view that "as it is the custom everywhere to stand while the Psalms are read in the Daily Services and in many congregations in London it is constantly

practised particularly at singing at the Sacrament, it is very commend-
able to promote a practice so decent". Clearly, then, by "Psalms" are
meant either the Bible Psalms read at Mattins and Evensong or the
Metrical Psalms, hymns as we call them, and it is difficult to say what
is meant in any given case.

CHURCH AUTHORITY

The Society's tradition has always been to pay extreme deference to
the wishes of the episcopate. The Archbishop of Canterbury appointed
the preacher at the Anniversary service, and all kinds of subjects were
referred to him. The successive Primates took an interest in them all,
especially in the East Indian Mission and Charity Schools; and all
details were approved by the Bishop of London. The diocesan Bishops
also were frequently consulted, for example in the election of corresponding members, if there was any scope for doubt as to their suit-
ability. It was an unusual occurrence when on 28 January 1710 the
Secretary reported that the Archbishop (Tenison) was too busy with
the executorship of his late sister to attend to a matter referred to him.
He, perhaps remembering the censorship over all books exercised by
Lambeth until recently, took special responsibility for the Society's
publications. On 2 January 1709 it was reported that he "had expressed
some resentment that a little book entitled *Further Instruction to those
who have learned the Church Catechism* had been recommended by the
Society to be used in churches", no doubt at catechizing. In September
1728 a deputation was appointed to wait on the Archbishop and
request his opinion of a work, *The Chief Truths of the Christian Religion*.
None the less, in 1718 Archbishop Wake's *Exposition of the Catechism*
had to be considered at four meetings according to the routine.

CONTACTS WITH FOREIGN CHURCHES

A surprisingly large proportion of all the letters, especially those
written by Henry Newman, were addressed to correspondents on the
Continent of Europe. This must have been partly due to Newman's
interests and competence. He disclaims the gift of speaking and writing
Latin "like an angel" and says he knows little of French, Italian,
Spanish, and High Dutch, but he seems to have made Latin drafts of
important letters. However, the chief reason for the numerous contacts

was the nature of the work, which included the Charity Schools (influenced by German models) and the Indian Mission, which involved frequent letters to Germany and Denmark.

Apart from these matters, the S.P.C.K. took a great interest in the Protestant Churches of the Continent. It was a time when Reunion was being seriously discussed, under the auspices of Archbishop Wake. Robert Hales constituted himself a kind of travelling missionary of the Society. The Dutch were difficult to convince that a Society was necessary. Hales visited Hanover, Berlin, and various centres in Switzerland. Relations with Professor Osterwald, Dean of Zürich, were particularly close. On 7 March 1714 the Dean and Pastors of the Sovereignty of Neufchâtel and Valingen wrote to the S.P.C.K.: "All the Reformed Churches ... have their eyes fixed on the Church of England as the bulwark of the Reformation."

There are reports of Charity Schools already set up or about to be in various countries, including Russia. On 30 March 1704 the Society was asked to recommend a book for the education of the Czar's son and at a later meeting they "pitched on *The Whole Duty of Man*".

THE HANOVERIAN SUCCESSION

Mr Hales in 1713 went on behalf of the Society to Hanover to see the future Royal Family. He reported on his interviews with the Elector and Princess Sophia, who were much pleased with the books he brought. He suggested that it would "excite the esteem and love of this illustrious House in regard to the most venerable Society if they should separately or jointly express their zeal for this House". Later he proposed that the Prince be made a member of the S.P.C.K. The Secretary's note on this was: "To thank Mr Hales for his good offices to the Society, and to let him know the reason suggested at the Society why this proposal is not complied with, which is because it might be thought a presumption for a voluntary Society to desire such an honour from the Heir Apparent to the Crown." When George I was proclaimed, and again when he arrived in London, Newman wrote ecstatically to Hales, describing the popular feeling. The enthusiasm of the S.P.C.K. for a not very estimable monarch was due to an instinct of self-preservation: only by the Protestant succession could the country be saved from a Roman Catholic Sovereign, under whom it was anticipated the Society could hardly survive. After the Jacobite rising of 1715 it was felt necessary to safeguard the loyalty of the Society. In August 1716 it was "agreed that, if it shall appear that any residing member has not taken the oaths to His Majesty King George, he be desired to withdraw from the Society, and if it shall appear that any corresponding member has not taken the oaths the Society will hold no further correspondence with him". In October 1735 it was ordered that two members should testify to the loyalty to King George of a subscribing member. As is mentioned elsewhere, strict tests were applied to the masters in Charity Schools, which were suspected of Jacobitism.

PRISONS

One of the activities of the Committee was the provision of religious services in the Marshalsea prison, associated with Dickens's *Little Dorrit*. It was financed by a public appeal. In August 1710 Mr Rawlins, Lecturer at Poplar Church, offered his services as Chaplain for a stipend of £40 a year, and an appeal was drafted. In October he reported that there was no shelter from the weather in the room provided. Those who attend have to pray "whilst others are blaspheming and ridiculing if not cursing them for their religious exercises". The appeal went badly and the salary, which did not cover expenses, was only £15. Rawlins wanted to celebrate the Holy Communion "if the place were in any measure decent enough for the purpose". Mr Arthur Bedford, of Bristol, one of the chief subscribers, offered 12s. each time for a monthly sermon, the preacher to be not under 35 and "a methodical plain preacher and a virtuous man".

SOME GRANTS

A few out of many grants of books may be mentioned.

The King in 1725 presented copies of *The Seaman's Monitor* to 4,773 sailors (out of 14,597 on the Admiralty lists). Mr Dickie, ordained by the Bishop of London for work in Virginia, was given books to the value of £50 (1730). The Reverend Samuel Walker of Truro, applying for books to give to soldiers, said that, having conversed with more than 100, he found not one of them instructed in the Christian religion, owing to lack of catechizing (1757). It was agreed to distribute in London and Westminster 20,000 copies of a pamphlet on *The Approaching Fast* (1776). Later, at the request of the Archbishop, several thousand books were given to the chaplain in charge of 700 convicts going to Botany Bay.

EDUCATION OF ORDINANDS

On 6 December 1763, the Society was informed that "a person of slender fortune" asks if it will accept a legacy in his will "for the benefit of a seminary in a remote diocese, there being at this time in that diocese and in a Corporation town, near the Bishop's Palace therein, a very useful and well conducted theological seminary, which doth credit and service to that poor country, by fitting out from time to time a set of serious and well disposed young men for the Sacred Orders of our Church", men unable to afford a University education. It was agreed that the Society would accept a trust for the purpose. Nothing seems to have come of the project. The identity of the seminary has not been traced.

In the will of the Reverend John Jones, in 1769, was a sum to provide 40s. in prizes "at the said Academy for the Diocese of St Davids", for ordinands; also £5 for Welsh Bibles to be given to the head Tutor for gifts of the Welsh Bible to those preparing to be ministers of Christ's religion, "who do not statedly join with the Church Established", if "in no way addicted to Enthusiasm". This seems to refer to the college at Carmarthen, originally a Unitarian foundation but having always an interdenominational flavour.

In June 1757 it was proposed that the following books be sent to all intending to take Holy Orders, on their taking the B.A. degree (also to the non-University candidates in Wales, and the north and north-west of England per the Bishop): Bull, *Candidate for Holy Order*, Burnett's *Pastoral Care*, Erasmi *Ecclesiastes Primus*, and Stearne, *De Visitatione Infirmorum*. Agreed that such a scheme must be approved by the Archbishops and Bishops before it could be considered by the Society.

MISSIONARY PROJECTS

A pathetic incident occurred in 1721–2, when two "African princes" were "trained" to be missionaries to their own people in Mozambique

(Portuguese East Africa). The story begins with a letter of 18 August 1721 to Dr Wilkins, for the information of the Archbishop. Colonel Towgood took them off the rocks at Cape Corinantes. He asked help from the East India Company, within whose Charter they fell. The Company paid him £500 to reimburse him for his expenditure and was willing to take them to England via Bombay. However the Colonel, who has the character of "a rattle and a rake" and gives a bad impression of Christianity, through the Duke of Chandos got the Africa Company to take them under its protection. They were brought to London and for six months kept like prisoners at the Spread Eagle Inn, Grace Church Street. On 5 October a Captain Sherow brought them to meet the Society. Whether they could return to Africa depended on an agreement being reached between the two Companies, Delagoa Bay being within the territory covered by the East India Company's charter. This difficulty was soon settled by the East India Company's agreeing to leave the matter in the hands of the Africa Company. On 19 October the schoolmaster of Sheldon reported that he had attended the two men as often as he could and Mr Crane, schoolmaster of Dr Bray's London parish, had attended them daily and they seemed to improve very much. In February 1722 the Society agreed to a proposal for sending two discreet persons to Delagoa Bay with the Africans ("princes" is now dropped) "in the same manner as the Malabar Mission is encouraged and that subscriptions be taken for such a purpose". It might be necessary to advance money from the Society's funds. Formal application was made to the Africa Company for leave to send two persons "with passage and suitable accommodation under the protection and at the charge of the Company" (and to return, if necessary, at the Company's expense). Only one person was found to go with the Africans, Marmaduke Penwell, who according to a letter written to the Archbishop on 16 June was unsatisfactory "but the best we could get". The Company asked £20 each for provisions on board.

Some interest was aroused and various donations were reported, including £50 from the Bishop of Chichester and £10 from Lord Perceval. A formal appeal was issued in March.

"Whereas James Macquillan Mussoom and John Chaung Mussoom [the name is a corruption of Mozambique], commonly called the African Princes of Delagoa on the south-east coast of Africa, have expressed an earnest desire to be accompanied in their return home by some person or persons capable of preserving and improving that knowledge in Christianity which they have happily acquired in London, and also of recommending the same to their countrymen, and the Society for Promoting Christian Knowledge being dispos'd to take upon them the care of sending such person or persons as should be found willing and qualify'd to go on such an errand to Delagoa if means could be rais'd for affording a suitable support to such persons. We under writing, out of a hearty desire to propagate the light of the Gospel into those dark regions of the earth, and in hopes that it may please God to bless an endeavour promising so great a harvest for his glory, agree to contribute annually the sums against our names subscrib'd, towards supporting such person or persons as now or hereafter may be sent to Africa for propagating the Gospel."

The list of stores sent with the missionary includes garden seed, 400 pens, 2 razors, 1 hour glass, 1 coffee mill, and the following books: 3 Wake's *Church Catechism*, 3 Gastrel's *Christian Institutions*, 1 Portuguese Dictionary, 1 Mortimer's *Husbandry* (2 vols.), 1 Perpetual Almanack, 1 Treatise of Eclipses for 26 years. A letter to the Archbishop later in the year says that the elder African died at sea, after curious behaviour due to disorder in the head. The story is completed by a letter to the Bishop of London (8 January 1740), enclosing Marmaduke Penwell's Journal for 1722–3. He "was sent thither as a catechist to inform the Society what might be done in that part of Africa for the service of Christianity, under the influence of the two pretended African princes. Penwell was a plain illiterate man as his journal will show, but honest and well recommended to the Society". He returned to England in 1723 and entered the service of the Africa Company.[1]

After this experience we are not surprised to read that the offer made in 1768 of a substantial sum with which to start a mission in

[1] This is the story as told in the S.P.C.K. records. It is supplemented by H. P. Thompson, *Thomas Bray*, pp. 93 f. The Africans had been enticed on board by a trader, who took them to Jamaica, where he sold them as slaves. Later, a Mr Bowles bought them, and eventually they reached England. They were put in the charge of a Captain Sherraw (*sic*) who lived in Bray's parish, and given a "princely education" at the cost of the Africa Company. Bray intervened and insisted that they be given Christian instruction and learn the practical arts of building, etc. When the surviving African reached Delagoa he deserted Penwell and went to his mother's home.

China led to no action. In 1767 a clergyman who wished to go as a missionary to the South Sea Islands at his own expense applied to be put on the Society's list of missionaries. He was recommended by Sir Joseph Banks, who promised to contribute £100 yearly plus a gratuity of £100 on his return. The Society was asked to find £50 a year and a gratuity of £100 on his return. The proposals were accepted, provided on inquiry he was satisfactory. Nothing more is recorded about the matter.

SIDELIGHTS ON CHURCH LIFE

The Society's correspondence abounds in references to contemporary conditions, from which a few extracts may be of interest.

On 23 January 1720 the Secretary writes to the Archbishop of Canterbury (Wake): "Don Emanuel of Minorca will be glad of the honour of waiting on your Grace; I have taken the liberty to tell him nobody expects an invitation from your Grace, to whom all mankind have free access." A very different picture from that sometimes drawn of proud Georgian prelates.

In 1795 the Society agreed to help pay for the erection of Christ Church, Walcot, Bath. The ground floor was to be free, the galleries to be let at such rents as would pay all outgoings, including the salaries of Minister, Clerk, and Sexton, also ground rent. The S.P.C.K. asked that the names of its three Treasurers be added to the list of Trustees. The church was opened on 7 November 1798, and was described as "the first attempt made in England of late years to provide free accommodation for the working classes and poor".[1]

A Mr Disney wrote from Lincoln on 31 October 1719. The Lord Chancellor has given him the living of Kirby-on-Bain, Lincs. The fees for the seals are these: The Secretary £5 16s. 6d., his clerk 10s., the King's stamps £4, the great seal £3 18s. 6d., private seal £2 6s. 6d., the Chancellor's porter 5s. If the living exceeds £50 a year, then these extra fees are charged: My Lord's two gentlemen £2 2s., the seal-bearer £1 1s., two sealers 10s., engrossing the patent £2 2s., the engrosser's clerk 10s. In all £16 16s. 6d. plus £6 5s.

A number of letters illustrate conditions in the provinces. The Reverend A. Pimlowe, Rector of Great Dunham, Norfolk (5 April

[1] S. D. Major, *Notabilia of Bath*, p. 69.

1740): neglect of the Lord's Day is due to the custom of paying wages on Sunday morning, so that the labourers go to the public houses for change; also the numerous fairs are a hindrance to religion, for everyone gives up work and goes to other villages, where every house sells liquor. Mr Carpenter, Rector of Sheldon (11 May 1741): there have been no converts to Popery lately in the Birmingham area. "At Birmingham their Presbyterian minister is a hot and zealous Arian and Socinian; he both preaches and prints his heretical opinions and they have spread very much". "The Freethinkers there are chiefly among the Bankers' and Attorneys' clerks." The Reverend James Cranston of Hastings (24 March 1713): of 5,000 in the parish not more than ten are Dissenters. He seldom has a congregation of less than 2,000 on Sundays; he catechizes 200 to 300 children every Wednesday and Friday. The Reverend John Hutton writes from Standford, Berkshire, in December 1709: The children are backward in coming to catechizing in church, so he catechizes them every Saturday afternoon and gives them his tithe fruit; "the effect is that the children come in good numbers and learn with eagerness and emulation". Mr John Tatam, near Derby, writes (27 February 1710): Mr Arnold Wilson and he succeeded in getting the Mayor to put off the market fixed for Good Friday and require the shops to close; congregations were larger than ever before.

SIDELIGHTS ON SOCIAL HISTORY

The Secretary was frequently asked to procure lottery tickets for members of the Society. In 1740 Henry Newman received tickets from the Bishop of London to be sent to his seven Commissaries in America and the West Indies. In the same year he wrote to a Mr Gibb (26 January) to say that his tickets "came up blank and you are among the benefactors to our bridge (Lambeth, which was built of the proceeds of a lottery), for which posterity will be indebted to you and your lady".

On 13 September 1708 Mr Bedford wrote from Bristol to say that the players had been driven out of the liberties of the city, the justices of Gloucestershire having made an order that no plays should be acted in the county. The Society was much concerned with the health of missionaries and schoolmasters. On 19 April 1720 the Secretary described a remedy. "To cure an ague. The late Bishop of Ely (Patrick) advised. Take ½ dozen cobwebs, roll them into a pill with sugar, and give it to the patient an hour before the fit." Servants are abundant, owing to the importation of French, Irish, Swiss, and Indians (1737). No ships are allowed to leave the Thames till the King's press for the Navy is finished. "Coals are three guineas a chaldron and hard to come at in the river by reason of the ice." (29 January 1740.) An officer named Hudson writes from Houndsditch to say that he has had the courage to prosecute a soldier before the Provost Marshall for profanity, a thing that has not been done for many years. He was sentenced to be loaded with firelocks on his shoulders and to parade in front of the whole regiment with the particulars of his crime placarded on him.

RELIGIOUS SOCIETIES

A few references from the Society's records to these bodies may suggest to someone a line of research: they are arranged in chronological order.

1700. Agreed to help Religious Societies that want advice through the "agent for schools"—evidently this refers to their work for Charity Schools.

Correspondents to urge clergy and laity to form Societies "to promote the designs of this Society".

Agreed to circulate "Mr Wesley's Letter in vindication of the Religious Societies".

An Account of the Societies to be sent to all Correspondents.

500 copies of the Account to be sent to the Bishop of Worcester.

Agreed to keep in contact with the Societies.

A Committee appointed to inspect the proceedings of the Religious Societies.

Agreed to inform the stewards of the Societies that in the opinion of the S.P.C.K. they should co-operate with the Societies for the Reformation of Manners by giving information.

The Bishop of Chester has started a number of Societies.

1701. A Committee of Divines appointed to inspect the Orders of the Religious Societies in order to answer objections laid against them.

1703. Letter from the Bishop of Bath and Wells concerning the opposition met with in Wells by a Religious Society.

1708. The Society having discussed Training Schools for teachers, it was decided "that the Religious Societies have hitherto furnished the Charity Schools in and about London with discreet masters at far less charge, and to better satisfaction, than by any other method that has been try'd".

1704. A letter from Gittisham, Devon, refers to a Society of Clergymen who meet in their houses by turn to confer about the duties of the ministry, beginning with prayers in church.

The subscribers to St Michael's School, Bristol, have formed themselves into a Society which meets once a fortnight.

A letter from Bristol says that the clergy are too much divided to make a Religious Society possible.

1755. Mr Gawthorpe writes from Ripley: thirty persons have formed a Religious Society, which meets every Saturday night in his house; also at four distant houses on Tuesday, Thursday, and Friday, and on Saturday nights in the church.

Finally, a letter dated 20 January of this year refers to the Bishop of Oxford's sermon at the Anniversary of the Religious Societies.[1]

---

[1] Probably information about the organization at this later date is in print somewhere, but I have not been able to find it.

8

Foreign Literature

"FOREIGN" literature is used in the sense of "non-English", being a convenient term employed by the S.P.C.K., though it is an unsuitable description for the languages of the British Isles, with which we begin.

I. THE BRITISH ISLES

Welsh. As we have seen in connection with education, Wales was very near to the heart of the founders of the Society, and in fact during the eighteenth century Wales and South India were the fields in which its funds were mainly spent. Yet the popular impression is that it was negligent, at least so far as the Bible in Welsh was concerned. An Anglican Church historian[1] wrote in these terms. The S.P.C.K. in 1787 refused to part with more than 500 copies, at a prohibitive price. In 1791 it offered to print 10,000 if the sale of 4,000 was guaranteed. "It was not till 1799, twelve years after the question was first raised, that the Society for Promoting Christian Knowledge issued editions of the Bible, New Testament, Prayer Book, and New Version of the Psalms in Welsh." It then refused to print any more. A little girl, Mary Jones, saved up her pence and walked thirty miles over the hills to buy a Bible, only to find that none was obtainable.

The facts may have been as stated, though that a book is not to be obtained is not rare now and must have been a frequent occurrence a century and a half ago. But the story has a very different aspect when told in full. It begins with the S.P.C.K.'s ordering an edition of 10,000 copies of the Bible in 1714 from Basket, the King's Printer, who with

[1] F. Warre Cornish, *A History of the Church of England in the Nineteenth Century*, I, 37.

the approval of the Welsh Bishops was printing an edition.[1] The copies were delivered in 1716, from which date until 1804 the Welsh Bible was apparently always to be had from the Society, if the Annual Reports are to be trusted. This does not exclude the possibility of its being "out of stock" sometimes. In 1743 the Society ordered an edition of 15,000, which was delivered in 1748, "This impression, large as it was, fell exceedingly short of the universal demand that was made on it." Another 15,000 were ordered in 1752, and 5,000 New Testaments. In 1768 a book with larger print and marginal references was published in a 20,000 edition, which used up all the available money and left a debt of £2,000 to be recouped in part out of sales. A further edition of 10,000 followed in 1799. These were the Society's private enterprises, carried out so far as funds would allow; they were dependent on getting sufficient support from the public. The responsibility of keeping Welsh Bibles in print rested with the Privileged Presses, who possessed the monopoly and from whom the Society would buy when its editions were sold out. Real hardship accrued to the poor people of Wales when S.P.C.K. cheap editions were unobtainable. The 1726 Report states that the Bible with the Prayer Book was sold at 3s. 6d., the New Testament with Prayer Book at 2s., all orders being carriage paid. In the 1800 Report we read that the selling price was half the cost of printing in sheets. The Bible with Prayer Book and Psalms (metrical), bound in calf, was priced at 2s. 9d. (binding alone costing 2s.), the New Testament in calf at 6d. Earnest appeals were made that no one should make a profit by adding to the price. So far back as 1741 we find Griffith Jones writing to say that 15s. was being charged for a Bible.

The real causes of the B.F.B.S.'s taking the place of the S.P.C.K. as the chief distributor of cheap Bibles were two. First, the Society was

[1] Those interested in business details may like to know the estimate: Composition £375, Printing £375, Paper £975, Binding £500—£2,225 in all, about 4s. 5½d. a copy. The S.P.C.K. Appeal in 1713 was entitled "Proposals for reprinting the Holy Bible and Common Prayer Book in the British or Welsh Tongue, in Octavo". It referred to more than 500 parishes where most of the people speak only Welsh, to their deep poverty, and to the great desire for Bibles —people "would even pawn the implements of their houses, or even their clothes, to purchase them"; also to 6,000 Welsh in Pennsylvania, etc., who demanded Bibles. The octavo Bible was to follow the text of the Oxford folio book of 1702.

perennially handicapped by lack of funds and in justice to other claims could not press the provision of Welsh Bibles at the expense of these; it lacked the driving force of a society devoted to one object alone. Secondly, the strict Anglicanism of the S.P.C.K. must have stood in the way of its appeal to a Wales which was by now predominantly nonconformist. The Society's leaders looked on the Bible as the indispensable companion of the Prayer Book, which was its authorized interpreter, and therefore concentrated on the provision of a Bible which included the Apocrypha and was bound up with the Prayer Book and the Metrical Psalms, making a very cumbrous book. Griffith Jones in 1717 wrote to tell of the dislike of the Bible's being unobtainable apart from the Prayer Book. So far as the Apocrypha went, the Society's position was that it must be printed and that, if it were not taken by purchasers, the stock would remain unsold.

The S.P.C.K. continued to print the Welsh Bible for a long time. In 1808 an edition of 10,000 cost £2,288. The 1828 Report quotes from a pamphlet about the claims of the S.P.C.K. "So far has its forebearance gone that its very existence is unknown even to many of the Established Church"; it had been outpaced in this field by the Bible Society but continued to spend largely without public gratitude. In 1839 it yielded to the inevitable and decided that the Apocrypha be not included with the Welsh Bible except on application.

The first Welsh Prayer Book was published in 1567, edited by the four Welsh Bishops and the Bishop of Hereford, in whose diocese Welsh was largely spoken. The first S.P.C.K. edition was in 1727. When the Welsh Church was disestablished in 1919 the Privileged Presses lost their exclusive right to print its vernacular Prayer Book, which had become a financial liability rather than an asset, for it had to be sold at prices corresponding to those of the comparable English editions, of which much larger editions were printed. Up to the time of writing the Church in Wales has not produced its own revised Prayer Book.

A fair amount of other religious literature in Welsh has been published by the S.P.C.K., which in 1701 sent its correspondents a list of 37 books and pamphlets, to which it added steadily. The work has had to contend with difficulties arising out of uncertainty as to the form of the language, on which North and South Wales[1] were not always

---

[1] An early eighteenth-century correspondent from the South wrote to say "send no more North Wales books, we can't understand them".

agreed, and the fact that Welsh literature has always been predominantly poetical and devotional, those who appreciate theology preferring to read it in English.

Manx.[1] The Celtic language of the Isle of Man was first reduced to writing in the reign of James I. Though practically the same as Irish and Gaelic, it was made to look very different owing to unskilful transcription. The first translation of the Prayer Book was finished by Bishop John Philips in 1611 but remained in manuscript until 1895, when it was printed for philological reasons. Thomas Wilson, Bishop of Sodor and Man 1697–1755, said that it was "of no use to the present generation"; the clergy preferred to translate into the vernacular as they read from the English Prayer Book. The S.P.C.K. took up the matter in 1762, sending Bishop Hildesley (who was responsible for the new version) £100 with which to print parts of the Bible and Liturgy. Subscriptions were raised, Cambridge University sending £48 16s. 6d., of which Trinity College gave £21, and the New Testament and the Prayer Book were printed by the Society in 1765, the Old Testament following later. The Society presented 1,500 copies of the Prayer Book with fifty large size copies for use in church by the clergy. In place of the prayer for Parliament was one for the House of Keys, and for the Lord and Lady of the Isle. Other editions followed, including one of 5,000 copies in 1808, sold at one-third of the cost price. In 1804 the Bishop's request for 5,000 Bibles, to cost £2,562, was refused for lack of funds. In 1825 the Bishop wrote to say that the Bible and Prayer Book were no longer required, since the teaching of Manx was forbidden by Act of Parliament; however, at the request of the next Bishop the Prayer Book was reprinted in 1837 for the benefit of people over 50, after whose death he said Manx would become a dead language.

Irish. The first edition of the Book of Common Prayer in Irish was printed in 1608, before which date the Latin version had been used. The completion of the first S.P.C.K. edition was reported in 1712, the Catechism being sold separately; the book was announced as being for Ireland and Scotland. Various editions of the Bible and Prayer

---

[1] See for Manx and other versions of the Prayer Book W. Muss-Arnoldt's massive work of learning, *The Book of Common Prayer among the Nations of the World*, 1914.

Book followed; among them we may note that of 1820, the printing of which caused great difficulty, for the Oxford and Cambridge University Presses refused the work and when at last a London printer was found he abandoned the work half-way through the Old Testament, the corrector having refused to continue and no one being found to take his place. Eventually the printing was transferred to the University of Dublin Press. The 1822 Report says that the reprints of both books were for the benefit of the Irish poor in London as well as for Ireland itself. An Irish-English edition was published in 1832 and reprinted in 1861.

Gaelic. The Gaelic language, still spoken in parts of the Highlands of Scotland, early attracted the notice of the S.P.C.K., which contributed generously towards the production of the Liturgy (1793) and the Bible (1803). The former was several times revised and reissued during the nineteenth century.

French. The first Prayer Book of Edward VI (1549) was apparently at once translated into French for the use of the King's subjects in the Channel Isles and Calais (1551), though no copy is extant. It was revised in 1550 to conform to the text of the Second Prayer Book. This edition was used during Mary's reign by the English exiles at Frankfurt and with the Latin version was the source of the foreign reformers' knowledge of the Prayer Book. Further editions were put out in 1616 (of the James I book) and in 1665 (of the 1662 Book), the latter becoming the authorized version. The S.P.C.K. in 1720 sent 200 copies for use in the Ambassador's Chapel in Paris. The Society's first edition appeared in 1839, after revision by the clergy of Jersey and Guernsey. In a slightly altered form the book was reissued for French-speaking congregations elsewhere, which were found in Mauritius, the Seychelles Islands, and Quebec.[1] The Bible version to be used presented difficulties. The 1835 Report says that four different versions were used in the Channel Isles and ten among French Protestants. In 1841 *Seigneur* was substituted for *Éternel* as a rendering of "the Lord" in the Old Testament. An S.P.C.K. version of the New Testament appeared in 1840, of the Old in 1849, it being stated that it was not for

[1] In the eighteenth century there were a good many French immigrants into England, who conformed to the Church of England when they were in groups too small to form Huguenot congregations, and who for some time demanded French Prayer Books.

Jersey or Guernsey, each of which had its own version. There were several reprints later.

A curious controversy arose towards the end of the first world war. Some Army Chaplains objected to God's being addressed as *tu* instead of *vous*, the normal Catholic form, which seemed to stamp the Church of England as Protestant; it was irreverent to *tutoyer* God. The Society refused to make a change, which would indeed have been unacceptable to the users of the book. Hymn books and small devotional books have often been published by S.P.C.K. There is little scope for other books, since those capable of profiting by Anglican theology either prefer to read it in English or, as in the case of ordinands and clergy in French-speaking dioceses such as Madagascar and the Gambia, are too few in number to provide a sufficient demand. Little notice was taken of Bishop Luscombe's appeal from Paris in 1836, asking the Society to promote "the religious improvement of France, by means of translations of standard English theological books".

In the present century there has been some output of small popular booklets, both religious and educational, for use by missions in Africa and in the Pacific. The Book of Common Prayer continues to be reprinted for use in Canada, Mauritius, Madagascar (with State Prayers for the President of France instead of the English Sovereign), and elsewhere, but the present translation is still not entirely satisfactory.

From 1934 until the fall of France cut off its main public *Oecumenica*, a quarterly review intended to provide not only information about the Anglican Communion but an organic link between Anglicanism and "the vast world of French-speaking Christians", was published under the auspices of the Church Assembly Council for Foreign Relations. *Bulletin Anglican*, a similar venture but on a smaller scale and without official backing, was taken over by the S.P.C.K. in 1954, but had to be given up after three years for lack of support.

2. OTHER EUROPEAN LANGUAGES

The development of publishing in Continental languages was due to the setting up of a Foreign Translation Committee in 1834 with a mandate to superintend and promote publication and circulation of the Bible and the Liturgy of the Church of England. The Archbishop nominated twenty-seven members, to which the diocesan Bishops were added *ex officio*; Dr Pusey, Professor of Hebrew at Oxford, was one of the original members. Hitherto the General Meeting had dealt with all proposals in this connection, which indeed formed an important part of the Society's work. Later, when applications arrived asking for other books, they were sent to the Standing Committee to deal with, accompanied by the recommendations of the Translation Committee. The two Literature Committees, Tract and General, published in foreign languages to a small extent, confining themselves to translations of books for which they were responsible. In 1855 the Foreign Translation Committee's accounts were ordered to be kept separately, and in 1884 its powers were enlarged so that it could undertake any work required by the Bishops abroad. Finally, in 1920 its name was changed to Foreign Literature Committee in recognition of the fact that original works had become at least as important as translations.

Considerable interest was aroused by the inauguration of the new Committee and in the following year (1835) the existence of a number of local associations to raise funds for its work was reported. The enthusiasm was no doubt caused, so far as Bibles were concerned, by the desire that the Church's own Bible Society, and not a new inter-denominational one, should do the work. The Society went its own way and references to the B.F.B.S. are seldom found; in any case mixed responsibility was to be avoided. There was also the problem of the Apocrypha. Its inclusion was rare, but the Society did not like its exclusion to be enforced. The policy adopted by the Translation Committee in 1837, with the approval of the Archbishop, was, if the Apocrypha was included, to print it in different type and to paste inside the cover a translation of the relevant words of the sixth of the Thirty-nine Articles. As time went on the Society's funds proved inadequate to meet the strain of independent Bible-publishing and it tacitly withdrew from the field. Wherever possible the B.F.B.S. versions were produced by representative Committees, on which Anglican missionaries, if available, served. The Society frequently published books containing lessons from the Apocrypha, and in some cases individual books in full or even the whole Apocrypha. No one seems to have raised the question of the authority attaching to the Anglican definition of the Apocrypha.

Prayer Books stood on a different footing. No one disputed the S.P.C.K.'s claim to be the Prayer Book Society of the Church of

England. After 1815 the national prestige stood very high and Anglicans believed that their Liturgy had only to be known to be appreciated, or even adopted, by other nations. District Committees were formed on the Continent to promote the sale of S.P.C.K. books, notably Bibles and Prayer Books, and considerable success was achieved. It was a pre-critical period and Prayer Books, without note or comment, were expected to do their beneficent work in the same way as Bibles.

Latin. The Act of Uniformity of 1662 allows the use of the Latin Prayer Book in the Universities, in the Colleges of Westminster, Winchester, and Eton, and in the Convocations; the Latin sermon still preached at the opening of Convocation carries on the tradition in part. This was an obvious provision at a time when Latin was commonly understood by educated men. Though there have been many versions, the S.P.C.K. has never published one of its own, being content to buy and put on its list editions of other publishers. An unsuccessful attempt to produce a new translation illustrates the difficulties of the task. In 1864 Dr Jacobson, Regius Professor of Divinity in the University of Oxford, agreed to make a translation, for which he wanted no remuneration. On his becoming Bishop of Chester in 1865 he relinquished the work and Dr Stubbs, then Librarian of Lambeth Palace Library, was invited to take his place. However, he could not agree to make the Psalter conform to the Prayer Book Version; he might be willing to substitute readings from the Old Latin, or from Jerome's version from the Hebrew, for Vulgate ones, but would not make his own translations; Jacobson had said that the distinctive character of the English Psalter should be preserved. Stubbs was unwilling to eliminate *sacerdos* from the Ordination Service but would use *presbyter* for the order, keeping *sacerdos* for the minister. Jacobson's line was that *presbyter* in the Scottish Prayer Book of 1637 satisfied Laud and should be kept. Other scholars who were consulted advised that any divergence from the Prayer Book in what purported to be an exact translation would be dishonest. The Committee deferred the matter in view of the difficulties and no further action ensued.

Greek. In the early eighteenth century England had many business contacts with the Turkish Empire, and the Society's attention was naturally drawn to the Near East. In 1708 Mr S. Hayward wrote from

Zante to say he had been distributing New Testaments in "vulgar Greek" and asking for a further supply. "I am mightily tormented by these bearded ignorant priests"; "they say it is a gift from heaven, now they have the light of the Gospel to know what they read in their churches".

By the Peace of 1814 the Ionian Islands came under British protection, and the Church of England began to take an interest in Greece, which was still under Turkish rule. A preacher at the Society's Anniversary Service, Dr W. S. Goddard, late Headmaster of Winchester College (see Report for 1819–20), said: "Look at Greece, or even Italy . . . what a wretched spectacle these countries now present of imbecility, and sloth, and ignorance, and sensuality."

A translation of the Prayer Book into Modern Greek, made by A. Calbo, of Zante, was included in Bagster's Polyglot edition of 1821. In 1840 the Society sent its Secretary, George Tomlinson, on a visit to the Near East to ascertain how it could render assistance. On his advice it was agreed to print the Greek Old Testament (the Septuagint), the New Testament in Modern Greek, and if possible Eusebius' Ecclesiastical History and the Homilies of St Chrysostom; the books to be printed in Athens and sold at a very low price or else given away. Of this programme only the Septuagint and the Homilies were put in hand. An independent edition of the Prayer Book had been already produced by the Society in 1839. Mr Tomlinson in 1842 was consecrated first Bishop of Gibraltar and was able to arrange for distribution of the books through the Holy Synod of Greece, which in 1846 received 1,500 copies of the first two volumes of the Septuagint and 500 of Chrysostom. Its Secretary's becoming Bishop of Gibraltar helps to account for the great interest taken by the Society in spreading knowledge of the Anglican way of worship on the Continent. Prayer Book and Bible both were criticized. The Prayer Book was condemned for its use of the word *hiereus* for priest instead of *presbyteros*. It was replied that *hiereus* was the commonly understood term for a Christian minister. The Septuagint controversy was more serious. Codex Alexandrinus had been printed and the Apocryphal portions of Daniel and Esther appeared in the midst of the canonical books. That they were clearly distinguished by the printing was not deemed a sufficient explanation, and a new edition was therefore put in hand, to be "free from all objections" and to be printed in England instead of

Athens. This eventually appeared in four volumes, edited by Dr F. Field. St Chrysostom seems to have been edited by Dr Pusey, who in 1860 urged the S.P.C.K. to buy 1,000 copies of a further volume, which it felt unable to do.

In 1923 the S.P.C.K. published the definitive edition of the Prayer Book in Greek—neither ancient nor modern but ecclesiastical. The translation was made by Greeks under the direction of Dr F. E. Brightman.

Danish. An edition of 2,250 Danish Prayer Books was printed for prisoners of war in 1808, i.e., their own Lutheran Book.[1] The S.P.C.K. translation of the English Prayer Book was published in 1849 and several editions followed. The object was to provide for Danish and Norwegian Sailors in Hull, who it was expected would take them home and stimulate a demand. The book proved useful in the Danish West Indian islands of St Croix and St Thomas, also in Canada, where many immigrants to New Brunswick became Anglicans in 1876.

Dutch. Archbishop Laud insisted that Dutch and Walloon immigrants should conform to the Church of England and therefore arranged for a Dutch translation, which was published in 1645, the year after his execution. The S.P.C.K. took up the subject in 1710, with a view to the needs of the Dutch in New York (which had been ceded to Britain in 1665) and produced a Dutch-English edition in 1711. A copy was left at Lambeth Palace, when Archbishop Tenison was ill. When he recovered he examined the book and on 22 June the Society, owing to his intervention, rescinded an order to send 500 copies to New York. On 19 July the Archbishop's criticisms were sent to the Society. Socinian influences had been at work, so that in the Preface for Trinity Sunday the words "without any difference or inequality" were omitted. Also the Ordinal was omitted. Tenison was gentle in his dealings with the problem: the mistake might have been due to lack of thought, he would subscribe towards the cost of a true edition. He ordered the erring edition to be burned, an order carried out in February 1716 in the kitchen of Lambeth Palace.[2] The new edition

---

[1] Not, as Allen and McClure's History, p. 206, might suggest, a translation of the English book. Frequent grants of Swedish and Finnish Bibles and Prayer Books were also made to the Swedish pastor in London for distribution to seamen in the British Service, stated in 1811 to number 5,000.

[2] E. F. Carpenter, *Thomas Tenison*, pp. 309 f.

was issued in 1718. A revised edition appeared in 1838, made by Dr Bosworth, English Chaplain in Holland, in 1858 Professor of Anglo-Saxon in the University of Oxford. According to the S.P.C.K. records it was revised by eight Dutchmen in the newly legalized form of the language; no doubt they worked under Bosworth's direction. Later editions of the book and a Dutch Bible (1843) continued to be printed for South Africa, until in the twentieth century Afrikaans gradually replaced Dutch as an official language in that country. The Society still has a Dutch hymnal in print, which was in use there as well as the Prayer Book, as late as the 1940s.

German. If the close connection of England and Holland in the reign of William III favoured the Society's interest in a Dutch Prayer Book, we should expect much more importance to have been attached to a German one. However, although members of the Society were concerned, the actual production was due to Frederick I of Prussia and his Chaplain Jablonski, who cherished the plan of uniting the two Protestant Churches, Lutheran and Reformed, on an episcopal basis and with a liturgy similar to the English Prayer Book. The translation was published at Frankfurt on the Oder in 1704 and copies were sent to Queen Anne, who acknowledged hers suitably, and to Tenison, Archbishop of Canterbury, who remained silent. It had been supposed that he did not relish the part played by Archbishop Sharp of York, in the preliminary negotiations.[1] Another version appeared in London in 1707 for the German Lutheran churches, which later in the century numbered six, and a German-English book in Dublin (1710), intended for Protestant refugees from the Palatinate who had settled in Ireland. The first S.P.C.K. edition was in 1845; it and its successors were meant primarily for the first generation of German immigrants in British Colonies. The Society had to settle the controversial question, whether in the Creed "Catholic Church" should be translated as *katholische* or *allgemeine Kirche.* Dr Littledale's *Plain Reasons against joining the Church of Rome* (1882) was thought to be an unsuitable book for the Society to produce in German but was justified as being asked for by the Old Catholics. The Society's German Bible followed Luther's text.

Italian. Littledale's book was also produced in Italian as well as in

---

[1] See A. Tindal Hart, *The Life and Times of John Sharp, Archbishop of York,* pp. 261 f.

French (both in 1881), in spite of objections by members to "stirring up schisms in other Churches". The Committee had made a valiant effort to make Anglican theology known in Italy, publishing the first Homily in 1856, Jewel's *Apology* (1853), Bull's *Corruptions of the Church of Rome* (1864), besides tracts for navvies (1853). Depots were opened in Milan and Naples (1862) and educational books were exhibited in Turin (1863); in the latter year a special fund was opened for Italian literature. However, in 1859 the Committee refused the request of the Archbishop of Dublin to produce Whateley's *Evidences* for Italian soldiers visiting Irish ports. Earlier attempts to circulate the Bible and the Prayer Book had met with success. The 1853 Report says that the Bible "promises ... to be a powerful instrument for the diffusion of Scriptural light and truth among Italian readers"; one of the charges brought "against the Tuscan confessors of the Lord Jesus" was that they possessed copies of the S.P.C.K. Bible. Large numbers of the New Testament were distributed to the Sardinian soldiers in the Crimea (1858 Report). The Prayer Book had a wide circulation in Piedmont and among the Vaudois (Reports of 1860, 1861; the 1862 Report says that the Prayer Book is an example to Italians of how to reform their Church).

The first translation of the Prayer Book was said to have been made by Bedell, Bishop of Kilmore, when he was Chaplain to the English Ambassador at Venice (1607–10). He died in 1642 and the book, which probably owed something to his initiative, was published in 1685, edited by Edward Browne of Clare College, Cambridge. The first S.P.C.K. edition was in 1841.

Maltese. This is a Semitic language, akin to Arabic. Thanks to the initiative of Bishop Tomlinson, the S.P.C.K. financed editions of the Prayer Book (1845) and the New Testament (1848).

Polish. In 1853 the Society distributed the New Testament, in roman script, in Silesia; also a Polish edition of Whateley's *Evidences*.

Portuguese. As is narrated elsewhere,[1] the early S.P.C.K. missionaries to South India did some publishing in the Portuguese patois spoken there. The first Prayer Book in the correct language produced by S.P.C.K. seems to have been published in 1844, and to have been a revision of the book put out by the East India Company in 1695. In 1861 the

[1] P. 65.

Society decided to leave future editions to the American Episcopal Church, which had missions in Brazil.

Russian. Except for a few tracts and a small book of prayers published in 1942 for Russian-speaking Canadian Servicemen, nothing has been done in this language. In 1835 a translation of the Prayer Book was received; the 1838 Report says that printing had been suspended because the difficulties in the way of circulation had become apparent.

Serbian. When in 1915 Serbia was overrun by the Austrian army, those who escaped, both military and civil, became the special responsibility of Britain. A remarkable priest, Father Nicolai Velimirovitch (afterwards a bishop, who died in America in 1956), persuaded the S.P.C.K. to produce service books for the religious needs of the exiles. One of these service books was reprinted for use in Yugoslavia just after the end of the 1939–45 war, but political conditions making this impossible, was distributed to refugees.

Spanish. As early as 1710 the publication of Spanish tracts was urged, but no action seems to have been taken. In 1826 we find Blanco White reporting that the Spanish translation of Paley's *Evidences of Christianity* is unsatisfactory. In the same year a number of small educational books in Spanish and English (also in French and English) were sanctioned for the West Indies. The whole Bible was published in 1862, following several editions of the New Testament. The scheme was announced in 1856 as providing a version translated from the Hebrew and Greek, not from the Vulgate; reference was made to the toleration existing in Spain. The first Spanish edition of the Prayer Book was published at the cost of John Williams, afterwards Archbishop of York, in the reign of James I, to enlighten Spanish public opinion at the time when a marriage was proposed between Prince Charles and the Infanta of Spain. The S.P.C.K. interest was stirred by the Protestant congregations that met in Gibraltar, for whose benefit an edition was first published in 1839. Revisions of this book made by Juan Calderon, a former Francisan priest who became preacher to a congregation of refugees in Somers Town, in London, were brought out in 1852 and 1854. The latter has continued in print until the present day, when it is supplied chiefly for congregations in the care of the South American Missionary Society.

Ukrainian. To complete the chronicle we mention a Ukrainian edition of the Canadian Prayer Book, published by the S.P.C.K. in 1924, for recent immigrants to Canada.

The culmination of the Society's efforts in this field came in 1851, the year of the Great Exhibition. Bishop C. J. Blomfield in his 1850 Charge spoke of the vast influx of foreigners expected. Our duty is to give them a chance "of profiting by the opportunities of the Christian Sabbath", with the help of the Prayer Books provided by the S.P.C.K. in their own languages. Legal difficulties prevented the reading of services in languages other than English in consecrated buildings and so, with the help of the S.P.C.K., which provided chaplains, proprietary chapels were used for the purpose. The Society also put out a great many tracts for free distribution to foreigners in Arabic, Dutch, French, German, Italian, Portuguese, Spanish, and Swedish.

3. THE NEAR EAST

When the Society was founded the vast Turkish Empire, in which Christians and Muslims lived side by side, was accessible to English merchants and there was a reasonable expectation that by helping the Christians a bridge might be built and influence brought to bear on Muslims.

Arabic. The first translation of the Prayer Book, made by Edward Pococke, Laudian Professor of Arabic at Oxford and formerly chaplain to the English "Turkish merchants" at Aleppo, was published by the Oxford University Press in 1672. This did not meet with approval in the Levant, and at a meeting of the Society in 1700 proposals were submitted for "the instruction of the Greek Christians" of the Turkish Empire by the publication of something that would give them "the elements of the Christian religion". Not till 1720 did the Society issue an appeal for funds. The programme included 10,000 New Testaments, 6,000 Psalters, 5,000 *Catechetical Instructions* and an edition of *Abridgement of the History of the Bible*, at a cost of about £3,000. The books were distributed through the correspondents and Indian missionaries to Persia, Russia, and India, as well as to the Turkish dominions. This was a large scale undertaking for those days, and details are worth recording. Copy was obtained from Aleppo; that for the Psalter had been corrected by the Patriarch of Antioch. It was necessary to get an assurance from the Lord Chancellor that a private collection might be made without obtaining a Royal Licence. King George I gave a Royal Bounty of £500, the Society paying the requisite fees (£45 12s. 6d.) to officials. The Bishops subscribed liberally, headed by the Bishop of Llandaff (£100), the Archbishop of York (£50), and the Archbishop of Canterbury (20 guineas). The Duke of Bedford gave £50 and the Presbyterian congregation of Nottingham £21 15s. 7d. The preparation of the manuscript and seeing it through the press was entrusted to Mr Solomon Negri, who was paid 9s. 3d. a week for his food, plus 5s. for wine, 2s. for coffee and 1s. for tobacco. The first plan of paying £6 a quarter for his lodging at the printer's house was not satisfactory because of his "weak stomach".

Two estimates for production were received.

	Van de Water, Utrecht £	Palmer, London £
Printing the New Testament	800	933
Freight and customs	60	
Psalter	215	233
	1,075	1,166

Common to both were: expenses of getting copy from Aleppo £50, payment to learned correctors £250, binding the N.T. in calf at 1s. each £400, binding the Psalter £300, contingent charges £125. Paper was not included; the Society would buy it from the stationers, or the printer would include it in his bill. The work was given to the London printer, who agreed to use better and larger type, cast from matrices cut specially by William Caslon. The "learned correctors" may refer to the Reverend Dr Wilkins, Librarian of Lambeth Palace, who agreed to read the final proofs. The Society had difficulty at first with Basket, the King's Printer, who claimed the right to print all Bibles; apparently he was unwilling to get the type desired.

The Society in 1857 produced a new version of the Bible, but when it sold out preferred to leave the field to the Bible Society. Its first Arabic Prayer Book was published in 1850, a revision of one published in Malta (1840). A new edition appeared in 1844, edited by F. A. Klein, the discoverer of the Moabite Stone, and yet another in

1886, revised by Dr Klein. A curious controversy troubled the Society at this period: should "Sacraments" be translated by the Arabic dual or plural? The Committee had various other ventures in publishing, including Bishop Wilberforce's *Agathos and other Sunday Stories* (1854), a selection from the Homilies (1856), and the first eight of the Thirty-nine Articles (1858), the last on the assurance that they would be "perfectly intelligible to Muslims".

After the first world war the C.M.S. in Cairo arranged to hand over its publication department to a newly formed S.P.C.K. for the Near East, with separate Committees for the dioceses of Jerusalem and Egypt, continuing to provide the skilled literary workers and collaborating in distribution. The inspiration of the venture was Canon Temple Gairdner and his friend Miss Constance Padwick. Gairdner was an Arabic scholar of great distinction; the bibliography at the end of his life gives thirty Arabic works written by him. At his request the S.P.C.K. engaged an artist missionary, Miss Elsie Anna Wood, to illustrate the Society's Arabic books. Living in Egypt, and later for a time in Palestine, she was able to catch the spirit of the East with success and, in particular, to avoid the features introduced by European artists into religious pictures that offend Muslim taste. At one time the work was promising and the Society's Cairo branch has continued publication on sound lines, but the difficulties at present are very great.

Nevertheless, in 1956 the Society was able to put an exceptional gift of £3,000 to an interesting and promising use. The time seemed ripe for seeking to improve understanding between Muslims and Christians, particularly at the scholarly level. Largely as a result of the S.P.C.K.'s grant Dr Kenneth Cragg, an Arabic scholar and theologian, was enabled to take up a canonry at St George's, Jerusalem, for three years, and to devote himself completely to this purpose. At the time of writing, in spite of the great difficulties created by the Suez Canal episode, he has already achieved remarkable success, and the Society hopes to take a leading part in enabling him to continue his work in the future.

Amharic. This is the language of the dominant race of Ethiopia (Abyssinia). A short-lived mission of the C.M.S. was staffed by men of outstanding gifts, among them K. W. Isenberg and J. L. Krapf, who produced various Christian books, including the Amharic Prayer

Book, published by the S.P.C.K. in 1842. Anglican missions came to an end in Ethiopia in 1865.

Armenian. Portions of the Prayer Book had been printed in 1827 for Bishop's College, Calcutta. The complete book was published for the S.P.C.K. at Constantinople in 1847 and revised in 1867. The Society disavowed any intention of proselytizing and stated that the book was for information only.

Coptic. To help the Copts of Egypt, the S.P.C.K. published the Gospels in Arabic and Coptic (1847) and the complete New Testament (1852).

Hebrew. Between the two wars Dr P. P. Levertoff, a distinguished Jewish Christian of Russian origin and a priest in the Church of England, induced the S.P.C.K. to embark on a modest publishing programme of books in modern Hebrew. It was hoped that they would be useful in Poland, where the Church Mission to Jews had several stations, as well as in Israel, but the difficulties in the way of getting an adequate circulation were too great.

Turkish. The S.P.C.K. published the Prayer Book in the Arabic script of Turkish in 1883 and in the Armenian script in 1880. At the time of the Crimean war the hope was cherished that the way would be opened for Western missions, and the Society therefore published a few small books and tracts.

In 1838 the Royal Geographical Society sent an expedition to explore Kurdistan, to which the Society contributed £750, in the hope of getting information which would lead to helping the Nestorian Christians. As a result, ninety manuscripts were brought to England, which in 1887 were given to the Cambridge University Library.

4. PROBLEMS OF PRAYER BOOK PUBLISHING

Hitherto we have been considering the Society's efforts to make the doctrine and worship of Anglicans known to Christians of other obediences rather than directly missionary literature; even the Arabic publications did not come under the latter heading, for it was hoped to influence Muslims through the Eastern Churches as intermediaries. We now come to missionary literature as generally understood, and this will be a convenient place at which to discuss the problems of translating the Book of Common Prayer.

The early missionaries had no doubt that their duty was to give converts the Prayer Book which they esteemed so highly. Today some experienced leaders take the same line. Our duty, they say, is to give the Young Churches as faithful a translation as possible of the book we know and love. Later they will make their own liturgies, which we shall welcome. The thing to be avoided is our making adaptations to suit what we imagine to be their needs, a task beyond our competence. A version once launched is apt to hold its own tenaciously, the forces of religious conservatism rallying to its support.

Some kind of Prayer Book is a necessity for a young Church. Indeed it comes before the Bible, since a framework of public worship must be provided before the converts are prepared to read the Bible —at least in the normal mission-field, where until lately adherents have been in the main illiterate. Probably the early versions in new missions were often very bad. The pioneers' knowledge of the language was imperfect and their native helpers were slow to criticize their efforts. With improved linguistic knowledge continual revisions were necessary, which shows how expensive this side of the Society's work must be. In some places, where converts are drawn from a variety of races, it has been necessary to have services in English, the second language of nearly all.

The total number of languages in which the S.P.C.K. Prayer Books have been published cannot be determined accurately, for no one knows where to draw the line between a language and a dialect. Suppose a large tribe, in whose area a pioneer English mission is working in the north and a Continental one in the south. Each takes down the language—which differs slightly in vocabulary and pronunciation—phonetically, as its workers understand it, and uses different methods of transcription. An impression of two kindred languages is given, and they may be called by different names. In reality the difference may be no more, or may even be less, than that which would have been presented by versions in the speech of Devon villagers and Yorkshire ones made a century ago by foreign visitors who transcribed them phonetically. Then there is the difficulty of the *lingua franca* of a given area and the local vernaculars. Is each to have its own literature or is the *lingua franca* to prevail? The latter may be a convenience to the missionaries but may hinder the work of evangelization. An example of this is provided by East Africa, where Swahili is widely understood but in many areas is not the mother tongue. Government action has eased the problem, for often school teaching above the primary stage is given in Swahili only. But then comes the conflict between English and Swahili. It is impracticable to supply books in Swahili for all the needs of higher education, and from every point of view it seems best to many to take the child direct from the vernacular of his home to English. This policy is favoured by Government officials, and by Africans, who want an education that will fit them for the better paid jobs; besides, to force a child during his school days to be taught in three different languages is to put an intolerable strain on him, such as would certainly not be put on an English child. The general belief has been that English will eventually be the only language that matters in education, but the new African states now arising may not all share that view, and indeed in some areas there seems to be a reversion to tribal languages, so that works long out of print may have to be revived. Where the Church's work is concerned, the mother tongue will always have the preference. The answer to the question put above as to the number of Prayer Book versions published by the home Society or its branches, or independently with its assistance, depends on our definition of a language; perhaps 170 would be a fair estimate.

The Society's policy in regard to translations of the Prayer Book has been governed by its rules. The Foreign Translation Committee was appointed directly by the Archbishop of Canterbury, who used to give personal attention to the problems that arose. The mission which sent the manuscript had to fill in the answers to an elaborate schedule of questions, dealing mainly with the principles of translation. The chief problem was whether to find equivalents for technical terms at the risk of associating them with heathen ideas in the minds of the users, or to transliterate them and trust that the process of education would make them intelligible. Experience has shown that the latter policy is better. Archbishop Davidson, in particular, took a deep personal interest in these matters and was very anxious that hasty action on the part of missions should not prejudice the unity of the Anglican Communion. However, in 1920 he informed the Society that he no longer expected to be consulted about versions that had the authority of a province. The problem of the independent diocese, directly under Canterbury, remained. The Lambeth Conference of

1920 set up a Consultative Committee to advise on liturgical matters, but not much use was made of its services.[1] The 1930 Conference did not reappoint the Committee, and the Consultative Body, which functions between the Conferences, took over the work, with the help of such liturgical experts as it might care to consult. This refers in the main to past history, for few independent dioceses remain outside the provinces now formed.

The Evangelical missions founded and supported by the C.M.S. have generally been satisfied with the 1662 book, supplementing it with non-liturgical services and extempore prayer. Those who adhere rather to the Catholic tradition have wished to enrich their liturgies and in particular to have a fuller Canon[2] in the Communion Service, in line with the Scottish and American Canons. In South Africa a complete revision has been carried through, at first published by the Society in several parts, each section being put out separately as the work of revision progressed. When it was eventually ready for issue in one volume, however, the Society found itself without the necessary capital to underwrite so large a project. The Oxford University Press was accordingly invited to take over the publication, which it did in 1954, the S.P.C.K. simply retaining its imprint upon the title page, and its right to publish the various African translations which are being gradually made to conform with the English. A Central Translations Committee, with local sub-committees for each major vernacular, has been set up for this purpose by the Province with the aid of S.P.C.K. grants.

An example of how things were done elsewhere is provided by the diocese of Zanzibar.[3] Faced by a bewildering variety of use in the churches of his diocese, Bishop Weston drew up a liturgy, which was accepted by the Synod. With its details we are not concerned. But Archbishop Davidson's treatment of the matter illustrates our problem. After much consultation with the Bishop, by correspondence, and personally in 1920, Davidson decided to raise no objection to the publication of the diocesan Prayer Book in Swahili, provided that the 1662 book was used in English services held in the Cathedral at

---

[1] *Walter Howard Frere* (S.P.C.K. 1954) shows how largely an eminent liturgist was consulted by overseas bishops, independently of Lambeth.

[2] Prayer of consecration.

[3] See H. M. Smith, *Frank, Bishop of Zanzibar*, p. 288.

Zanzibar. However, as he explained to the Secretary of the S.P.C.K., he was not prepared to sanction its publication by the Society, which would seem to give it more official approval than he wished to appear. This book, with some revision, was eventually published by the S.P.C.K. in 1950. It included the Psalter and a collection of Office Hymns as well as Daily Offices, etc., and was followed in 1954 by the Communion Service and Occasional Offices with Collects, Epistles, and Gospels. These are used by all three Swahili-speaking U.M.C.A. dioceses in East Africa, while the C.M.S. dioceses use the "standard" translation of the 1662 Book also published by the Society.

The recent liturgical experiments of the Church of South India show what may be expected from a wholly independent body. The Communion Service drawn up for that Church is a bold and satisfying attempt to enrich the traditional Anglican Service from various sources, including the liturgies of the Eastern Orthodox Church, which in view of the presence of the Syrian Church of Malabar, claiming descent from St Thomas, is obviously desirable. Whatever happens, the predominant influence of Cranmer is unlikely to disappear from the Anglican Prayer Books of the future. The S.P.C.K. throughout has acted with self-effacement. As a Society it expresses no views on the problems of high ecclesiastical policy; but in justice to its supporters, who have found the money for publishing unremunerative editions, it has tried to ensure that any book purporting to be a translation of the Book of Common Prayer shall be what it professes to be.

5. INDIA, ETC.

Here we find the Society's work growing out of that done in the eighteenth century. The means adopted was that of trusting District Committees, which was a natural extension of the substantial amount of local initiative allowed to the early missionaries and their local supporters (East India Company chaplains, Governors, etc.), who could not get speedy answers to their letters and so had to be trusted; the Committees were an extension to the Mission Field of the method found useful at home. The large grants given to the first Bishops overseas were intended, at least in some cases, to be administered by the Diocesan Committees. This seems to have been the origin of the nineteenth-century missionary grants, which were originally meant primarily for S.P.C.K. work—the production and circulation of books, the founding of libraries, and the running of schools. The first Calcutta Committee was formed in 1815 and consisted of those members of the Parent Society residing locally with others nominated by them, who had to make an initial donation of two gold mohurs plus a yearly contribution of that amount. The work of the Committee included the publishing and circulation of books, and the opening, maintenance, and management of schools. In 1822 we read of depots established at Calcutta, Cawnpore, Chittagong, Dacca, Dinapore, and Meerut. The Annual Report of that year refers with pride to the "Establishment" of India and to the co-operation of Church and State. The Committee began publishing at once, putting out Mrs Trimmer's Spelling Book for the use of European children; in this case the Government repaid the cost. With a magnificent sweep of vision they extended their operations in 1819 to New South Wales, then in the diocese of Calcutta, and even to Pitcairn Island, both being supplied with books. A consignment of £558 worth of Family Bibles was sent from London and had a ready sale; Europeans, it was reported, would only buy expensive books. The substantial grants made by London largely took the form of books, the sales of which financed new purchases. Publishing began in Bengali and Hindustani. In 1820 six schools were run by the Committee and another school was about to be transferred to the Society by the Marchioness of Hastings, with an adequate endowment. The supervision exercised by the Committee is illustrated by a letter written from Calcutta in 1823 by the Reverend J. Hawtyne. He is obliged to give up his superintendence of the native schools. He leaves home at 6, rides a long way, is cooped up in a hut with native children; then he rides on to other schools and returns at 11 in stifling heat. Conditions are even worse in the rainy season.

The Madras Committee (1816) regularized and put under the new plan for District Committees the work already being done by local supporters of the Society who had for a long time been supervising some of the missions. The constitution was the same as that of Calcutta, but the subscription was ten pagodas (a pagoda being worth about 8s.). The Vepery Press was its chief concern and there were six depots for the sale of books. The 1861 Report says that the Press was opened in 1751[1] and had in the past made large profits from the sale of school books. The profits were made possible by a large annual grant of stores from the Home Society and were devoted to the support of schools and especially girls in boarding schools. In 1847 the grant was stopped, and the local Committee made an urgent appeal for its renewal. The decision was reaffirmed and the Press was closed, to be reopened before long as the Madras Diocesan Press. The comparatively large Christian population of South India ensured a steady demand for Tamil and Telegu books, which was met with the help of the Home Society. An example of the difficulties confronting publication is given by a volume of sermons in Tamil (1830). The Society whose name was used felt that it must know the contents of a book published under its auspices and so insisted on being furnished with a literal translation of the manuscript. This remained the rule within living memory for books the original English edition of which was not published by the S.P.C.K., though it could be evaded by putting the responsibility on the Bishop.

The Bombay Committee on its foundation in 1816 began at once to publish in Marathi and Gujerati; all the schools connected with the Bombay Education Society were supplied with books. In 1825 the S.P.C.K. granted £500 to the Committee for printing school books. Libraries were opened, mainly for soldiers and their families; books were carried from England free of charge in the East India Company's ships. Two interesting letters from Mr Barnes, Archdeacon of Bombay, written in August 1820, say that the Committee have agreed not to publish religious books, owing to pressure from the Governor, who fears that they will cause disturbances, but this does not apply to translations of Bible portions for use in schools; the name of the Society in the imprint is a handicap. The Colombo Committee was formed in the same year and in 1825 received a grant of £500 with which to produce school books. Its first activity was the publication of a Tamil Prayer Book, the language of the Madras book being "too high and refined" for Ceylon. By 1837, seventeen books in Sinhalese and Tamil had been published.

On the basis of these beginnings a considerable body of literature was built up, especially in Madras and, later, the Punjab (Urdu). No

---

[1] A printing press had been sent from England before that date, see p. 65. The press got into difficulties in 1820, but was soon reopened.

consistent plan was pursued and production depended on the existence of individual missionaries with the necessary qualifications and driving force. What surprises us is the type of theological book which was thought suitable for translation. The list includes Butler's *Analogy*, Pearson on the Creed, Whateley's *Evidences*, etc. However, in 1822 the Home Society refused to sanction a translation of Bishop Porteous' *Evidences*, saying that Bishop's College, Calcutta, was the place where books designed for Indians should be written. On a different level, in 1871 the Society made a grant for the production of twenty little books by A.L.O.E. in Persian, Punjabi, and Urdu. The initials stand for "A Lady of England", a popular writer for women in those days. It is easy to criticize the Committee, but it had always to work through the missionaries, whose knowledge of English books was often small and who would fall back on those known to them in their student days. One difficulty in getting religious books written in Indian languages is that the educated have preferred to read theology in English and few have felt a call to interpret the ideas to their own people in their mother tongue by rewriting an English book in the native idiom.

The Society's publishing in fairly recent years was disappointingly small. An enlarged output is almost useless unless there is an organization for sales, and until there is a sufficient number of books to be sold setting up machinery for sales seems a useless expense. This difficulty cannot be said to have been solved so far, but some progress has been made. In 1920 a meeting held in London of Indian Bishops and representatives of the S.P.C.K. decided on a plan which led finally to the setting up of an S.P.C.K. in India, whose governing body was the Church of India, Burma, and Ceylon, which was to work in close relation with the Christian Literature Society in Madras. At last, in 1949, it was possible to send an S.P.C.K. Secretary for India, the Reverend J. D. M. Stuart, who made his headquarters at Delhi with the Cambridge Brotherhood and began to organize production on a sound basis, concentrating at first on books intended for Anglican worship. His work has continued to expand; in 1956 Mrs Esther Mullins went out to assist him by taking over the work for the Marathi area, and in 1958 Sri John Henry Anand was appointed as full-time assistant for the Hindi work. An annual grant of £1,500 is being sent from London to help finance this publishing, most of which still has to be heavily subsidized. In 1953, moreover, an S.P.C.K. bookroom and sales depot was opened in St James's Church Hall, Delhi, which has steadily increased its turnover year by year, and which is developing also a healthy mail-order business to serve other areas.

When the Church of South India came into existence, it naturally preferred to use its own institutions for the development of literature, but its relations with the Society have been cordial, and there has been co-operation in certain fields.

6. THE FAR EAST

China and Japan differ from most of the foreign fields in which the S.P.C.K. has worked, for the Anglican missions were based on the United States and Canada as well as on England. The Japanese Prayer Book accordingly is a compromise between the English and American forms. The S.P.C.K. helped the Japanese Church from the first, but not till shortly before the first world war was any attempt made to publish theological literature in a bold way. A considerable number of good English books were then published by the aid of the Society's grants. In 1920 a new start was made, and the Church Publishing Society of Tokyo, the official body of the Japanese Church, was made the Society's agent. The S.P.C.K. supplied nearly all the funds and the American Episcopal Church the services of a Secretary, a priest who had reached pensionable age and preferred to live on in Japan. He built up a considerable trade in English theological books besides developing a programme of Japanese works. The years immediately preceding the second war witnessed the retirement of foreign missionaries, and the cessation of contacts between Japan and the West was made complete when the war came. The Society could congratulate itself that the work had been built up on national lines, for everything had been done through the local Church; the withdrawal of foreign help no doubt crippled the work but did not end it. Since the renewal of contacts after the war, the Church in Japan has turned to America for any outside assistance it might need, but the S.P.C.K. has nevertheless been able to make one or two grants for specific Japanese publications in recent years.

The immense size of China and the consequent difficulty of communications made it necessary to deal with the individual dioceses rather than with the Church as a whole. Here, too, dioceses were founded by different branches of the Anglican Communion. Each diocese had its own Prayer Book, printed locally. The situation was regularized in 1920, when, under the guidance of Bishop Scott of North China, a Church Literature Committee of the (Anglican) Church in China was formed which reported yearly to the National Synod. A list of about a hundred theological books was built up, but the perennial difficulty of circulation confronted the Society. It was felt that, by the side of the specially Anglican books, we ought to be contributing to the general stock of Christian literature. So an arrangement was made with the Christian Literature Society of Shanghai, which published a number of books for the S.P.C.K. A promising start had been made when the war and political difficulties severed contacts. The last help which the Society was able to give to China proper was to provide £400 towards the Fukien Prayer Book in 1949. In 1956 a Prayer Book in unified Mandarin was printed in Hong Kong and published by the Society in Singapore for the use of Chinese in that diocese and in Borneo, and in the same year £650 was granted towards the cost of a Cantonese book for Hong Kong.

7. AFRICA

In the early days of African missions a great deal of pioneer work was carried on by the Society, of a type that is no longer necessary. Languages had to be reduced to writing, and grammars and dictionaries compiled, a work which was done almost entirely by missionaries. Some, like the great Bishop Steere, were men of supreme ability, and by their skill the more important languages became literary vehicles. They had to teach children themselves and the elementary readers which they compiled had an enormous sale. In quite early days the S.P.C.K. printed an edition of 100,000 of an elementary Reader for Uganda. Today, there are energetic Education Departments everywhere, and much of the work originally done by the Church has passed into other hands. The Society's work has been costly, for the various languages have evolved rapidly, and official orthographies have been introduced, necessitating constant revision of books. But in Africa, at least, there has been the advantage of a large potential public, for both educational and directly religious books, and in some areas the school books can be priced profitably enough

A proof page of the Arabic Psalter with type designed by William Caslon, and a page of the Chinese (Mandarin) Prayer Book published in Singapore

"As faithful a translation as possible"

Bath, the first of
the 20th century
provincial shops

A Tanganyika branch bookshop

"The most important development . . . has been the opening of bookshops"

to contribute to the large subsidies that are usually needed for Prayer Book work.

In the last generation much thought has been given to the planning of literature for Africa, and frequent conferences, at which the S.P.C.K. has been represented, have taken place at Edinburgh House, the headquarters of the Conference of British Missionary Societies, and elsewhere. So large is the reading public now that the leading English educational publishers have taken up African literature on a considerable scale, thus easing the pressure on Missionary Societies. Nevertheless this continent remains one of the main fields of the Society's work, and African vernacular liturgical books alone normally account for more than two-thirds of the total overseas publishing budget.

8. RECENT DEVELOPMENTS

The most important development in recent years has been the opening of bookshops, owned and managed by the S.P.C.K., overseas. Among these may be mentioned Baghdad,[1] Rangoon,[2] Singapore, Johannesburg, Salisbury (Southern Rhodesia), Dar-es-Salaam and its branches, and a chain of shops in the West Indies. The problem of making a Church bookshop pay its way, in a far off land remote from London, is very difficult. The managers have to be trained and supervised from home. Prices have to be kept down to a level which the local population can pay. A happy mean has to be observed. By offering a plentiful supply of general literature customers are brought to the shops and culture is spread, but it is easy for the manager to become absorbed in this and neglect the specially religious end for which his shop exists. Broadly speaking, it may be said that the shops, after growing pains, are settling down to their proper work and becoming self-supporting. But, as is inevitable in the present condition of the world, they are a cause of anxiety as well as of pride, for, apart from the problem of management, at any moment a political convulsion may cripple the work of an admirably run business. Recently, a policy has been introduced whereby the entire management of a bookshop and its finances has been handed over to the diocesan authority, with some supervision from London, in order to meet the difficulty, if not impossibility, of transmitting profits to London.

[1] Now locally owned.   [2] Now run by the autonomous "S.P.C.K -Burma".

The writer can look back to things as they were in 1915, when he joined the staff of the S.P.C.K. The foreign literature work was then almost entirely on a charitable basis. A book was printed and the edition, in whole or in part, was granted to a mission, which was supposed to return the sales as a charitable donation to the Society. The objections to this plan were obvious. People don't value what they get for nothing; they naturally ask for a liberal supply and so there was waste; also the missionaries had to devote much time to the keeping of accounts. There was a certain romance in the work which has now passed away. The Eskimo Prayer Book and Hymnal were supplied to people who had no money and on one occasion made dolls out of the skins of Polar animals and sent them to the Society as a gift. An island in the Pacific paid for a book in sharks' teeth, the local currency. In one mission a Prayer Book was acquired by doing a week's work in the mission garden. This phase was evidently passing away and the first step was to fix a price such as the prospective user could be expected to pay and to insist on receiving it. The next step was to divert the business to Mission bookshops, and, where they did not exist, to encourage their formation. Finally, as we have seen, the Society began to found its own shops; and during the last ten years experiments have been made, notably in East Africa and Jamaica, in "mobile distribution": book-vans that can take literature up-country to the schools and missions and can reach people in their distant villages who would never be likely themselves to make the journey to a shop. In forty years we have seen a money economy become universal. The old "charity" has come to an end and publishing and bookselling on modern lines have replaced it. High profits cannot be expected; indeed, much of the work must still be carried at a loss; but the mechanism of business must be used, inspired all the time by Christian idealism.

In conclusion, something should be said about English books written especially for the needs of Africans, etc. There are various systems of simplified vocabulary, such as "Basic", "Simplified", etc. English, which have served a useful purpose. One objection to these is that Africans are apt to be suspicious of attempts to write down to their assumed intellectual level, and to the African leaders of the future any system of simplification may be repellent. But a greater problem than that of vocabulary (which can after all be overcome by the use of a dictionary) is the difference in background and experience, and in patterns of thought, between the European writer and the local reader, at whatever level of education. Increasingly, collaboration between Europeans and Nationals is seen to be necessary in the preparation of new books, so as to ensure that the material is presented in a form relevant to the local need. Similarly, adaptation or reinterpretation is likely to be more successful than direct translation in making books of theology and Christian teaching available in other languages, and here too some measure of collaboration can be of the utmost value, until the time comes when Indian and African writers and theologians will themselves be producing the literature that is needed for their own people.

9

Other Activities

(a) FRENCH PROSELYTES

JOHN CHAMBERLAYNE in his book *The Present State of Great Britain* (1718) describes the help given by William III to the Protestants who fled from France to Britain after the revocation of the Edict of Nantes in 1684. £15,000 a year was charged on the Royal Bounty, and confirmed by Act of Parliament, for their relief. George I added £400 annually to be confined to converts from the Church of Rome. This was administered by the Archbishop of Canterbury, the Bishop of London, and the Lord Chief Justices of the King's Bench and the Common Pleas, who added others and had authority to raise voluntary funds to augment the grant.

Books relating to the Charity are found among the Society's archives, the minute books of 2 May 1717 to 10 September 1729, and the Treasurer's book of 25 April 1724 to 8 March 1728. Chamberlayne had been the first Secretary of the S.P.C.K. and Henry Newman, the third Secretary, was Treasurer of the fund 1724–8. Both belonged to the Commissioners, 86 in all, who administered it, and they were present at practically every meeting. The personnel was drawn largely from the members of the S.P.C.K. and seemed to regard themselves as acting on its behalf. A number of French names occur in the list. The circle of philanthropists was evidently limited, for it was ordered that the general meeting fixed for the first Wednesday in the month be postponed till the next day if it clashed with meetings of Queen Anne's Bounty or the Directors of the Lottery. The attendance at meetings was usually very small, but copies of the minutes were sent to the Archbishop and the Bishop of London. Many cases were referred to the former for approval.

In 1724 the Royal Bounty is said to be £500 a year and in 1728 a supplementary grant at the rate of nearly £300 a year is reported, to be spent on laity and clerics in the proportion of four to one. The voluntary subscriptions amounted to £506 in 1717: Princess Anne subscribed 10 guineas, the Archbishop 6, the Bishop of London 5, Sir Isaac Newton 2. In 1724 it was ordered that the Royal Bounty be spent on permanent pensions of £5 to £20, benefiting 50 persons in all, emergency cases to be helped from the voluntary funds. The Commissioners in May 1717 agreed that "the debates be regular and without heats, that no member interrupt another, and that he who speaks first be first heard". A proposal made by Lord Perceval in 1720 to lend £100 "towards entitling them to a subscription in the South Sea for the benefit of the proselytes", evidently a lottery, was rejected on the ground that "it would not be for the honour of the Society [i.e., the Commissioners] to engage in such a way of helping them".

Like all such bodies the Commissioners found difficulties in establishing the *bona fides* of applicants, and in 1721 examiners were appointed at a salary of £30 a year to investigate motives and the degree of instruction in Protestantism attained. Great care was taken and a full description of each case is entered in the minute books. Some were found employment, after training if necessary, some were helped to emigrate; others had to be given alms simply. For the most part the proselytes lived in and about London. Inquiries made in 1720 into the yearly cost of boarding a person outside the capital produced these figures: Bangor £7, Beverley £10, Carlisle £9, Lincoln £12, Neath £6, Tiverton £12. The Isle of Man, according to its Bishop (29 December 1718), would have welcomed proselytes, but it has become a kind of asylum, things are as dear as in England, and there is plenty of wine and brandy to corrupt them.

Recipients of help were expected to attend Divine Service every Sunday, those living in Westminster at "the great Savoy church". The difficulties of the Commissioners are illustrated by a letter written by Newman to Mr du Fresne of Twyford (17 October 1721): "the last printed list of proselytes contains the names of fifty that are detected of having been spies or are now returned to Popery." One of the rules ran thus: "Any proselyte in orders who shall put on the gown without the leave of the Ordinary and first acquainting the Commissioners shall be excluded from any assistance."

(b) GEORGIA

The Society played a minor part in the colonization of Georgia, to understand which the background must be briefly described.[1]

General Oglethorpe (he was promoted to the rank of general in 1765) as a soldier, landed proprietor, member of Parliament, and philanthropist, had an almost unique knowledge of the practical problems of his day. He was particularly concerned with prisons, the treatment of debtors, and unemployment; he also strove continuously for consideration to sailors. His desire to restart prisoners and workless men in life led him to think of emigration. In 1730 a Mr King had left a legacy which was dormant. He was able to get possession of it for his charitable purposes and to add a further fund "for the conversion of negroes". In all £6,000 was available and a body of trustees was formed to administer it. Oglethorpe as a soldier wanted to form a colony which would protect South Carolina from aggression on the part of the Spaniards in Florida; he was also a philanthropist benefiting the unemployed. In 1730 a Society, later called the Trustees for Georgia, was formed and in 1732 a Charter was granted. The Trustees were authorized to hold land but not to derive any personal benefit; they had to publish annual accounts and after twenty-one years the new colony, which was to be separate from South Carolina, was to be vested in the King. Mr H. Verelst was appointed Accountant. The first party of poor Englishmen with wives and families, 114 in all, arrived at Savannah in January 1733, accompanied by Oglethorpe. Food had to be guaranteed for the first twelve months at least. In the first fourteen years of the experiment about 2,000 people were settled, of whom nearly half were foreigners. Some Salzburgers, with whom the S.P.C.K. was concerned, sailed in January 1734 and a further stream of Scottish Highlanders followed in 1735. In 1739 a Parliamentary Grant of £20,000 was received. The foreigners made the best settlers, the British often proving indolent and inefficient; the necessity of military service to guard the frontier prevented their giving full attention to agriculture. Oglethorpe had a very difficult time, the complaints against him being as follows:

[1] See L. F. Church, *Oglethorpe: a Study of Philanthropy in England and Georgia*, on which the following paragraph is based.

1. He was too friendly with the Indians.
2. He prohibited negro slave labour.
3. Rum, etc. was not allowed.
4. Land was granted on the condition that on the owner's death it went to his sons; daughters were excluded since they could not give military service.

In 1750 the last grievance was rectified, grants of land being made absolute. Serious charges were made against Oglethorpe, but he was completely vindicated by court-martial in 1744.

The persecution of Protestants arose out of the passions excited by the wars of religion and the particular one with which we are concerned began with the appointment of a new Archbishop of Salzburg, in Austria, in 1727. They were punished with fines and confiscation of property for reading the Bible. They therefore appealed to Frederick William, King of Prussia, who offered to accept them. Nearly 30,000 in all found new homes in 1732 and following years, and more could have gone if George II had not been willing to take some.

The S.P.C.K. was stirred by the news of the persecution and the General Meeting held on 9 March 1732 considered the matter. A thousand copies were ordered of the pamphlet *An Account of the Sufferings of the Persecuted Protestants in the Archbishopric of Salzburg*, the approval of the Government was sought, permission was obtained for making collections, and a treasurer was appointed. In October an "Extraordinary Committee" for the Salzburgers was appointed. Exactly how responsibility was shared between the Society and the Trustees for Georgia cannot be determined. Newman, Secretary of the S.P.C.K., was also a trustee and the two bodies were in close touch. In December 1735 it was reported that £9,317 had been received by the treasurers of the fund.[1] The Bishop of Winchester sent £100 in 1732. The Bishop of Norwich in 1734 directed his clergy to preach on the subject and have a collection, followed by a house to house collection in Norwich, if authorized by the Mayor and Corporation. The University of Cambridge sent £172 10s. in 1733 from the Colleges, plus £40 from the University chest. Certain expenses were shared by the two bodies in agreed proportions. The Trustees, being responsible

[1] These were Archdeacon Denne, Rector of Lambeth, Mr Benjamin Hoare the banker, and Mr Ziegenhagen, the King's German Chaplain.

for the enterprise as a whole, naturally had larger resources. Dr Church states that between 1733 and 1740 they received £94,000 in Parliamentary grants and raised £18,000 by their own efforts.

However, the preliminary correspondence of the S.P.C.K. with Urlsperger and Münch, ministers in Augsburg, shows that the Society was regarded as the source of benevolence. The conduct of the refugees was exemplary. Urlsperger preached to a congregation of several thousands in an Augsburg cemetery. Daily meetings for prayer and psalm-singing were held. Urlsperger made all the arrangements with the S.P.C.K. for the escape to England, and in December 1732 approved of the Georgia plan. Shortly after this he asked for a description of Georgia to print and distribute; we learn from his letters that 300 families went to Holland, where they were at once accepted as citizens, and 800 persons to Hanover, of which the English King was Elector. The Society financed the refugees so long as they were in Germany and paid for their transport to Rotterdam. Exact descriptions of them were sent to London. The number, which had been fixed at 300, fell short of this, but later parties may have made it up to the original figure. The first party was fetched from Rotterdam in a specially chartered ship. Arrangements were made for their food, which included beef and pudding four days a week, pork and peas two days, and fish and butter one day: beer, rum, sugar and spices, and candles, had to be provided. The party arrived at Dover on 18 December 1733 and were invited to dinner by the magistrates. They marched through the town singing psalms and hymns and were fed with beef and plum pudding. The two ministers, Bolzius and Gronau, at once set to work to learn English. These chaplains by previous agreement were to be paid £50 a year,[1] the same salary as that paid by the S.P.G. to its ministers, until the emigrants were able to undertake their support. Later, a catechist was paid £30, and a schoolmaster £10 plus 20 acres of land.

The first transport to Georgia sailed in January 1734, with 53 persons, who were settled at their new home, called Ebenezer, by 7 April. The original idea was that each settler should have 50 acres of land, the townships to consist of 100 persons each. Conditions at first were very difficult. The Society had to send stores of all kinds: bedding, shoes, handsaws, coppers for boiling beer, mill stones, fishing tackle, livestock,

---

[1] However, the actual figure seems to have been £30, soon raised to £40.

firearms, and especially silver and copper coins. Chemical apparatus was sent for Mr Zwiffler, apothecary. Newman, however, wrote to a German correspondent on 3 December 1734 that the trustees could not sanction bringing to Georgia workmen skilled in the manufacture of glass and earthenware, which would interfere with the makers of such things in England. The financial burden laid on the S.P.C.K. is illustrated by the bill presented on 27 September 1734 for 50 Salzburgers for twelve months plus freight.

	£	s.	d.
Owing	619	1	3½
Passage from Gravesend to Georgia at £5 each	250	0	0
9 months' provisions in Georgia at £4 10s. each	225	0	0
	1,094	1	3½

Frugality and industry enabled the colonists to overcome the initial difficulties. On 20 June 1740, George Whitefield wrote from Savannah after a visit to Ebenezer, which he approached through four miles of fruitful plantations: "Surely the Salzburgers are a happy people. . . . When I reflect on them and the inhabitants of the other part of the Colony, it puts me in mind of the great difference God once made, when there was darkness among the Egyptians, but light in the land of Goshen." The piety of the refugees, who on board ship were instructed twice daily by their chaplains, with prayers and hymns, continued in the new land, where they had a service lasting half an hour every evening when work was done. The quality was very good; the Society had refused to take anyone that had not freely volunteered. The first mention of a church is in 1737; in 1740 a letter from the S.P.C.K. to Bolzius and Gronau says that Mr Whitefield has collected £52 9s. 9d. towards the cost of building the Church at Ebenezer. We hear of the Sacrament of Holy Communion being administered every six weeks, the vessels having been provided by the S.P.C.K.

The unlucky career of John and Charles Wesley in Georgia (1735–37) and the later visits of Whitefield are too familiar to need recounting here. John Wesley and Whitefield were frequent correspondents of the Society. A letter written by Henry Newman to Mr S. Quincy at Savannah on 19 October 1735, is worth quoting. Newman approves Quincy's plan for forming a Religious Society. "The Revd. Mr Wesley a corresponding member of the Society with other well dispos'd gentlemen go over volunteers with Mr Oglethorpe, and will doubtless be always ready to assist you in your labours to cultivate a sense of religion among the Europeans in your settlement and if possible among the natives, who for many ages have lived in the utmost darkness.

"N.B. The names of the volunteer missionaries were Mr John Wesley, Fellow of Lincoln College, Oxford, Mr Charles Wesley, Student of Christ Church College, Mr Ingham or Ingram of Queen's College, Oxford, who sailed in the *Simonds* with Mr Oglethorpe."

In 1761 the Society published a letter from Mr Bolzius, in which he stated that communicants at Ebenezer numbered 1,098. In 1771 a document in its archives gives the Salzburgers' numbers as follows: original emigrants 29, children 96, grandchildren 33, 158 in all. Obviously some had moved away and there had been a considerable influx from outside into the prosperous community. When the War of Independence broke out in 1776, Georgia was at first in the hands of the American rebels, but surrendered to the British in 1778, to be handed back at the peace. The last missionary, Triebner, narrated his troubles in a letter to the Society dated 4 March 1779 which broke a silence of nearly three years. In 1781 he fled to Savannah, but had to leave America when the British forces left, being threatened with death if he remained. He found other work, finally as a Lutheran Minister in London. Later (1796) the Society granted him £100 plus a pension of £50, increased to £70 in 1812.

(c) THE SCILLY MISSION

Until 1836 the Scilly Islands were considered extra-diocesan and no one was responsible for the spiritual welfare of the inhabitants except the Lord Proprietor, the Earl of Godolphin, who appointed and maintained a chaplain at St Mary's, one of the six inhabited islands. In 1752 the Reverend R. C. Hartshorne, Rector of Broseley, Shropshire, gave the S.P.C.K. £250 for the purpose of providing a schoolmaster in deacon's orders for Tresco. This was treated as a trust fund, to which the Society added money of its own, until in 1765 £400 had been accumulated. The Society then opened a school in each island under the supervision of the minister of St Mary's. In 1774 an appeal produced enough money to proceed with the original plan. A Mr Coxon was ordained deacon by the Bishop of London, having given an undertaking that he would not exercise his ministry elsewhere. His salary, paid by the S.P.C.K., was £40 a year and he received an initial gratuity of £20 to "provide himself with a gown and cassock and other apparel necessary to support the dignity of his profession".

Conditions on the islands were very hard. Fresh fish was abundant and corn and potatoes were obtained locally, but everything else was imported and very expensive. Frequent deaths by drowning reduced the male population. Storms often prevented the missionary from visiting the islands other than that on which he lived and his position as a missionary by the side of the legal chaplain led to quarrels. At last, in 1796, the Society sent its Secretary, Dr Gaskin, to visit the islands. His report was on the whole favourable. The schools were better than he expected. The salaries paid were incredibly small. One can only suppose that the teachers had other sources of income. But the obvious way of increasing earnings, by taking paying pupils, is referred to in some cases. Thus the master at St Martin's had £3 a year plus £6 from these. As a result of his visit, which cost the Society £83 18s. 6d., salaries were doubled or trebled, and incompetent teachers were pensioned off. Dr Gaskin reported that the inhabitants were "inoffensive, well-disposed persons, desirous of instruction, respectfully attached to their ministers". Of the one Methodist teacher he said: "there did not appear either in him or among his followers any enmity to the Church of England, or any disaffection to Government." By 1806 the two missionaries were paid £100 a year, which was raised to £150 in 1821. The difficulties of a missionary are illustrated by the application of Mr Woodly in 1822 to be refunded the cost of going to Exeter to be ordained priest (£19 4s. 9d.) and by the necessity of relieving starving islanders out of his own pocket.

Shortly before the Secretary, W. H. Coleridge, was appointed Bishop of Barbados in 1824 he visited the islands on behalf of the Society. He reported that things were in an unsatisfactory condition and the Bishop of Exeter had no power to intervene. The Bishop invited the Society to draw up a memorandum which he would present to the Government, urging that the islands be annexed to the diocese of Exeter. This was done and in 1836 the desired action was taken. The anomaly of "missionaries", responsible to a Society, working in an English diocese had now to be ended and in 1840 the mission was wound up. The clergymen became curates to the Chaplain of the Lord Proprietor (since 1834 Augustus Smith). The Society paid £4,000 to Queen Anne's Bounty for an endowment fund, pensioned its two missionaries with £75 a year each, and continued its existing pensions to school teachers. The connection ceased finally at Christmas 1841.

The diary of Henry Phillpotts, Bishop of Exeter, for 1831 (see his Life by G. C. B. Davies) gives a description of his visit to the islands, in anticipation of which the Society had ordered its missionaries to prepare the population for Confirmation; hitherto Communion of the unconfirmed had been inevitable. Except for the salary of the minister of St Mary's, paid by the Proprietor, everything was done by the S.P.C.K. The population was 2,465. "A man, his wife, and a child can live on 5s. a week." At Tresco 250 to 300 attended in the morning, 100 to 130 in the afternoon, when the parish clerk and schoolmaster read prayers and sermon, Mr Lane having gone to another island. The Bishop confirmed 163 females and 76 males.

10

District Committees

IN THIS chapter we shall attempt to chronicle a spirited attempt to cover England and Wales, and even the overseas territories of the Empire, with Church bookshops, and the gradual realization that the impossible was being attempted—at least on the lines laid down.

The story begins with the corresponding members of the Society, that is the country members whose absence from London debarred them from taking any part in the administration of affairs. These people, who already had a link with the S.P.C.K., were the obvious ones to whom to appeal when extension was being planned. In 1808, at a meeting presided over by the Archbishop of Canterbury, it was resolved to appoint a Committee to consider increasing the influence of the Society by forming associations of clergy and laity. The members included Dr Dampier, Bishop of Ely (Chairman), to whom a later report gives the credit of originating the scheme eventually approved, Archdeacon Pott, Dr Christopher Wordsworth, Van Mildert, H. H. Norris, and Joshua Watson. By June 12, 1810, the plan had matured. The General Meeting of that day agreed to try to get Committees formed in every Cathedral city consisting of the Bishop, the Dean and Chapter, and such clergy and laity, being members of the Society, as were willing to co-operate. The response was immediate, Ely and Lincoln Committees being formed in July, Bristol, Winchester, and Durham in August. Next June, a meeting at which both Archbishops were present adopted a forward policy on the initiative of the Norwich Committee. All members were invited to inquire into the needs of prisons, workhouses, hospitals, and the poor generally, in respect of Bibles and Prayer Books. Depots should be opened everywhere, with help from the Parent Society and local sources. A Committee of Correspondence with Diocesan and District

Committees[1] was appointed, consisting of the Archbishops, Bishops, and twenty others, three to be a quorum. Two-thirds of all money raised locally was to be transmitted to London and credited to the District Committee in books, at member's prices. These were according to a tariff. Thus Bishop Andrews's *Devotions*, nominally 3s., was 1s. 3d. to members; specimens of other prices are 2½d. (for 8d.), ½d. (for 2d.). Some Committees allowed members and supporting parishes the full value in books of the amount received. The first account of the Bath Committee, published in the 1812 Report, is instructive. All local institutions (hospitals, penitentiaries, prisons, etc.) have been supplied with books gratis. A tariff has been fixed for the labouring poor—Bibles 1s., Prayer Books 6d. No depot has yet been opened. In spite of great efforts to raise money for local needs, 64 new members have been obtained for the Parent Society. Some places went to an extreme of cheapness. Thus Winchester sold for 3s. a Bible priced at 5s. 2d., itself one-third less than the original cost price. So successful was the drive that in 1815 Committees numbered 100 and members of the Society 11,746 as against 3,560 in 1810. Foreign Committees are described in Chapter 8. It will be understood that the operations of all these bodies were confined to books, etc., on the S.P.C.K. list, that is the Society's own publications, and those of other publishers approved for circulation. Everything was done on strict Church lines, each Committee being "under the sanction and by the direction" of the Bishop of the diocese; indeed the readiness of the Bishops to co-operate and the practical interest they showed are very unlike the conventional picture of episcopal supineness at this period.

The Committee for Correspondence sometimes had the Bishop of London in the chair, but in 1812 a Sub-Committee was formed consisting of Christopher Wordsworth, H. H. Norris, and Joshua Watson. They were very co-operative and would make up local funds if insufficient to launch new ventures. At first reports were required twice a year and the proceedings of the Committees were read and approved at headquarters. The Committees were treated with the greatest consideration except when they showed signs of trying to become independent societies.[2] In December 1817 the Salisbury report was

[1] Districts were areas within the larger dioceses.

[2] "Parent Society", the current phrase, might suggest that children would grow up.

read and passed except for a passage "expatiating on the private character of individuals, which the Committee considers to be foreign to the purposes of the Society". In no case would headquarters accept responsibility for the financial affairs of a Committee, the object being to call forth the maximum of local initiative and effort. Co-operation with other Societies was ruled out, as for example at Gateshead, where to a proposal to co-operate with a Religious Tract Society the reply was sent that the S.P.C.K. "cannot, from its peculiar constitution, enter into connection with any independent society". The 1813 Report mentioned a new rule that in future clergymen may become "corresponding members" without an annual subscription. Clearly the intention was that the local supporters should be a continuation and extension of the original corresponding members.

The movement begun with such enthusiasm soon ran into difficulties. In 1817 District Committees were asked to make local subscriptions at least 10s. 6d. a year, and it was decided that they be supplied with publications at three-fifths of the prime cost, with an obligation to sell to members at the same price (carriage was often added). One-third of the local funds was to be sent to London, unless designated for local uses; it would have been a simple matter to influence the donor in this direction. All these arrangements were subject to frequent changes. The number of Committees continued to rise, until in 1820 it reached 216. The tendency to become independent must have been encouraged by the Society's authorizing the Committees in 1827 to receive contributions of any amount "to be applied to the use of their respective districts in conformity with the designs of the S.P.C.K.". The difficulties were as follows.

1. The poverty of the general population and the desire to propagate Christian knowledge led many to give books away. Thus in 1820 the Bishop of Chester wrote to say that in large parts of his diocese the people were too poor or too ill-disposed to buy books at all, and the Society replied that it would ask for no payment in such cases.

2. If not parting with books for nothing, some Committees undersold the London Society, which caused trouble.

3. It was often difficult to get Committees to pay for their books, owing to mismanagement by amateurs or even sometimes defalcation by shopkeepers. Subscriptions intended for the Parent Society had to

be held back to meet local obligations. Naturally it was argued that the Society was one.

4. Getting books so cheaply and not being forced to pay for them, for the Society could not sue itself, Committees over-ordered and piled up unsaleable stock, adding to the loss at headquarters, which in 1836 was £19,393 on £55,354 worth of books supplied.

The Society tried many expedients to solve its problems. In 1825 local funds were left entirely in the hands of the Committees. In 1836 they were asked to send to London the difference between cost and the amount obtained by sales to non-members. The following year a different plan was adopted, that they should donate 10% of all sales, whether to members or non-members.

The expansion continued until in the middle of the century the number of Committees reached nearly 400. Methods varied from place to place. Some Committees, such as Bath, aimed at reproducing in miniature the arrangements of the Parent Society, but the usual practice was to make arrangements with a bookseller or stationer, who sometimes devoted little more than a shelf or two to the Society's books. The Society itself continued to foster self-help and in 1861 refused an urgent plea to take over the management of the Leeds depot. Many such requests came in later years but nearly always as the only alternative to the closing of a business that had failed. In 1824 the cumbrously named Committee for Correspondence, etc., was dissolved, its functions being taken over by the Standing Committee. The latter in 1836 recommended that the request of the District Committees that they be consulted on all important matters be declined as impracticable; the Society must be trusted.

In spite of all difficulties these local agencies did useful, if limited, work. Nearly all sent exact details of sales. For example, in 1843 Liverpool sold 2,015 Bibles, 1,350 New Testaments, and 3,148 Prayer Books. The necessity of creating outlets for the Society's publications is illustrated by a curious correspondence in *The Guardian*. On 4 April 1855 a correspondent complained of the miserable display of books in S.P.C.K. depots; booksellers generally get only a 5% commission, so have no inducement to stock. Why not put literature first instead of giving vast sums to Colonial bishoprics? (But the Society had spent vast sums on literature; the 1855 Report says that in the last twenty years the losses on publications have amounted to £228,612, almost entirely in respect of cheap Bibles and Prayer Books.) On 2 May Mr W. H. Smith, Treasurer, founder of the bookselling firm of that name, replied that no inducement would get the ordinary bookseller to stock S.P.C.K. books; the Society must find its own methods of distribution. Probably as a result of this complaint a travelling Secretary was appointed to supervise the depots and keep in touch with the District Committees; other appointments followed until the ground was covered. A clerical officer was added in 1860. We are not surprised to read that in 1863 the experiment was pronounced to have failed. In that year a purely commercial man was appointed, to advise only. That he had no better success may be gathered from a note in 1865 that of 384 depots controlled by Committees 16 had been inspected at their request.

For the rest of the century difficulties continued and even increased. As Committees came to order more from other publishers, they naturally paid them first, and the S.P.C.K. only as funds allowed. Many depot-keepers went into liquidation, and this reflected on the Society, from which publishers demanded payment, asserting that they had supplied goods on the strength of its name. In 1890 the Archbishops and Bishops wrote a letter to the Society calling attention to the failure of the depot system and asking for improvement. Renewed efforts met with no success. The local bodies had no hold over the booksellers they used and resented interference from headquarters. In 1898 a report to the Finance Committee said that on paper there were 266 District Committees, of which 142 were practically non-existent; of the other 124 only 64 sent any money to headquarters. Abolition was not recommended, but a renewed attempt to arouse keenness on the part of Secretaries. A further report in 1903 urged that steps were needed to arrest the dying out of the system. The fact was that the original Committees had focused the energies of the clergy and provided one of the few ways of acting corporately then open; when Ruridecanal Chapters and other opportunities of meeting developed, this *raison d'être* disappeared and they became redundant. Bookselling was becoming a skilled profession and there was no longer a place for amateurs. When in 1939 recognition was withdrawn from "depots" (the word had become obsolete) not owned by the Society, centrally or locally, the action was a formality, since the system had died a natural death. The story is a pathetic record of "might-have-beens". If the business genius of W. H. Smith had established a chain of Church shops owned and managed by headquarters the Society might have won a position of considerable influence; as it was, the Committee clung too long to a noble but impracticable plan. The distinction between members and non-members and the privileges given to the former, by which the S.P.C.K. was in effect a co-operative book society, became almost meaningless with the coming into force of the Net Book Agreement (after 1899), which should have been the signal for ending the system.

The picture will be rounded off if we add some notes based on the minute books of the District Committees, some of which survive.

Chichester. The depot was founded in 1814 and, though the local S.P.C.K. was responsible, it was regarded as the National Society shop also. This was a common arrangement, and the supply of books to Church Schools was an important part of the modest business done; as a result of the Education Act of 1904, these schools henceforward procured their books through the local authorities. In the period 1873–82, the Bishop of Chichester often took the chair at Committee meetings and the Duke of Richmond attended sometimes. Development of the business was frustrated by the unwillingness of the clergy to offend local traders.

Exeter (founded 1815). Between 1875 and 1900 the business averaged rather less than £1,000 a year. In 1874–5, £182 was raised for the Parent Society, £167 for the local Committee. Here the S.P.C.K. and the S.P.G. joined forces and shared the Anniversary Service. The business was built up on preferential buying by the clergy of a very small range of publications—Bibles, Prayer Books, hymn books and Sunday School prizes. For profit the shop (owned by the Committee) had to rely on sales to non-members at full prices and on charitable contributions.

Leek, Staffordshire. This is an example of a very small enterprise. On 10 February 1836, three clergymen and one layman, being members of the S.P.C.K., formed themselves into a District Committee, having obtained the consent of the Bishop. The method was for one member to attend at the Grammar School on Wednesdays and Saturdays to sell books. The sales were about £50 a year.

Lewes. A meeting held on 19 August 1816 established a Committee, with the consent of the Bishop and the Archdeacon. Annual Meetings were held at Brighton, jointly with the S.P.G. Two depositories, at Brighton and Lewes, were opened. The 1819 Anniversary Service was held in the Chapel Royal, Brighton. Hymns were sung by the National School children, accompanied by the private band of the Prince Regent, lent by him gratuitously. It was resolved that no money be paid for seats and no gifts made to the pew-openers. The S.P.G. was associated in the Service, and in 1830 the Clergy Orphan Corporation, collections being shared between the Societies.

Maidstone. By 1830 there was a financial crisis, since subscribers had obtained unlimited numbers of books at 25% below members' prices. The remedy adopted was to increase the price to 20% below, the value of the books thus bought not to exceed three times the amount of the subscription—which some "members" did not pay. Finally, the S.P.C.K. agreed to take back the stock in order to meet the heavy debts. A new start was made in 1833, the Reverend T. Harrison offering a room in the Grammar School for a depot. In 1861 the S.P.C.K. again took back the stock. Next year 1d. in the 1s. was added to the prices charged to members living outside the Deanery.

Salisbury. In 1853 a lady was paid £25 a year plus the use of the house, one room of which she had to keep for the use of subscribers. She was enterprising enough to set up a stall in the market place. Later there was the difficulty that members authorized others to buy at privileged prices. There was a succession of financial crises, culminating in the discovery in 1909 that there had been no stock-taking for some years. The shop was closed in 1913.

11

The Society in the Nineteenth Century

(a) PROGRESS AND POLICY

IN THIS CHAPTER we propose to give a general sketch of the Society's operations, referring the reader to later chapters for accounts of the Literature Committees, business methods, etc. The survey will extend to 1914; the opening years of the twentieth century witnessed no important change in methods.

In 1800 there were approximately 2,000 members, whose subscriptions produced £12,025; donations, amounting to £322, came mostly from the fees paid on admission by new members. The Society existed for the diffusion of books and tracts; nothing was spent on Charity Schools except £50 towards the expenses of the Annual Service. The East India Mission was in theory a separate work, not completely identified with the Society. By 1810 the number of members had risen to 3,560, by 1820 to 14,530. In 1822 the figure of 15,000 was passed but never rose much above this. In 1820 the total receipts were over £60,000. This remarkable progress may be described as the success of a Church co-operative book society rather than as an evidence of missionary zeal, except in the form of spreading religious knowledge among the largely heathenized masses of England; the clergy and others who bought books at greatly reduced prices did so with the purpose of giving them away and must often have made great sacrifices.

In 1813 the initial benefaction on becoming a member was excused in the case of curates and incumbents with small incomes and was soon to be abolished altogether. The 1812 Report shows how membership was made popular. Corresponding, or country members had been discouraged, it being felt unfair that they should benefit in the same way as full residing members. In future they were to be allowed to buy books on subscribers' terms to the extent of two-thirds of what they collected, the other third to go to the General Fund. This concession, coupled with the formation of District Committees, turned a London Society into a national one. The phrase "corresponding members" lasted for a long time to come, being as late as 1880 applied to parochial clergymen with small incomes specially recommended by their Diocesan Bishops. In 1863 the practice of sending publications priced 6d. and under to subscribers of two guineas was introduced. This, which had the effect of making the Society's publications widely known, was to continue for nearly a hundred years; one disadvantage was that the Literary Committees, knowing that a sale of from 2,000 to 3,000 was guaranteed, had no reason to look narrowly into the intrinsic merits of pamphlets.

Members were entitled to attend the General Meeting, often called The Board, and on special occasions took advantage of their privilege in large numbers. Thus in 1868 the meeting voted for nine candidates for the Standing Committee: the highest number of votes cast was 355, the lowest 157. A system of voting by post seems never to have been considered. In the same year the highly controversial question of grants to the diocese of Natal, whose Bishop (Colenso) had been deposed by the South African Church, came up. A motion to vote £2,000 to be expended by the Standing Committee at its discretion produced a packed meeting, at which 1,439 votes were cast. The motion was accepted after amendments had been rejected; it was made clear at this meeting that the members had no power to make grants other than those recommended by the Standing Committee. However, in 1870 Counsel's opinion was obtained that the Board could deal as it liked with resolutions submitted by the Standing Committee. No difficulties appear to have arisen subsequently, and it was understood that only the Standing Committee could decide what money could be spent on any particular object. Shorn of its powers, the General Meeting lost its attraction and by the beginning of the twentieth century the attendance had become sparse; even the inviting of speakers, generally Missionary Bishops, did not revive it. In earlier days a proposed new member (or a tract) was sometimes blackballed. That is, one adverse vote, cast secretly, could exclude him. The notorious case was when Charles Simeon was blackballed. This did not imply that the Society was hostile to Evangelicalism, but merely that a method, appropriate to the little group of friends who founded the Society, was continued too long. (The box with its supply of white and black balls was passed round at meetings until recently.) In the end Simeon was elected, thanks to the personal influence of the Bishop of London (Blomfield).

Let us now see what the S.P.C.K. stood for during the century. There were a number of definitions of its objects. In 1815, when it was still responsible for the Indian Mission, its work was defined as the distribution of the Scriptures, the Prayer Book, and religious tracts; the education of the poor in the principles of our faith; and missions. The third object was expanded in 1824 to read: "The establishment and support of Christian influence in the Scilly Islands and India." However, in 1821, H. J. Rose, associated with the meeting at Hadleigh Rectory that led to the *Tracts for the Times*, in a sermon preached for the S.P.C.K. in Brighton parish church, had mentioned these objects: (1) the diffusion of Scriptures; (2) the explanation and illustration of Scripture; (3) promoting the use of the Prayer Book; (4) providing books for Christian education. "These are the claims which the Society presents."

The 1839 Report prints the sermon of Bishop Maltby, of Durham, who defines the objects thus: "(1) The education of poor children in the doctrines and duties of Christianity, as taught by the Church of England. (2) The gratuitous supply and cheap distribution of the Holy Scriptures, the Book of Common Prayer, the Homilies of the Church, and Religious Books and Tracts; as well as of books of general instruction. (3) Translations of the Scriptures, the Common Prayer Book, and other books into foreign tongues."

However, in statements of 1832 and 1834 block grants to Bishops of new dioceses were added. As we have seen elsewhere, these began with the enthusiasm aroused by the appointment of the first Bishop of Calcutta and were intended to be used on S.P.C.K. work, i.e., on schools and literature, with the help of the local Committees. An 1847 statement includes among the objects the founding and endowment of Training Colleges for the clergy overseas, meaning grants towards this—it was not the Society's intention to undertake work that demanded further grants for maintenance. The most authoritative utterances were those heard at the opening of the new S.P.C.K. House in Northumberland Avenue on 3 November 1879. There were four speakers, who dealt with the various branches of work in this order: religious literature, general literature, foreign translations, and missionary work. Some of Bishop Lightfoot's words in his sermon on that day may be quoted: "The Society has been from the first essentially sober. Sobriety was stamped upon it from its birth ... all combined to impress upon it that calm, unobtrusive character which it retains to this day." So far, then, the primary importance of literature is evident. By 1892 other departments of work had come to the front, for at the Annual Meeting the following resolution was moved: "That the efforts of the Society to supply wholesome literature for the masses, to provide for the spiritual care of emigrants, to promote medical missions, and increase the efficiency of the Church generally in her many colonial and missionary dioceses, deserve the increased support of all members of the Church at home."

The general policy of the Society in the second quarter of the century is illustrated by a statement made in 1853. In the preceding twenty years these sums had been spent:

	£
Loss on publications, almost entirely due to the sale of Bibles and Prayer Books at members' prices	228,812
Grants of books	62,234
Educational purposes at home	31,980
Building of churches in the Colonies	89,339
Building of colleges in the Colonies	40,220
Founding bishoprics	27,000

Finally, the speech made by the Archbishop of York (Lang) in 1912 may be mentioned. The S.P.C.K. was the "wise, kindly, resourceful maiden aunt of the Church of England". This was kindly, and true enough; but nephews and nieces do not subscribe to support maiden aunts, rather they expect help from them. Some years later, another Bishop at the Annual Meeting describes the S.P.C.K. as the "Cinderella of the Church Societies, who never wore a party frock". An exhaustive study of the Society's records confirms this impression: except in one instance, to be mentioned later, no one would suppose from them that High and Low Church parties existed.

The real turning point in the Society's history was in the early nineteenth century, when in 1811 it promoted the founding of the National Society to be wholly devoted to religious education, and in 1825 handed over its Indian Missions to the S.P.G. Had it been directed with foresight and skill, a critic might urge, it might have developed as the main organization of the Church of England, taking education and missions as well as literature under its wing; and eventually being recognized as an official agency. There is no hint that anyone considered such a development possible or desirable; the Church of England for the next century was to be served by a number of Societies organized for different purposes and advancing on parallel lines.

The Annual Meeting of the Society in London is a comparatively recent institution, as distinguished from the meetings of District Committees. When in 1892 arrangements were made for a public meeting it was stated that none had been held for 25 years. In December 1899 it was agreed to make it a yearly event. At first the date was fixed by "the meeting of Bishops", which indicates the importance of the Society in official estimation. Before long the Archbishop of Canterbury alone chose a date, when as President he could take the chair. After the 1914–18 war the date was changed from May, the traditional month for Societies' meetings, to 8 March, which was termed Founders' Day; the idea had occurred to Canon G. L. Gosling, General Secretary, soon after his entering into office in 1910. It was a reversion to what was done in 1849, the 150th Anniversary of the founding of the S.P.C.K. In December 1848 it was reported that the plans for observing the third Jubilee had been abandoned, for fear of interfering with the 300th Anniversary of the publication of the first English Prayer Book. But the Archbishop had written to say that the objections to commemoration of the 1549 Book were very serious and the plan had been abandoned. He then promised to preach for the Society on 8 March following; the service was held in St Paul's Cathedral and a special Thanksgiving Fund realized more than £3,000.

The Society, or rather its Committee, had a touching faith in the efficacy of petitions. These are some of those recorded in the minutes.

1812. To the Government, presented by William Wilberforce, praying for the establishment of Christianity in India with an Archbishop of Calcutta, three other bishops, and four archdeacons.

1829. To the East India Company, for new bishoprics.

1832. To the East India Company, concerning the tax on pilgrims to heathen shrines, which implied State approval of idolatry.

1837. Another Memorial to the Company for additional bishoprics, after the death of Bishop Turner, the fourth Bishop of Calcutta.

1839. All to the British Government: Against the grant of public money to any scheme which allowed people hostile to the Church to teach religion in schools established under the authority of the State, or to introduce versions of the Bible other than the Authorized Version. This was advertised in the Press;

—On religious education in the Colonies and urging State help for Bishops and clergy;

—Against the Prisons Bill, which gave power to appoint non-Anglican chaplains if as many as 50 non-Anglicans were in a prison.

We turn now to the Society's accommodation. In 1824 it was clear that Bartlett's Buildings were too small for the increasing business, and in any case there was not enough room for the meetings of the Board. The Society therefore left its house, where it had been since 1777, and bought No. 77 Lincoln's Inn Fields. There must have been some spare room at first, for in 1835 the Clergy Mutual Assurance Society (now merged in the London Life Association) was said to have been for a long time housed at the S.P.C.K. However, in 1844 the arrangement was terminated. In 1836 a building in the neighbouring Great Queen Street, formerly occupied by the S.P.G., to whom it was let at a peppercorn rent, was adopted by the Society as a bookshop.

In 1876 the Lincoln's Inn Fields premises proved too strait for the enlarged activities of the Society and courageously the Committee decided to buy a site in Northumberland Avenue, a new business area which was being formed on the land formerly occupied by the town house and grounds of the Duke of Northumberland. This was the last of the palaces on the south side of the Strand, a huge and inconvenient house which had to be demolished. The Metropolitan Board of Works, which had acquired the ground for £500,000, so it was said, sold a small piece of it to the S.P.C.K. for £40,500. The Board of Works insisted on a handsome building in the Italian or classical style, made of stone, marble, or granite, so that the ecclesiastical style desired by the Committee was impossible. The ground was excavated to a depth of 40 feet before putting in the concrete foundations. The plans were approved by the Board of Works, the Royal Institute of British Architects, and the Charity Commissioners. The total cost of £82,880 was defrayed by the sale of stocks held by the Commissioners for the Society as part of the Van Vryhouven Trust, as was a further £4,635 required in 1891 for two additional floors, Subsequently two large hotels (used at the time of writing as Government offices) were built on adjacent sites and the hope that the street would become a shopping centre was not realized. To all appearances this was the final solution of the Society's housing problem and the Committee of that day would have been greatly surprised at the step taken in 1956.

The Society has never enjoyed a large income from which important enterprises could be financed. Subscriptions and donations as given in the 1898 Report were £18,357 compared with £18,977 ten years previously. Legacies varied, but at the close of the century averaged £7,000 a year. Transfers from the Publishing Department for rent and allocation of profits were about £9,000 a year, almost all of which generally went back to the business as payment for books granted by the charitable side. The Bicentenary year, kept in 1898, stimulated interest and led temporarily to an increased income, but, after that, little improvement is recorded.

The natural reaction to the increasing demands upon an almost stationary income was an effort to raise more money by energetic propaganda, for which the services of Organizing Secretaries were required. Not till 1890 do we find the beginnings of a proper Organizing Department. Twenty years later a Home Organization Committee was set up and the number of Secretaries was increased.

Two minor activities of the Society deserve mention at this point. In 1894 a Church Year-Book Committee was formed to supervise the production of the Official Year Book of the Church of England, which, started by the Reverend F. H. Burnside as a private enterprise, had been taken over by the S.P.C.K. An important part of the publication was the statistics of Church work, which were collected by the Society in deference to a resolution of Convocation forwarded by the Archbishop of Canterbury in 1905. This involved the appointment of a staff of four or five clerks, towards whose salaries and incidental expenses bishops, archdeacons, and rural deans were invited to contribute in return for copies of the statistics relating to the areas for which they were responsible. Shortly after the passing of the Enabling Act of

THE OPENING

OF

THE SOCIETY'S NEW HOUSE

IN

NORTHUMBERLAND AVENUE, CHARING CROSS,

MONDAY, *November 3rd,* 1879.

SOCIETY FOR PROMOTING CHRISTIAN KNOWLEDGE,
NORTHUMBERLAND AVENUE.

"The new S.P.C.K. House in Northumberland Avenue"

Cathedral of the Redemption, New Delhi; the last to receive endowment funds from the S.P.C.K.

Gateway Film Productions

U.M.C.A.

St John's College, Lusaka: classrooms

"Grants to school and church building in the Mission Field continued"

1919 and the setting-up of central Church Institutions this work was taken over by the Central Board of Finance.

The men who held the key positions in the Society during the nineteenth century are shadowy figures except for Joshua Watson, a biography of whom in two volumes appeared in 1861, written by Edward Churton, Archdeacon of Cleveland; a recent life by A. B. Webster was published in 1954. Born in 1771, he retired from the family business in 1814, having made a modest fortune, which he gave away with profuse generosity. He was the outstanding layman of his time and was connected with most of the Church movements. With two others he planned the formation of the National Society; he was instrumental in founding the Incorporated Church Building Society and the Additional Curates Society; was one of the first donors to King's College, London; was largely responsible for the spending of the Parliamentary grant for new churches (1818) and for the transference of the S.P.C.K. Missions to the S.P.G. He was also a moving spirit in the plans for rehabilitating Germany after the Napoleonic wars. In 1834 he drafted the letter reasserting their Churchmanship, which was signed by 230,000 heads of families and presented to the Archbishop of Canterbury. The help of such a man was invaluable to the S.P.C.K., whose Treasurer he became in 1814. He at once set to work to reorganize the office, and the great advance made by the Society in the following years was mainly due to his inspiration.

In a letter of 1811 written to Christopher Wordsworth, Watson refers to a proposal submitted to S.P.C.K. "which awakened all the fears and all the prejudices of our worthy Secretary [Gaskin]". In April 1821 the Bishop of London presented Dr Gaskin with his portrait which hangs in the Society's house, saying that he had held the office for 35 years, during which income and expenditure had increased ten times. In his reply Gaskin said: "As my name and my portrait will probably be handed down to distant posterity, associated with those of my invaluable predecessor and father-in-law, the late Rev. Dr Broughton[1] ...". An autograph letter from Gaskin, dated 4 March 1823, is preserved: he resigns since "at my advanced age" he was unequal to the work; he wants to devote the rest of his life "to the discharge of my ministerial duties"—he was Rector of Stoke Newington.

[1] Whose portrait, as well as Gaskin's, hangs in the Society's house.

Two Secretaries became Bishops: W. H. Coleridge, first Bishop of Barbados (1824), and G. Tomlinson, first Bishop of Gibraltar (1842).

(b) EDUCATION

We take up the story of the Society's educational work from Chapter 4, which describes the Charity Schools. In 1811, when the National Society was founded, education was in a deplorable state. Whether in more favourable circumstances an improvement would have been effected we cannot say; certainly the S.P.C.K. showed little sign of being shocked at the state of affairs. But the war which ended in 1815 after nearly a generation made such demands on the national energies that progress was not to be expected. The great increase of the population coupled with high prices made it necessary for children to work for wages. The S.P.C.K. Report of 1810 says that two-thirds of the children of the poor have no schooling. Lord Brougham's Commission of Inquiry into the Education of the Lower Orders reported in 1818 that of 13,500 parishes in England 3,500 had no school. William Otter (afterwards Bishop of Chichester) in his sermon before the S.P.C.K. that year, when there were already 230,000 children in the National Society schools, spoke of "sickly half-naked children" and quoted Malthus freely.

However, in spite of the war consciences were stirred, and in 1811 Dr Marsh, Margaret Professor of Divinity at Cambridge, afterwards Bishop of Peterborough, preached a sermon at the S.P.C.K. Anniversary which urged clergy and laity to combine to promote the education of the poor on definite Church lines. The way seemed open for a forward move, for the hitherto insuperable difficulty of providing teachers for a largely increased number of children had been overcome. Since 1797, when Dr Bell, who had been chaplain at Madras, published his account of "An Experiment in Education", interest had been aroused. His method was simply to use the elder children as monitors. The master gave orders to the monitors, either personally or through the usher; they first copied the teacher and then taught without a model. It was argued that the elder children could explain difficulties to the younger ones better than an adult. To us the method may seem naïve, but when education consisted largely of learning by heart it was a useful expedient; certainly in no other way could the schools have been rapidly expanded. One of Bell's devices was to have the children standing round in a semi-circle. If you corrected a boy you moved up into his place; if you misbehaved you went down to the bottom of the class[1]; a boy who remained steadily at the top was made an assistant teacher. The S.P.C.K. report of 1808, referring to the new method, says that if it is to be a success constant supervision and visiting by the Patrons (modern Managers) of the school are necessary. Mr Lancaster had independently invented a similar system; he wished the schools to have undenominational religious teaching, whereas Dr Bell insisted on the teaching of the Catechism. Professor Marsh's sermon was a call to the Church of England to be loyal to its own principles.

As a result of the sermon the Archbishop of Canterbury (Manners Sutton) took the chair at a meeting of the members of the S.P.C.K. held on 16 October 1811, when it was decided to form a new Society for religious education on a national basis. The dead weight of tradition was probably too strong for the S.P.C.K. For more than a century it had maintained the principle of being an advisory body only, leaving to the local trustees the task of managing their schools. When a new departure was called for, it seemed best to found a new Society. The "National Society for the Education of the Poor in the Principles of the Established Church throughout England and Wales" was the title chosen. The Society was incorporated by Royal Charter in 1817. The supporters of Lancaster's schools formed themselves into a Committee, which in 1814 became "The British and Foreign School Society".

The Charity Schools were gradually transformed into the new "National Schools", which at first the S.P.C.K. could hardly realize had passed out of its hands, to judge by the sermon preached to the Society in 1818, in which it was said that "the mechanism, and government, and superintendence of our schools" are left to the National Society, but we supply materials of instruction and information on very favourable terms. Books were charged at a rate below cost price, and many free grants were made. The newly founded District Committees administered the help and looked upon the supervision of Church Schools as part of their work; in some cases they were joint committees of the two Societies. Thus the first Report of the Preston Committee states that of 8,305 books issued, 5,376 were school books,

---

[1] The method was used at a well-known Grammar School to which I went in 1891. It had the advantage of ensuring constant movement.

and adds that the new system of education was being spread by training teachers (five men and two women) at the Preston National School. The National Society opened its own depot for books and school material in 1845, a step welcomed by the S.P.C.K., which was not so much losing profitable business as avoiding a loss which threatened to be serious in view of the terms of supply. The original stipulation that only S.P.C.K. religious literature should be used in schools connected with the National Society was dropped after a few years.

The Church of England was heroically trying to shoulder the burden of educating a large part of the nation and, it must be confessed, failing in its impossible task.[1] Until 1870 the theory was that the State supplemented the efforts of the religious bodies. In 1833 statistics, probably unreliable, gave well over 1,000,000 as the number being educated in Church elementary schools and about 5% of that figure for those in the Dissenters' schools. Teachers' pay was very low, and the teaching was correspondingly unsatisfactory. The best minds of the day had no illusions. Thus Dr Hook in 1846 published an Open Letter to the Bishop of St David's, in which he exposed the inefficiency of most Church teaching. Many of the clergy did everything in their power to support schools, making up deficits, paying for poor children (1d. a week was a usual charge, but "school pence" tended to rise), and teaching themselves. A pamphlet on religious education published at Salisbury in 1838, by "a clergyman of South Wilts", states that he has a small endowed school, not connected with the National Society. Some tradesmen pay 1s. or 1s. 6d. a week for a better education; he has a night school from 6 to 8 every weekday in the winter. A neighbouring clergyman uses his parsonage for a school: he, his wife and daughters, and four servants, are the teachers.

Prior to 1839 small grants had been made by the Treasury to elementary schools working in conjunction with the National Society and the British and Foreign School Society. In that year the Committee of Council of Education was set up, which was in future to administer all Government grants. The Committee proposed to start Training Colleges and Practising Schools, in which the religious teaching would be given to all alike so far as the common basis of Christianity went,

[1] In 1833 Joshua Watson resigned from the National Society rather than sanction acceptance of Government grants.

the special teaching of the different religious bodies being in the hands of teachers provided by them. Strong opposition to this proposal was expressed by the Archbishop of Canterbury in the House of Lords, which carried an address of protest to the Queen by a large majority. The S.P.C.K. sent petitions to both Houses objecting that "the authority of the State ought not to be given to any scheme of education which involves principles contrary to the Church, as established by the laws of the land" or "which may remove the education of the people from the pastoral care and guidance of the clergy". The National Society adopted a similar petition. The proposals were withdrawn, and the National Society set up its own Training College, towards which the S.P.C.K. voted £5,000. It was high time something was done. As an Anglican pamphlet said, "In England we have no normal schools deserving the name".[1] The Committee of Council gradually established a system of inspection and grants, but many schools remained out of it. According to a report of a Committee of Convocation in 1870, in 1866 Church of England schools not aided by the State had 609,168 children.

Having disclaimed any share in the establishment and management of schools, the S.P.C.K. pressed on with its publishing work and in 1831 the Committee of General Knowledge and Education (described elsewhere) was appointed, in connection with which school lending libraries were set up on a wide scale. The subscription was fixed at 6d. a year per child and a grant of £5 worth of books, to meet an equal sum raised locally, was offered to all schools in connection with the National Society. These books, which were obtained from the S.P.C.K.'s new depot, opened in 1836, provided it with a large accession of business. In 1848 the first of the many grants to Training Colleges was made, when £1,000 was voted to Carmarthen.

Mr Forster's Education Act came in 1870 and the State now undertook responsibility for the education of the nation. About a quarter of all children of school age attended no school, and less than half the children were in schools under inspection. Power was given to local authorities to set up School Boards and to erect and maintain schools at the expense of the rates. This measure, which forbade the giving of distinctively denominational teaching in the new schools, was a challenge to the Church of England, which built many new schools of

[1] *Recent Measures for the Promotion of Education*, 16th edition, 1839.

its own. Indeed in 1881 it was stated that the new Board Schools had provided 1,082,634 places since 1870, a figure substantially exceeded by those in new or extended independent schools. To some extent, it must be acknowledged, these Church Schools, mainly Anglican, were financed by the contributions of those who wished to avoid a School Board with the consequent addition to the rates; but the loyalty of parishes to well known and loved Church Schools was inspired by the desire to avoid what was somewhat inaccurately described as "godless teaching" and evoked real generosity. The S.P.C.K. in 1870 voted £10,000 for Church Schools maintained under the auspices of the National Society. Out of 977 applicants 326 were helped. A further £5,000 was given in 1874.

A sudden crisis arose when in 1870 H.M. Inspectors were no longer allowed to inspect religious knowledge either in Training Colleges or elementary schools. The Society voted £300 towards the expense of appointing Canon Norris to examine and inspect Church Training Colleges in religious knowledge; also £3,000 to inaugurate a system of diocesan inspectors of schools. This was shared among 23 dioceses; not more than one-third of the inspector's salary was to be paid out of the grant or more than £100 to any one man. Canon Norris in 1875 reported that the standard in Training Colleges was very low, many of the answers being shocking. Out of 1,874 candidates $3\frac{1}{2}\%$ got a first class. In the same year (1875) the S.P.C.K. relinquished the work to the National Society in accordance with its policy of initiating work but not assuming permanent responsibility.

Another beneficent work done by the Society was the help given to the many pupil teachers in London Board Schools who were unable to receive Church teaching. This, which entailed Saturday morning lectures, began in 1876 with a grant of £500 for one year and continued for many years. Scholarships for the more promising pupils at Church Training Colleges were awarded, and all pupil teachers who obtained a first class in the Archbishop's Examination in Religious Knowledge were given a prize of £2, at a cost in some years of over £1,000. Continual grants were made to the various Church Training Colleges, and in 1894 £5,000 was voted to the Endowment Fund of King's College, London. A further £10,000 was given to the dioceses in 1872, to help Church Schools in danger of extinction.

In 1877 the Society voted £10,000 to found a College for training schoolmistresses, in conjunction with the National Society, which contributed £5,000. It was then decided that the latter should withdraw from the scheme, leaving the sole responsibility to the S.P.C.K., but making a donation of £2,000. The buildings of St Katharine's, Tottenham, designed by Sir Arthur Blomfield, were erected at a cost of over £33,000; they included accommodation for 104 students and practising schools holding 400 children. A chapel was added in 1888, and many subsequent additions were made. The Government Inspector of Training Colleges reported to the Education Department that "nothing could be more satisfactory than the buildings, which are model premises, admirably ordered, and complete in every way". Needless to say, subsequent inspectors found fault with what was then praised. The first Council, appointed in 1879, consisted entirely of men and it was agreed that the Principal should always be a priest. The Reverend Edwin Hobson, who was appointed (the only male Principal), began his work in temporary buildings in 1878 and continued until 1919. The cost per student was considerably under £50 a year; the fees were £15, and the expected cost to the Society was stated to be a maximum of £500 a year. Present day students will be amused to read that, at the opening of St Katharine's on 24 June 1880, the speaker congratulated the girls on "having obtained admission into this peaceful dwelling place". In 1889 the Society queried the item of pew rents in Tottenham church. The Principal said that the girls could not sit together in the free seats and, unless they did, discipline could not be maintained. The average starting salary for a trained woman teacher in 1891 was said to be £77.

In 1880 St Katharine's College was situated in what was practically a rural area. Today with its adequate playing-fields it forms an oasis in an industrial and dormitory suburb of London. The lack of amenities, in comparison with some other colleges, is in a measure compensated for by the abundant opportunities for practice in all kinds of schools within a small distance.

In 1895 the Society made a grant of £10,500 to buy the freehold of St John's College, Battersea, managed by the National Society, besides giving £2,500 towards its enlargement. The College paid rent to the S.P.C.K. After the 1914-18 war the property was sold and the College was amalgamated with the Chelsea College, now known as the College of St Mark and St John.

In 1888 a Committee was appointed to consider "by what means the Society can assist in the work of spreading Christian knowledge among the masses in our large towns". It recommended the founding of a college in which to educate lay workers. It was felt that working men could best be approached by members of their own class, for whose training there was at present no institution available. Some of the language used reads curiously today—in view of "the fall in clerical incomes; the undesirability of increasing the number of ordained clergy, many of whom can never hope to become incumbents". The College began, in January 1896, in a converted boot factory in Commercial Road, Stepney, with 7 students, and with the Reverend Paul Petit as Warden. The number rose to 17 by the end of the year. A permanent building was opened in 1898. The cost to the Society of a student was £50 a year, towards which he paid £15. The demand for Readers was in excess of the supply, and after a year's training the salary offered was £75 in London and other large cities, and £65 in the country. In 1903 it was reported that about 250 had been turned out: 10 had died, 20 had been ordained, a few had dropped out, and 200 were doing paid lay work. By 1912 the resident students had fallen to 16 and it was becoming hard to place them. After the 1914–18 war it proved necessary to close the college. Conditions had changed in various ways. The type of man who previously offered himself was now thinking of Holy Orders; the shortage of clergy was being met by a considerable extension of voluntary Lay Readers; in the difficult intellectual surroundings of the day a man of little or no education and only one year's training was not required; and bodies like the Missions to Seamen and the Church Army were giving a more effective training to those who felt a call to full time lay work, besides providing the security of a well-established Society.

(c) MISSIONARY GRANTS

The origin of missionary grants has already been described. The first noteworthy gift was £1,000 to Bishop Middleton on his consecration as Bishop of Calcutta, to promote the objects of the Society in his diocese, which, seeing that S.P.C.K. Committees already existed in India, meant the maintenance and development of their work. The endowment of bishoprics overseas made great demands on the Society's resources, and by 1912 £120,000 had been spent on this object. When the Colonial Bishoprics Fund was inaugurated £10,000 was subscribed by the S.P.C.K. In some cases as much as £5,000 was given, but towards the end of the period, £1,000 to meet £9,000, the money not to be paid until the balance was raised, became a customary amount. In some cases the endowment money was invested overseas, earning a much higher rate of interest than at home, but was lost owing to bank failures; so in 1898 it was decided to insist that endowments be invested in England.

The training of the clergy was always an object dear to the Committee and large donations were made for this purpose. Thus in 1847 £2,000 was granted to Adelaide for a College, £1,500 to New Zealand for the completion of St John's College, Auckland, and £2,000 (promised) to Melbourne for one. In 1873 interest shifted from the buildings to the men trained in them, though many grants for the former were still made; in that year the policy of helping individual candidates being trained overseas was adopted. And in 1913 it was decided to give priority to training rather than to churches. The payment of stipends to the clergy was outside the Society's scope, but endowment funds were frequently helped; for example £5,000 was given to Nassau to meet £5,500.

The number of churches which the S.P.C.K. grants helped to build is surprising. For example, in 1864 Huron diocese reported 40 churches erected with the help of the Society. That a few thousand pounds a year could do so much is explained when we remember that a large proportion of them were humble pioneering efforts—wooden shacks in Canada or glorified reed huts in Africa—and were built by voluntary labour. The Society's help was used to buy things that could not be provided locally, such as a corrugated iron roof for an African church, or perhaps window frames.

Schools, too, were often helped, as in 1884, when £5,000 was voted for Christian schools in Tinnevelly. And there were continuous appeals, always responded to, when disasters like hurricanes struck a poor diocese, especially from the West Indies.

The Society's work for Medical Missions began in 1885, when £2,400 was voted for the training of medical missionaries, who were to be (1) doctors who wished to be ordained; or (2) priests who wished to be trained as doctors; or (3) doctors who needed a year's training at a theological college before going out as missionaries. What was to become the chief item of expenditure, the cost of training in medicine those who wanted to go as lay missionaries, and had been provisionally accepted by a bishop or a Society, was added later.

The next year (1886) the offer was extended to women, £1,200 being voted for the purpose. In the following year the plan was enlarged, £5,000 being set apart for buildings and maintenance of Medical Missions in addition to further expenditure on training. The needs of the mission field were limitless and the possible demands on the Society were very great. Of the value of the work there could be no doubt—the only question was whether the S.P.C.K. was the appropriate body to undertake it.

A very different piece of work was the support of the Archbishop's Mission to the Assyrian Christians, formerly a Nestorian Church whose adherents lived in what is now Iraq, then part of the Turkish Empire. It began in 1875 with a visit of friendship and inquiry paid by a well-known scholar, the Reverend E. L. Cutts, on behalf of the Archbishop. If help should be acceptable, it was to take the form of educating these Christians along their own lines, any idea of prose-lytism being ruled out. The visit was warmly welcomed, but the funds subscribed did not allow of more than a very modest start. The Society gave £250 a year towards the cost of this Mission of Help until 1886, when its contribution was increased to £500. This con-tinued until the first world war, on the eve of which the total income of the Mission was about £3,000 a year. The unfortunate little Church was largely dispersed by the tragic events of 1918 and the following years and it proved impracticable to continue the Mission.

This section gives the briefest possible description of a series of beneficent works to which the Society contributed. In practically every case the major share of the cost, and as a rule the responsibility for administration, was in other hands, and a description of the various branches of missionary endeavour which were helped is outside the scope of this book.

Leaving later developments to another chapter, we may summarize the position as it was in 1914. The 1902 Report quotes the speech of a bishop at the Annual Meeting: "The S.P.C.K. always helped him whenever he asked it, and it sent what he asked for." Meant as a compliment, it was really a criticism of the Society's methods. Such indiscriminate giving was possible only if the Society was very wealthy. The Committee had no background of knowledge of a mission acquired over a period of years by careful administration and first-hand acquaintance with the workers such as the Church Missionary Society would have of a diocese like Sierra Leone. It had therefore to trust the bishop who asked for help, and the bishop who was most skilful in describing his needs probably received most help. There was no waste; every part of the Mission Field could make good use of all the money it received. But the question was bound to be asked, whether the best use was being made of the scanty funds available.

In 1913 an attempt was made to improve the Society's methods by dividing overseas dioceses into three classes:

1. Those which can be reasonably expected to be self-supporting or are the special care of some other Society.
2. Those which should receive help but not on the same scale as those in Class 3 (45 in number).
3. Those in special need (about 40).

This was an improvement, but the task of discrimination remained difficult. A good case could often be made out for disregarding the classification and it was hard to define what "the special care of some other Society" meant.

(d) WORK AMONG EMIGRANTS

In March 1836 a letter was read to the meeting of the Society, written by W. E. Gladstone, M.P. for Newark, asking the S.P.C.K. to take up the care of emigrants, in view of their spiritual destitution, beginning with the supply of books.[1] A list of fifty books, of the average price of about half-a-crown, was compiled and grants of these were made to appropriate ships. The books were calculated to supply wholesome reading rather than to teach religion, and not until 1846 was the latter work undertaken seriously. In that year £1,000 was voted to supply emigrants with Prayer Books and other religious books;

[1] Mr Gladstone was always a good friend of the Society. When I became Secretary in 1915, I asked an old member of the staff whether anyone used the books in the so-called Library—editions of the Fathers, etc. He replied: "Only one person, and that was Mr Gladstone, who I remember came sometimes in the lunch hour to consult them."

the offer was taken up with eagerness by Mr T. C. Childs, Vicar of St Mary's, Devonport, who was the pioneer of the new methods. He described them as follows.

"Little could be done until the passengers got on board, for they were at various centres in the town, but when news of embarkation reached him he went to the ship with boxes of Bibles, Prayer Books, tracts, and school books, and began to address the crowd. "The ship itself is divided into three compartments (I speak now of ships fitted out by Government).[1] The hind-part is for the single women, separated by a sort of Venetian screen, with generally a separate hatchway leading to it; the midships are occupied by the married people; and the fore-part by the single men; each of these compartments is separated after the same manner, the berths are upper and lower, ranged along the sides of the ship; the tables run through the middle, dividing the one side from the other, with seats attached.... The people themselves are divided into messes, generally equal to eight grown people in a mess; one of which is termed the Captain, and transacts all the business, such as getting the provisions, etc. There are also constables appointed, who have to preserve order, and to carry out the regulations of the Commissioners and the instructions of the Surgeon, such as seeing to the cleanliness of the floors, etc."

He then describes his addresses and individual work, which included asking each person whether he could read and whether he possessed a Bible and a Prayer Book. He urged them to meet for family prayers each morning after breakfast and to read the lessons for the day, pasting up a Churchman's Almanack so that these might be known. Bad weather sometimes held a ship up for a long time and gave an opportunity for such pastoral work.

In 1849 the work was extended to Liverpool, a small stipend being given to the Reverend J. W. Welsh, and also to Mr Childs. Here, the docks being spread over four miles, conditions were harder. Mr Welsh, in December 1849, reported that since May he had addressed 40,000 people and met 9,000 for private religious conversation. Perhaps this

---

[1] Charles Dickens sailed to America in 1842, and his *Martin Chuzzlewit* was published in 1843. *American Notes* also describes the voyage, which was in a smart ship of 1,200 tons, intended for a good class of traveller. In the novel he transfers his experience of seasickness, etc., to an emigrant ship, of which he will have known by hearsay.

voluntary work stirred up the public conscience; anyhow, in 1852 a
new Passengers Act came into operation, and a Government depot
was established at Birkenhead, at which emigrants were assembled
before embarking, and conditions began to improve. The chaplains
sometimes had to provide ministrations during a period of prolonged
waiting due to unfavourable weather. He gave an address and conducted evening service every day at the Birkenhead depot. The
number of emigrants was enormous by modern standards, reaching
368,764 in 1852; of these perhaps one-third was Irish, or of Continental, mainly German, origin. Of the 1852 total, 244,261 went to the
United States, 32,876 to Canada, and 87,424 to Australia and New
Zealand; by now the rush to the Australian goldfields had begun. The
early emigrants were predominantly male, but in the '50s unmarried
women began to go in large numbers. Mr Welsh, recognizing that idle-
ness was a snare to them on the long voyage, organized ladies' committees in Liverpool and Birkenhead, who provided material for sewing.

In 1852 the first of the long voyage chaplains was appointed, C. J.
Abraham, who in 1858 became the first Bishop of Wellington. These
chaplains at first were called "teachers of the emigrants" and teaching
the illiterate to read was an important part of their work. The length
of the voyage to Australia and its consequent monotony gave the
chaplains many fruitful opportunities, and, in contrast to the North
Atlantic crossing, long periods of fine weather could be expected.

Liverpool continued to be the most important port; in 1854 210,742
persons sailed from the Mersey in 957 ships. But chaplains were
appointed also for Southampton, Greenock, and London in 1855-7. In
1862 the Liverpool chaplain said that Canadian emigration had become
important, the United States being closed. He described the joy caused
by the services: "often have I seen the tears of thankfulness wiped
from the eye of the emigrant when he found the old familiar words
'Dearly beloved brethren' fall once more upon his ear." This may
almost strike the modern reader as humorous, but to a village labourer
who had never left home before and was bewildered by his new surroundings, the link with the past must have been precious. Next year
we find Mr Welsh saying that in general the skilled artisan preferred
the United States, for whose institutions he had unbounded admiration; he left provided with subversive literature, and "with underground feelings of disloyalty to our Queen". The rural labourer was

loyal and more likely to go to British Colonies. This is worth noticing, because it throws light on the traditional anti-British sentiments of the U.S.A., generally attributed to memories of the War of Independence reinforced by Irish immigration. At least in part it must have been caused by the feeling of British immigrants that they had been badly treated in their own land.

Occasionally the Port Chaplains undertook a voyage, but normally the only persons available were priests going to serve overseas. In the present century large ships have often had priests on board travelling for various reasons, who have offered their services. A specimen log sent by a chaplain travelling in 1901 shows the kind of work done. On Sundays he had Holy Communion at 7.30, Mattins and Sermon at 10.30, Sunday School and Children's Service at 2.30, Evensong at 7.30. In the week he had daily prayers at 11 a.m. and every evening "a service of song and story". On Easter Day there were 113 communicants. We may add that in the later nineteenth century the Society provided matrons whenever possible, to look after the unmarried women, and that in 1894 the Plymouth Chaplain baptized 102 emigrants.

In 1881 and 1882 the Archbishop of Canterbury (Tait) challenged the Society to increase its efforts in this field; and in particular to publish handbooks giving full information about the countries to which emigrants went. This was done on a large scale, additional Port Chaplains were appointed, great efforts were made to persuade the clergy to write letters of commendation, and gradually the Churches of the countries receiving immigrants formed organizations for welcoming them. Little remains to be chronicled in regard to twentieth-century developments. In 1902 a large number went to South Africa with the end of the war, and Canada in particular absorbed many in the years before 1914. In the inter-war years, 1919 to 1939, immigration was taken very seriously by Canada and Australia, though during the economic crisis that began in 1929 large numbers returned to Britain. After 1945 the Dominions encouraged and controlled immigration more than ever before, and for the first time Australia and New Zealand supervised spiritual ministrations. In England, the problem confronting the S.P.C.K. was complicated by the formation in 1955 of the Church of England Council for Commonwealth and Empire Settlement, which at first sight seemed to overlap with the work of the Society.

At the time of writing the situation is so different from that described above that re-thinking is necessary. The heroic age has passed; the adjective may seem out of place for work on so small a scale but it is undoubtedly appropriate for the little band of heroic men who laboured amid such difficulties. Government control or supervision is everywhere in operation now, and there is no longer any need for philanthropy. Comfort, recreation, contact with the outside world are provided by the large ships of today, and the forlorn people welcoming a friendly voice and a shake of the hand hardly exist. The opportunities open to a faithful priest now are probably very much the same as in a parish: his ministry will be welcomed by the few and what he can do for the outsiders in three or four weeks will depend on his personality.

12

Nineteenth-Century Publishing and Bookselling

(a) BIBLES AND PRAYER BOOKS

THE BACKGROUND of the publishing of these two books is the privilege enjoyed by three English institutions, the Queen's Printers and the Universities of Oxford and Cambridge (who exercise it through their University Presses). It goes back to the restrictions originally imposed by the State on the new art of printing, which after 1640 were limited to "the King's books", in particular the Authorized Versions of the Bible and the Book of Common Prayer. No restrictions have existed in Scotland since 1890, but only one firm has availed itself of the liberty to print these two books. As there is no customs barrier between England and Scotland, the importation of Scottish-printed books into England must be allowed. In the eighteenth century Basket, the King's Printer, had exclusive rights which he tried to enforce, but in 1758 the Courts decided that Cambridge University had been "intrusted with a concurrent authority", a ruling which of course included Oxford.

It was out of the question that the S.P.C.K. should print its own editions of these books, but there was nothing to prevent its acting as a main distributor. It began systematic "publication", in this sense, in 1705, the chief motive being to facilitate the procuring of them by the Charity Schools. A Newcastle correspondent in 1712 complained that the booksellers had raised the price of Bibles to schools from 3s. to 4s.[1]

[1] An interesting letter from Mr Fox of Potterne, Wilts., dated 9 May 1723, reports the Master of the Temple, formerly Vice-Chancellor of Cambridge University, as saying that the privilege was justified, since without it the Bibles would be full of errors; the high prices were due to the duty levied on the large amount of paper used in books of this size.

The 1734 Report states that Bibles and Prayer Books are sold at the prime cost of the sheets, the Society paying for the binding; this in 1764 cost 1s. 8d. for the Cambridge demy octavo Bible, while that of the cheapest Prayer Book cost 9d. In 1751 the price of the cheapest Bible was 1s. 10d., with which may be compared the 1s. edition sold by the B.F.B.S. before the 1939–45 war. The Society's charitable work in this direction was an indispensable factor in religious education. Throughout the century we find periodical references to discussions with the Presses about errors in their books. The Society must have been in a strong position as a big buyer to be able to criticize in this way; anyhow in February 1745 Mr Basket, the King's Printer, agreed that it might appoint fit persons to examine his editions of the Bible. In 1791 the S.P.C.K. had 58 different editions of the Prayer Book on its list, the type of some being impossibly small by modern standards. The Report of that year mentions the "prodigious increased demand" from Sunday Schools.

In the early nineteenth century S.P.C.K. was the main provider of the Army and Navy. The Navy was supplied at cost price and every new ship was stocked at the Society's expense. The same was true of the Army, which in 1830 was stated to derive half its supplies, and in 1837 all, at cost price. The 1838 Reports says that all workhouses have their books at 10% below cost price. Later in the century there was a period of extensive Church building. The *Literary Churchman* of 1 February 1873 says that between 1868 and 1873 the number of London churches increased from 617 to 742, the new buildings presumably getting their books from the S.P.C.K. In 1864 the Admiralty agreed to pay 4d. a copy for the Prayer Book bound up with Tate and Brady's Psalms, to give to every boy entering the Navy, instead of receiving them gratis as heretofore. Some figures show the magnitude of the business at this time. In 1876 187,346 Bibles and 411,058 Prayer Books were distributed, in 1885, 135,254 Bibles and 344,529 Prayer Books.[1] The 1886 Report defines the objects of the Society as (a) "the circulation of Bibles, Prayer Books, and books and tracts, especially in England and Wales", (b) other designs calculated to promote Christian knowledge in the Colonies. At this time the amount spent in buying

[1] "There can be but few houses in England, where religion has any place, in which Bibles or Testaments and Prayer Books issued by the Society are not to be found." (1878 Report.)

Bibles and Prayer Books was about five-eighths of total purchases. Towards the end of the century sales began to diminish; thus in 1895 they were 17% below those of 1881. The reason was that the original publishers began to develop their own methods of distribution instead of relying on the S.P.C.K., which for its part was unable to spend so much on maintaining its position owing to other claims on its income. The tendency has continued until today the Society is little more than an ordinary bookseller in its dealings with the Presses.

The question of the Apocrypha was often debated. At first it was always included with the Bible, but after 1743 the purchaser was allowed to choose whether he would have it or not. The complete Bible then cost about 1s. extra. In 1845 it was agreed that the Apocrypha should always be supplied unless its omission was demanded. In some editions it was unobtainable, so the Presses printed specially for the Society; large editions had to be taken, which twenty-eight years later had not been sold out. A Church Services book which omitted the Apocrypha lessons was withdrawn in 1872 at the request of more than 300 members.

(b) RELIGIOUS TRACTS AND BOOKS

The rise and fall of the tract is an interesting bypath of religious history. Its vogue was due to the existence on the one hand of a large number of persons who had learned to read and on the other of many devout people anxious to help their less fortunate neighbours by giving them literature that would inculcate profitable lessons. It is easy to make fun of the missionary-hearted busybody and to picture the tracts being used to light pipes. But we must remember the scarcity of printed matter in the first half of the nineteenth century and the little opportunity that the "poor" had of keeping up the reading they had learned at school; also, the printed word as such was still treated with respect and presumably read. The tract varied from a short simple exposition of some point of faith or conduct to a miniature theological treatise.

Responsibility for tracts prior to 1834 rested with the Board or General Meeting, which dealt with the publications brought to it by the Standing Committee. In 1834 the Tract Committee was appointed, its members being drawn from the Standing Committee. At first its chief work was the revision of old tracts (see below), which proved so thankless a task that in 1836 it threatened to resign unless the Standing Committee took back the work of revision, leaving to it the provision of new publications. In 1838 a crowded meeting of members accepted a new policy by 210 votes to 65. The Tract Committee in future was not to be confined to members of the Standing Committee and five Bishops were to be appointed as referees; previously there were five referees, two of them being bishops, the Archbishop of Canterbury and the Bishop of London—they continued to act for some years to come.

The procedure was complicated; it applied for the most part to books published elsewhere which were recommended for listing on a catalogue of books sold by the Society. In the case of an original work, four members recommended a manuscript, which was referred to the Committee by the Standing Committee. After being read by members it was set up in type and proofs were sent to the referees. When their approval had been gained and the author had agreed to any proposed alterations, the amended document went to the Standing Committee, which authorized its going to the Board. Its fate was then settled by ballot, and a publication approved by the Archbishop was sometimes blackballed by the vote of an anonymous member who happened to be present.

The output of tracts was very large. In the 1859 Report 112 new ones were listed. The classification of the public for whom popular religious works were intended was minute. The 1874 Report contains the following among others: for self-educated persons of average ability, for semi-educated persons, for imperfectly educated persons, for infidels, for deists, for general distribution (the most common), for very plain people, for untidy wives; even, for those who have itching ears, wandering from church to chapel. In 1861 half a million copies of a tract on the census were distributed (as late as 1891 the vicar of a large Yorkshire town preached a sermon on the census, which was reported in full by the local press, assuring people that there was no fear of a pestilence following the census, as in 2 Samuel 24). Narrative tracts were very popular. A navvy is said to have wept over *Slab Castle*. *How William Temple rose in the World* (1874) is an alluring title. The type of publication to which the bishops paid attention is illustrated by *The Orphans of the Castle* (to which three objected), *Sally Jack's Secret*, *Mike the Donkey Boy*, and *Farmer Brown and his new Pew*.

The Society's publishing was scrutinized carefully by its many members, to whose views the Committee paid almost undue deference. In 1856 a reference to *Uncle Tom's Cabin* was excised at the wish of a Mr Smith. However, in 1843 Lord Ashley (afterwards Earl of Shaftesbury) resigned from the Standing Committee because his request that *A Lancashire Collier Girl* be removed from the catalogue was refused—the title, he said, implied approval of such employment. In 1841 the Wotton-under-Edge Committee protested against the alteration of a tract, which was a triumph for the Dissenters of the neighbourhood, who claimed that the Church of England had circulated what it owned to be false doctrine. In 1833 *Deathbed Scenes* was withdrawn from circulation because a District Committee raised objection. As a result of this careful sifting the tracts were declared by members to be "inanimate, dry and didactic" (1846) and a questionnaire sent to local Secretaries in 1870 elicited the criticism that the S.P.C.K. literature was colourless and dull; the time had passed for literature that would offend no one. Perhaps the most enlightened criticism was that of the Furness Committee in 1836; they have confidence in the Tract Committee under the Referees, but "they protest against the sentiments of known and respected writers being replaced by those of persons unknown to them".

The seriousness with which S.P.C.K. publications were treated is shown by a letter from Cambridge University Library reported on 1 July 1830, asking for a set of the Society's tracts "as the funds of the University were not in a position to meet the expense of their purchase".

The gallant attempt to preserve a system of episcopal control of Church publishing, and even of the sale of other publishers' books by the S.P.C.K., deserves a comment. The chief difficulty was physical—the distant homes of the Referees. Normally they did not attend meetings, though when a Bishop did come he took the chair. Everything had to be done by post and delays were inevitable. The Bishops often took different views and the Secretary spent much time in explaining the views of one to the others. Frequently a Bishop wrote to say that he had no objection but, if any one else objected, better not publish. The Bishop of London being accessible took the most active part, having frequent interviews with the Secretary and even in 1839 asking the author of a tract to come and discuss it with him. In 1843 the Committee asked that the unanimous approval of the Bishops be not required, but the Society refused to sanction this. On several occasions a Bishop vetoed the publication of a work written by one of his colleagues. Such importance was attached to the Society's imprimatur that a tract once sanctioned was reprinted automatically unless the Referees gave permission for its discontinuance; and leave was not asked unless the annual sale fell below 500. Eventually, the Referees became a Court of Appeal, only resorted to when the Committee could not agree.' Since the Board of Referees could never meet, the difficulties remained and, in the twentieth century, the Bishops, if consulted at all, were asked their advice as individuals, the advice being always taken. But the existence of Referees was a valuable safeguard against unwise decisions on the part of the Committee.

The question may be asked, how did the Society manage to get authors at all, if the conditions of acceptance were so severe? In the first half of the century, when few books, as distinct from tracts, were published, there was little difficulty. The pay was good, as will be shown presently, and the prestige of being published by the Society was considerable. The precautions ensured that publication was a testimonial to one's orthodoxy. In 1836 the Tract Committee suggested to the Board that a note be inserted in all publications: "The S.P.C.K. does not consider itself responsible for every expression contained in the publications placed upon its catalogue, but adopts them as being generally calculated to promote Christian knowledge upon the principles of the Church of England", but the suggestion was not accepted. In 1835 it was agreed that the author's name be put on the title-page when the book was good enough; no one seems to have noticed the implication that the Society was taking full responsibility for the inferior books.

Later in the century resolutions were passed that "the best writers" be invited, but little came of them. In 1867 the Committee invited "Mr Tischendorf", who replied that he was "preoccupied"; and Dr Westcott, who, when asked to write a popular work on the New Testament Canon, answered that it was impossible to treat the subject "in a striking manner fairly": the evidence before A.D. 175 was meagre and so capable of "ingenious distortion". The Society's business methods must have left a bad impression. In 1864 at the meeting on 13 July, 48 manuscripts were given out to the members of the

Committee, to be considered at the next meeting after the vacation —4 November.

A few notes taken from the Society's correspondence with authors are added here. In 1832 J. H. Newman was invited to write a history of England, but he was too busy to undertake the task. Long afterwards (1879) he offered the Society chapters of *The Grammar of Assent* for publication in pamphlet form. In 1832 also Dr Burton, Regius Professor of Divinity at Oxford, complained of omissions in Mrs Trimmer's *Abridgement of the Old Testament* and offered to arrange a more ample work of the same kind himself. In 1838 Dr Hook's famous sermon before Queen Victoria, *Hear the Church*, was declined.

The extent of episcopal supervision is shown by a letter from the Bishop of London in 1838 about a manual for use in workhouses: the Society, he said, ought not to put out any prayers for worship unless they were approved by the Bishops. The next year the Archbishop of Canterbury vetoed the publication of a form for the consecration of churches. A proposal made in 1856 to publish an edition of *The Pilgrim's Progress* was blocked by the opposition of the Bishop of Bangor. In 1866 the Society, which had been publishing an edition of Keble's *The Christian Year*, discontinued it when James Parker, the publisher who supplied it, stated that in all future editions the verse for 5 November (Gunpowder Plot)

> O come to our Communion Feast:
> Here present in the heart,
> *Not in the hands,* the Eternal Priest
> Will his true self impart

would read "As in the hands".

Dr Westcott in 1868 wrote a pamphlet on the Resurrection, which was declined on the advice of the Bishops of Winchester, Lincoln, and Llandaff, who feared it would cause criticism. The author had refused to correspond with the Society about alterations but gave the Committee a free hand in making them.

The prestige of the Authorized Version is illustrated by a complaint made in 1864 that Dean Alford, in a sermon published by the Society, had made his own translation of a Bible passage, which was described as a slur on the A.V.; he was asked to omit the quotation. In 1881 an author was told that a book holding the view that Isaiah 40–66 was

written in the Captivity and Daniel, in its present form, in the Macca-
baean period could not be accepted. The 1905 Report says that an
answer to S. R. Driver's Commentary on Genesis has been published.
The Society has always made a point of encouraging the circulation of
the Apocrypha; but a complaint made in 1846 that copies of the
Apocrypha had been bound with a label containing the Collect of
Advent II ("all holy Scriptures") was met by ordering the substitution
of the relevant words from Article VI. We are surprised to learn that
a religious work by Charlotte Yonge (*Key-notes*) caused a great deal
of correspondence with the Episcopal Referees and that she was
considered grasping in her financial demands.

Perhaps the Society's biggest venture in the nineteenth century was
the Commentary on the Bible, which was launched with the help of
a grant of £1,000 from its charitable funds. Walsham How, afterwards
the first Bishop of Wakefield, agreed in 1863 to write on the Four
Gospels: "If I have any qualification, it is only the power of putting
things simply—a very inferior talent." The New Testament was
followed by the Old Testament and the Apocrypha; How's volume
had a sale of several hundred thousand copies. Instructions sent to
authors in 1873 said that verbal criticism was not required: "When the
accuracy of a passage is a matter of scholarship, and the whole bearing
of a passage is little affected by it, it will be best in general to abide by
our Authorized Version, without suggesting deviation from it. The
harmony of the Old Testament with the New must, of course, have
a prominent place in the Commentary." In 1875 the Committee
instructed the authors to omit all dates before the call of Abraham. In
respect of educational method they were less enlightened, for in 1870,
commissioning a history of the Kings of Israel and Judah, they
demanded that it consist mainly of conversations and follow the
example of Mrs Markham.

In 1886–7 the author responsible for an edition of *The Imitation of
Christ* was told to add a note to various passages, "written for Roman
Catholics", and to give the book an Anglican tone.

The Society's policy in respect of hymns was never adventurous.
For generations the Church of England, like the Church of Scotland
and unlike the Congregationalists and Methodists, held that only
inspired words should be sung in the regular services of the Church
and therefore the (metrical) psalms were deemed sufficient. The early

collections of hymns made by Evangelical Churchmen seem to have been intended for non-liturgical evening gatherings. The turning point was in 1819, when the Archbishop of York sanctioned a hymn book for St Paul's Church, Sheffield, to the editing of which he gave personal attention. By custom a few exceptions to the rule of only having metrical psalms were allowed, such as "While shepherds watched their flocks by night" and "The people that in darkness sat", straightforward metrical paraphrases of Bible passages, and "*The* Morning Hymn" and "*The* Evening Hymn" of Bishop Ken. These served as a bridge to the fuller use of "non-Scripture" hymns. After 1819 individual churches began to publish their own collections, which by 1861, when *Hymns Ancient and Modern* appeared, had become very numerous.

In 1834 the Tract Committee consulted the Board as to the expediency of publishing a collection of Psalms *and Hymns*, and in 1837 it was agreed to add hymns for the festivals and the Sacrament as well as "the Morning and Evening hymns" to the Society's book of extracts from the new version of the Psalms. But not till 1859 did a book appear entitled *Psalms and Hymns*, in which hymns fairly balanced psalms, and even then the only book bound up with the Prayer Book was the Psalms in the Old and New Versions. In 1862 it was agreed not to sell *Hymns Ancient and Modern*, whether for doctrinal reasons or because it was a serious competitor is not stated. A new book on a more ambitious scale was proposed by Walsham How in 1870, to consist of *Psalms and Hymns* with an appendix of equal length, to be sold at 1d. John Ellerton was to be his chief assistant. Mr Arthur Sullivan, not yet famous, agreed to be musical editor for a fee of £250 plus £150 to be spent on the use of copyright material. In the next few years there were continual references of lines of hymns to Episcopal Referees, against whose strictures the Committee generally championed the authors. When in 1874 the book was published under the title *Church Hymns*[1] a large sale was secured, as was to be expected when the editors were men like How, Ellerton, and Sullivan, who hit the popular taste unerringly. But, as so often in England, private enterprise prevailed over semi-official action and *Ancient and Modern* outdistanced its competitors. So the S.P.C.K. began again, this time under an *ad hoc* Committee. The new book was edited with very great care but, admirable as it was in many ways, both on the literary and the

[1] The words alone had already appeared separately under that title in 1872.

musical side, it was a little behind the times when it was published in 1903 and compared with other books, or even with its predecessor, seemed a little dull. Anyhow, though for a generation it had a respectable sale, it eventually dropped out of the race.

Two subjects have been left for special treatment: the Anti-Infidel Committee and the revision of old tracts. The Committee was set up in 1819, to deal with the threatening movements among the working classes in London and the Northern manufacturing towns. It got to work in 1820 and subscriptions towards its work were invited; the University of Oxford gave £200, the Grocers' Company £100. In the history of the S.P.C.K. this Committee played an important part, for it was allowed to open a temporary shop in Fleet Street, the pioneer effort of the Society's retail trading operations—all previous bookselling had been from an office. In 1823 the Committee reported that 677,491 books had been sold and that the urgency had passed.

A report from the Standing Committee in 1830 referred to this effort. "The enemies of religion were foiled in their attempt and disappointed of their expected triumph." The emergency had arisen again. It was decided to revive the Committee. Next year it was reported that sixteen tracts had been published, including *The Shepherd of Salisbury Plain* and *The Infidel's Life and Death*. Yet another attempt was made in 1870, when a Sub-Committee on Infidelity was appointed, presently to be called The Christian Evidence Committee. Infidelity, said a special report, was alarmingly prevalent, especially among the working classes, while among the better educated "scientific infidelity" was the chief enemy. Existing literature was out of date and cumbrous. £1,000 was voted for the remuneration of authors, who were promised exemption from the customary supervision. Little came of the attempt. In discussing a programme members urged tracts on the character of Jacob, and Geology, and the Bible; also the modernizing of Butler's *Analogy* and Paley's *Horae Paulinae*. A number of manuscripts were rejected and paid for. Also substantial books which would have been published anyhow were offered to the Society, such as Bishop Alexander's Bampton Lectures on the Psalms, for which the author asked £350 and was refused. The Christian Evidence Committee, which seems unnecessary by the side of the Tract Committee, never flourished, though it lasted for about sixty years. In 1839 the Bishop of Lincoln had written to urge another revival of the original

Committee, to meet the propaganda of "the Socialists who swarm in Birmingham and its neighbourhood and whose atheistical and licentious principles are spreading with awful rapidity"; the Episcopal Referees advised against any action.

The revision of tracts provoked a lively controversy. In the eighteenth century the Society had freely edited portions of well known authors, especially the Caroline Divines, with the view of turning them into useful tracts; where copyright existed, the leave of its owners was obtained. This practice continued in the nineteenth century, tracts being revised from time to time to suit the changed circumstances. Doctrinal issues do not seem to have been raised until shortly before 1837, in which year five Essex incumbents published a book of 118 pages entitled *Two Memorials: addressed to the General Meeting of the Society for Promoting Christian Knowledge, on the alleged corrupt Character of some of its Publications*. This was a protest of militant Evangelicalism, which stated that the S.P.C.K. originated at a time when the pure doctrine of the Reformation had been forgotten, a "dry and unevangelical" period dominated by Tillotson; its publications taught salvation by good works and grace was left out of sight. The Society is described as being in "an awful condition". By their own confession Evangelicalism appears as an interloper in the Church of England, claiming to go back to the neglected Reformation Fathers. The subject had been discussed at a General Meeting on 5 April 1836, when the Archbishop (Howley) presided and three other Bishops were present. The result of the discussion was that no action was taken. In 1839, 73 Somerset clergymen petitioned the Society on behalf of the Essex Memorial and in 1841 a similar petition came from Plymouth. The reply to the latter was that out of 18 tracts containing 60 passages objected to, 8 were out of print and 3 had been revised. As to the other 7, passages taken out of their context may be misread but in their context are innocent. No theological writers could escape the charge of opposition to the Scriptures, Articles, Liturgy, and Homilies "if their works were subjected to the sort of test employed by the memorialists". However, two tracts were discontinued with a view to the Society's works being "perfectly unobjectionable". Paid revisers were then appointed to ensure fidelity to the original texts. This did not solve the difficulty. By now there were many counter-memorials against altering the text of such writers as Andrewes, Cosin, and

Nelson, and in 1844 the Society had to sanction some edited texts provided that the title page showed the character of the edition.

The Society's failure to make an impact on the educated part of the nation was largely due to its tenacious hold on the principle of stratification of classes. As late as 1871 it appealed to the local Committees to find writers who would produce books for all classes—"the old, the poor, the superficially educated, tradesmen, teachers, gentry, etc."; also for children, "adapted to their several stations". The Bishop of Bangor in 1858 and 1859 disapproved the publication of books treating of "a class of life above that of the persons to which the Society's tracts are applicable". So the attempt to widen the scope of publishing met with difficulties. By tradition its publications were intended to be bought by people who would give them to "the poor". Probably the inevitable note of patronage was not resented. We must own that the Society was slow in meeting the need for new methods. But, granted the self-imposed limitations, we cannot withhold our meed of admiration for the heroic efforts of the Tract Committee, which had to satisfy the Episcopal Referees on one side and on the other a suspicious and theologically-minded public, whose susceptibilities had to be considered, lest charitable subscriptions be withdrawn.

(c) GENERAL LITERATURE

After the foundation of the National Society in 1811 the S.P.C.K. was expected to provide books for the rapidly growing number of Church Schools. So far as religious literature was concerned, this was merely continuing the output of books for Charity Schools. For some years co-operation between the two Societies was so close that the only religious literature used in schools affiliated to the National Society was that published by the S.P.C.K. Such non-religious books as were circulated by the latter were those of other publishers that had been approved by the General Meeting. The kind of thing that won approval is suggested by a *History of England compiled from the Cottager's Monthly Visitor.*

However, in 1832 the outlook appeared so black that more vigorous methods were called for; it was the year of the Reform Bill, and the riots at Bristol and elsewhere were fresh in men's memories. A special Committee reported that the desire for knowledge had increased

greatly; the population of England was becoming a reading population. The available literature was harmful. The sale of penny weeklies
in London alone was nearly 300,000. Not one supported the established religion; they taught rebellion, sedition, and hostility to the
Church of England. There were societies to provide books; one sold
£27,000 worth in a year, another £46,000. The formation of a General
Literature Committee was recommended, to have a free hand and not
to confine itself to the S.P.C.K. as previously understood.

The new Committee began at once with immense energy. Two of
its members were particularly active: William Otter, friend of Coleridge and Malthus, the first principal of King's College, London, and
from 1836 to 1840 Bishop of Chichester; and George Chandler, Dean
of Chichester. Chandler was Vicar of All Souls, Langham Place,
London, and at this time did not reside in Chichester apart from three
months in the summer. He was the leading spirit on the Committee,
generally taking the chair, and reading and revising very many of the
manuscripts. J. W. Parker, a London firm, was appointed publisher,
and his professional skill must have been responsible for the immediate
success of the Committee's operations. In 1833 the Society was informed that no book had been a failure. The great achievement was
The Saturday Magazine, which reached a circulation of 70,000. It was
reprinted in the United States and the illustrations were reproduced all
over the world. The Society's organization contributed much to the
success. Correspondents were appointed in the large towns and as
many as eighty of the District Committees sent donations in aid of the
venture. A light is thrown on the Committee's methods by an objection raised to the appointment of a Dissenter as agent in Bedford—
they refused to make a change.

The Committee pressed on with their plans for books, which included commentaries, volumes of sermons, and metrical paraphrases
of the Collects, Epistles, and Gospels. Some of the projects were
"referred to the S.P.C.K.", which suggests that the new body, though
financed by the Society, was claiming independence. In any case it was
clearly proposing to compete with the normal religious publishing of
the Society. So in 1835, after the report of a special Committee had
been received at a meeting presided over by the Archbishop of
Canterbury, it was decided to make the General Literature Committee
a part of the Society's organization; it was instructed not to publish

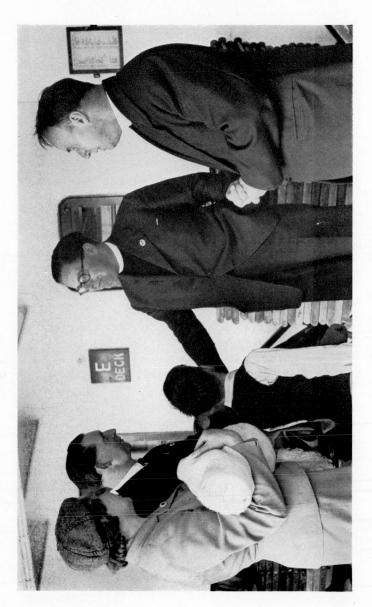

"The spiritual care of emigrants would continue"

THE
SEAMAN's
MONITOR;
OR,

Advice to Sea-faring Men,

With Reference to their

BEHAVIOUR

Before, in, and after their Voyage.

With Prayers for their Use.

Also an ADDRESS to the Officers and Seamen
in His Majesty's *Royal Navy.*

With a CAUTION to *profane Swearers,* and
a feasonable ADMONITION against
Mutiny and Piracy.

By JOSIAH WOODWARD, D.D.

Published by His Majesty's special Command.

The FOURTEENTH EDITION.

LONDON:

PRINTED FOR F. AND C. RIVINGTON,
BOOKSELLERS TO THE
SOCIETY FOR PROMOTING CHRISTIAN KNOWLEDGE,
No. 62, ST. PAUL'S CHURCH-YARD,

By Bye and Law, St. John's Square, Clerkenwell.

1799.

[Price 4d. or 25 for 7s.]

THE DEER.

"Literature . . . designed for special classes"

works on definitely religious subjects, and, if the two Committees disagreed on the interpretation of this rule, the Standing Committee was to delimit their frontiers. The new Committee's publications were to be in a separate catalogue.

In the following year the assets and liabilities of the Committee were handed over to Mr Parker in return for a yearly payment of £375 for 20 years; in 1837 Parker took over *The Saturday Magazine*. Exactly how the new agreement worked is difficult to ascertain. The Society provided the Committee with funds to buy the copyrights and to defray the costs of drawings and blocks and editorial expenses; Parker was supplied with manuscripts which he published at his own risk, the Society helping sales considerably by its free or assisted grants to members, schools, and parishes. When after a few years it became its own publisher, there was a long drawn out dispute, Parker complaining that the new books spoiled the sale of those he had bought and holding back his annual payments in protest.

The Committee's methods were by modern standards amateurish. For a long time there was no expert Secretary, the warehouse Superintendent being left to find people at his discretion to revise manuscripts and see them through the press. The members took responsibility for the contents of their books; a minute of 1841 records that pages 45 to 65 of a book were to be read in proof by seven of them, three pages each. Such care was necessary, for like the Tract Committee they had to consider public opinion both outside and inside the Society. As a specimen of the latter, at the General Meeting of June 1841 a vote of censure on the Committee was moved, condemning illustrations in a book which depicted the Hebrews in the wilderness with worn-out shoes, thus contradicting Deuteronomy 29.5: "Thy shoe is not waxen old upon thy feet". Examples of the former are resolutions condemning passages in S.P.C.K. books, passed by the Rural Deanery of Knebworth in 1861 and by the clergy and laity of Stevenage in 1864 —this time referring to a story entitled *The Errand Boy*. In the early days of the Committee books were commissioned in a casual manner. In 1841 one member remarked "I know a man who could write a book", and was authorized to commission him. In 1842 another told of an unnamed person who could write on Malachi to Our Lord and was authorized to offer him £12 a sheet. Payments in these cases were made to the member concerned, who passed them on to his friend.

Little needs to be said about school books on other than religious subjects. Long after the National Society had started its own educational publishing the S.P.C.K. continued its efforts to compete. There seems to have been no idea of planning according to changing ideas of education, so that the Society was always behind the times. The Committee evidently enjoyed their work, though only rarely had the members qualifications such as would have commended them for employment as readers by commercial publishers.

The first suggestion of an outside reader for school books was made in 1875. A special Committee reported in 1876 that the Society could not hope to compete with the Readers produced by other publishers. In 1872 Her Majesty's Inspector had written to ask that moral lessons be not introduced into Science Readers; this suggests a sufficient reason for the Society's relative failure in this field. As early as 1849 it had been criticized for giving too much natural history and physical science in its Readers, and not enough ethics and history, and in May 1850 it was agreed that ethics should predominate.

Ethics certainly predominated in the Committees' children's story books. Fifty or sixty new titles a year was no unusual number. The Catalogue pointed out the exact moral that each story was meant to inculcate. *Little Dora Playfair* was intended to induce little girls to go to school willingly. *Little Margaret Brown* (who died) was advertised as "for young children", presumably to prepare them for death. *The Cottager's Christmas Dinner* was "on contentment". *Leila's Quest* "shows the folly and danger of disobedience to one's elders". Many stories were labelled "for servants", often to discourage "the love of dress". One gets the impression of Victorian parents perusing an enormous list of books and picking out the exact antidote to their children's faults. How alluring the descriptions must have sounded! "Inculcates the duty of tidiness", "Shows the drawbacks of unpunctuality", etc. That this is not an unfair description of Victorian methods appears from the Summary of a tract put out by the other Committee: "to give to emigrants on first seeing the lights of the land they are going to".

Nothing is easier than to deride our forefathers; but putting ourselves in their place we may well doubt whether we could have done better. "The poor" had no purchasing power, at least not for books, and children's stories were bought by the upper and middle class to give away as school rewards or otherwise. They had therefore to be such as would justify the benevolent in doing good. If the stories depicted a sheltered existence with nurses and governesses (or working-class life seen through middle-class spectacles) and naughtiness of a very mild kind, that may have been the best way at the time to instil ideas of culture. At any rate, other publishers produced similar books. *The Literary Churchman* in 1857, reviewing *Charlotte Drew's Pinch* (Masters) said: "This is the story of a wilful schoolgirl, who gets into trouble with her schoolmistress by pinching the other children on various occasions . . . no very distinct moral lesson is conveyed." The same paper in November 1880 wrote: "The issues bearing the familiar device 'S.P.C.K.' have thrown off that character of elementariness, 'goodiness' (we do not mean *goodness*, for they have as much 'goodness' as ever), and general dullness which some people thought used to attach to them . . . we can hardly praise [them] too highly", and in October 1882 remarked that "the binding is more tasteful than ever". While the general run of fiction was redolent of mild domesticity, there were many adventure stories by the best writers of the day; a child restricted to the Society's books would not have done too badly.

At an early date in its career the General Literature Committee began to publish popularizations of history, science, and nature study, and with the coming of the Reverend E. McClure in 1875 as Editorial Secretary such books increased in number and excellence. His own interests were very varied. He was not a theologian but had many friends in scientific and archaeological circles, whom he persuaded to offer their books to the Society. Before graduating at Trinity College, Dublin, he had worked in the gold-fields of Australia and Peru, and served in the American Navy, and was admirably fitted to promote the publication of boys' adventure stories.

In the last decade of the century what was described as a crisis in publishing developed. The demand for cheapness was met by reprints sold through drapers, etc. The Society produced a series of penny books, including *Robinson Crusoe*, Scott's *The Talisman*, Southey's *Life of Nelson*, and Captain Marryat's books; also a 6d. series of famous books, running to 408 pages and strongly bound in cloth. These ventures had a very large sale but, as will be guessed, involved the Society in losses and had to be discontinued.

Finally, an episode of 1893 may be recalled. Fifty members of the Society, including three Bishops, objected to a book *Our Secret*

Friends and Foes, because experiments on living animals were described without reprobation and England was reproached for not having a Pasteur Institute. The General Literature Committee replied to the Standing Committee that "they had greatly modified the book to obviate criticism; in a work of science a distinguished author must be allowed to express his opinion; as for inhumanity that would exist if the discoveries consequent on infecting animals were withheld from benefiting human beings". The Standing Committee took no action and a number of resignations from the Society followed.

(d) TREATMENT OF AUTHORS

On two occasions the Society incurred public criticism for its treatment of authors.

In 1890 Mr (afterwards Sir) Walter Besant wrote a pamphlet on behalf of the Society of Authors, based mainly on the experience of one author, who had put her affairs in his hands; she had been paid for the copyright of a book and had received no subsequent payment, which she had been led to believe would be made. A Committee of Inquiry appointed by the S.P.C.K. reported that royalties were paid to authors who were recognized as authorities on their subjects or whose names on the title-page would enhance the sale of their books. The system was not suited to Sunday School prizes, the circulation of which was promoted by the special methods of the Society, or to tracts. The prize-books were often very short and could be written in a few days. They, and to a much larger extent the tracts, were largely given away by the Society. The controversy was caused by a misunderstanding. Having surrendered the copyright the author had no further claim to remuneration. But the Society had adopted the practice of making *ex gratia* payments to the writers of successful books, which came to be regarded as a right. The critics took this as a confession of guilt: no business firm would behave like this out of pure philanthropy. The Society's plea that it published many books that did not deserve to be put on a royalty basis naturally provoked the criticism that such books ought not to be published at all. The fact remains that the Society was overwhelmed with manuscripts of childrens' books, written mainly by ladies anxious to earn pocket-money, and that offers of modest sums for the copyright were gladly accepted. Other publishers of "rewards" behaved in the same way but did not as a rule make the supplementary payments which got the S.P.C.K. into trouble.

The other occasion was when a translator of an important work of scholarship made some alterations with the approval of the author, who naturally thought it best to respect her knowledge of the English public and its prejudices. Attention was drawn to the changes by scholars who were jealous of the Society's reputation and a slip was inserted to say that "certain passages in this version do not altogether represent Professor ——'s views"; the remaining volumes of the series were commissioned on the condition that they deviated in no way from the original.

One cause of friction was inevitable and arose from the Committee system. A manuscript was recommended by one or two members and with the author's consent was set up for further and final consideration by the whole committee. The other members not infrequently did not agree with the original readers and rejected the book. The author was told that the standing type was put at his disposal and he could offer the book elsewhere, the other publisher being saved a substantial part of the cost. In practice publishers did not take advantage of the offer, being suspicious of a book which had once been rejected; if the S.P.C.K. was prepared to lose money rather than go on with publication, it must be a poor book.

Examination of a good many examples of amounts paid to authors shows that, apart from Sunday School prizes, where competition to get into print inevitably forced down the sums offered, the S.P.C.K. paid very liberally. The figures mentioned must be multiplied by three or four in order to get the comparable figures at today's values. In the early nineteenth century £5–£10 was paid for tracts, even on one occasion £25. In 1839 it was agreed to pay 8 guineas a sheet, presumably of 16 pages. The following examples show the scale of payment for copyright: a book giving Scripture references to the Prayer Book, £300 (1845); zoology for schools, £100 (1851); epitome of Scripture history, £200 (1851); a very simple book on wild flowers, with coloured drawings, £240 (1857); a book on Palestine, £400 (1864). (The remuneration proposed in 1857 for a Bible Concordance which was not proceeded with was £700.) Supplementary payments were frequently made.

13

Business Methods

IN THE long life of the Society, we find at the beginning the admirable Secretary Henry Newman, with his clerk and messenger, and now, at the time of writing, a staff, at home and overseas, of more than 400 men and women. The personal interest we feel in the improvizations of the former is naturally greater than anything that the conduct of a modern business, which, if it is to survive, must follow the ordinary routine of its competitors, can hope to excite. In between the two extremes we can trace a Society gradually learning to do its business efficiently; served by good and devout men, themselves often versed in the ways of the world and at the same time wishing to put the things of God first; making many mistakes and often failing to read the signs of the times. To follow the successive generations as they toiled at the task of daily administration is impossible, but a few selections from the records may be acceptable.

The Society in 1800 had changed very little in the course of a century. It was still housed in Bartlett's Buildings, where readers of *Sense and Sensibility* (published in 1811) will remember Jane Austen makes Anne and Lucy Steele stay on their visit to London; she will have been familiar with the address in her clerical home. The bookselling business consisted of Bibles and Prayer Books, devotional works, and tracts, and was conducted by an outside firm, to whom customers, practically all members of the Society, sent their orders. When a new book was put on the S.P.C.K. list, it was usually by arrangement with the author or the publisher of a work already printed. On 3 October 1765 John Rivington was appointed publisher and bookseller to the Society. He was to purchase the stock from Mr Dod, his predecessor; the S.P.C.K. agreed to buy the stock at his death or retirement at a price fixed by arbitration. He was to attend the S.P.C.K. once a week to receive orders and to submit the names of binders and their prices for the approval of the Society, which was also to sanction all reprints. Mr Septimus Rivington in his book *The Publishing Family of Rivington* (1919) quotes from the Journal of John Rivington (1781); great interest was taken in the election, for which he canvassed freely; the Archbishop himself came to vote. When the connection was severed in 1835, the step had long been under consideration by the Society, which had received many complaints of bad service. There is no means of knowing what justification, if any, there was for them, but we may surmise that a business consisting largely of tracts was unlikely to arouse much interest in a commercial firm; also that dual control was unsatisfactory. Mr Rivington thinks that the real reason was theological. "In 1835 the S.P.C.K. removed their agency from the firm, no doubt owing to the tendency of the firm's publications towards views which were considered dangerous. The Reverend J. S. Boone, one of the Editors of the *British Critic*,[1] writes in February 1835: 'I much regret that the debate on Tuesday last has terminated unfavourably, and that I could do nothing more than give my poor vote against the motion. Yet perhaps, after all, you are well rid of a society which will, I fear become involved, sooner or later, in a hundred disagreeable scrapes through its book transactions.'" Mr Rivington adds that Joshua Watson and H. H. Norris had written to remonstrate with the firm about the *British Critic*.

Nothing in the S.P.C.K. records suggests any other issue than the purely business one. Great interest was taken in the matter. A General Meeting was held with the Archbishop of Canterbury in the chair. The debate was on a motion to end the agreement, the Society in future to be its own distributor. A proposal that the Society do not engage in commercial transactions was negatived by 57 votes to 35. The cost of buying Rivington's stock was about £35,000, that of erecting and equipping a shop in Great Queen Street, on the site of offices recently occupied by the S.P.G., a further £5,000. In 1837 it was reported that the Society was saving £7,800 a year by the change, which, however, had meant a serious depletion of its invested funds.

A few examples of salaries and wages may be of interest. When Henry Newman died in 1743, his successor in the post of Secretary was paid £105 a year plus £5 for coal and candles, presumably to

[1] Rivington's Review, on High Church and Independent lines.

cover the use of them by the Committee, and he lived in the Society's house. By 1870 the salary of a Secretary had risen to £400, £500 in 1878. The advertisement for an Editorial Secretary in 1870 asked for a man "of good theological and literary experience and acquainted with modern languages". It secured the Reverend J. M. Fuller, Fellow of St John's College, Cambridge, Tyrwhitt Hebrew Scholar, Crosse Theological Scholar, and Kaye Prizeman. The Reverend T. B. Murray, appointed Assistant Secretary in 1842, received £200. The Superintendent of the bookshop opened in 1836 was paid £400, later raised to £500. He was a responsible person, who for many years ordered reprints without reference to the Committee. When he gave up there were ninety-nine applicants for the post. Shop assistants received up to £2 a week, warehousemen 35s., packers 24s. These figures were considered satisfactory at the time, and it was common for sons to follow their fathers in the Society's service.

The costing system was curious, to say the least, to the eyes of a modern publisher. Thus Mrs Ewing, who kept the production of her books in her own hands, in 1883 supplied an edition of 10,000 copies of *Jackanapes*, with 13 illustrations by Caldecott, for 5¾d. a copy, the published price to be 1s. at a time when booksellers gave a discount of 2d. or even 3d. in the 1s. to their customers and expected a compensatory allowance from publishers. In 1864 an estimate was submitted to the Committee for a *Colonial Church Atlas*, as follows:

	£
Drawing and engraving 16 maps	400
Cost otherwise of printing and binding 1,000 copies	£130 10
Overhead expenses	19 10
	£150

The cost was 3s. a copy and the proposed price 4s. 6d. non-net. The non-recurring cost of £400 was disregarded, on the assumption that it would be eventually recouped by profitable reprints. Indeed, stereoplates, copyrights, woodblocks, etc. were in 1864 given a life of twenty years, the original cost being written off by 5% each year. In 1880 this depreciation was increased to 10% and the 1891 Report says that £3,000 has been written off the figure, for this item alone, of £30,000. In 1905 it was decided to write off these assets in five years and there was a general reserve of £1,000 to cover depreciation of ordinary stock valued at £58,111. The management went on too long on the assumption that it was living in a static society, in which books would continue to sell for a generation; the stock so valued was of course to a large extent unsaleable and the "profits" paid to the General Fund were fictitious. Up to 1915 the production manager was instructed to add 25% to the cost of a book to cover overhead expenses and to estimate that copies would be sold at an average discount of 25% from published price. Thus, if the printing, paper, and binding of a book cost 1s. or 1s. 3d. with overheads added, it was supposed that 1s. 6d. would be received (the published price being 2s.) and a profit of 3d. would accrue. Copyright was charged separately, as explained above. No publisher in fact can do less than treble the cost of production in order to arrive at the published price, and the difficulties experienced by the Society for a generation after 1914 were to a large extent due to the accumulation of unsaleable stock which had been valued in full. To give another example of the costing system in use. In 1887 a popular book of *Notes on Church History*, by C. A. Lane, was published, which was reckoned to produce a "profit" of £18 if 20,000 were sold, considered apparently an adequate return on a best-seller.

Otherwise, business methods were efficient, thanks to a radical reorganization carried out by Mr W. H. Smith during his time of office as Treasurer (1867–74), but he did not concern himself with the higher direction of publishing policy. In one direction, at least, the Society was on the right lines, the striving after cheapness, for towards the end of the century prices fell rapidly owing to the improvement of machinery and the development of the use of wood-pulp for making paper; but it was unable to compete with its rivals in the choice of the right books or in selling them to the trade.

The Treasurers have always played a great part in the history of the Society. In early days they kept the money in their own hands, and on one occasion in the middle of the eighteenth century the Treasurer, an esteemed Church dignitary, was unable to produce the cash at the annual audit. He resigned and the incident was declared to have been closed with blame attaching to no one. In 1880 the Treasurers received

a certificate of incorporation under the Charitable Trustees Incorporation Act of 1872, becoming Trustees. Previously the property had been
transferred to the new body of Treasurers whenever a Treasurer died
or resigned; also there had been difficulty in suing for debts.

The first traveller was appointed in 1850, being shared with the
Oxford University Press and J. M. Parker (of Oxford) and paid £100.
A full-time traveller dated from 1865, when it was decided that it
might be possible to open accounts with booksellers "without great
loss". A professional auditor was employed for the first time in 1879,
the Committee having previously examined the accounts themselves.

Relations with the trade were not always harmonious, for booksellers disliked the system of depots, where a member could buy a book
more cheaply than at an ordinary shop. On the other hand, members
began to complain that their privileges were illusory, since with the
increase of the practice of giving discounts they could buy as cheaply,
if not more so, elsewhere. This applied mainly to the Supplemental
Catalogue, at least in the earlier part of our period, which included
books of other publishers bought from them in order to make them
available to members at a lower price. The Society could disregard
complaints so long as the depot system flourished, having made its
own channels of distribution. But the District Committees looked
with disfavour at the comparatively small amount of trade done with
general booksellers; as early as 1839 the S.P.C.K. agreed to give booksellers the "usual 25% + 10% for ready money", although the step was
said to be likely to embarrass the District Committees.

Profits during the last third of the century were generally good on
paper, though the real meaning of the figures is another matter. In
1875–6 the profit of the Publishing business was £6,592, out of which
£4,000 was paid to the General Fund, which had paid £19,133 in
purchases and subsidies. How difficult it was to combine profits with a
policy of cheapness and philanthropy is illustrated by a letter from the
Committee of the Council on Education (which eventually developed
into the Ministry of Education) in October 1847, inquiring on what
terms the Society would supply educational books, to which the reply
was sent: orders of 20,000 at cost; of 10,000, cost plus 2%; of 5,000,
cost plus 4%.

14

The Twentieth Century,
1914—44

URING the long and exhausting war of 1914–18 practically all the staff of military age were called up; every man volunteered without waiting for conscription, so that the effect of war on the Society came early. Mercifully the casualties were not many.

The chief domestic event was the commandeering of the S.P.C.K. House in 1916, to provide Government offices. As a result, some unbound stock was left in the basement of Northumberland Avenue; a warehouse for the rest of the sheet stock was provided not far away in Great Suffolk Street, Southwark, on the site of the old Marshalsea prison so vividly described in Dickens's *Little Dorrit*; a building for the bound stock and the staff engaged in distribution was found in Wilton Road, near Victoria Station; and the shop and offices were housed in No. 68 Haymarket. This building was commandeered in 1918, the shop being moved to No. 64 New Bond Street, the offices to the Vicarage of St Martin-in-the-Fields. The business of the Society, which had been economically run from one centre, was thus distributed among four or five centres, which added greatly to the overhead charges. The substituted buildings were provided by H.M. Office of Works, but the cost of removal and fitting up new premises was borne by the Society, which claimed repayment from the tribunal that assessed war damages. Heavy losses were incurred: for example, to meet one claim of £2,500 the Office of Works offered £1,250 and the sum awarded by the tribunal was £371. However, 90% of the main claim was conceded, though no allowance was made for the extra cost of working in a divided state. After the war, when the question of return was considered, it was decided to let part of the ground floor to the Standard Bank of South Africa. Then for the first time it was debated whether it would not be better to go elsewhere, but the cost of suitable accommodation was prohibitive. When some years later the question was again raised it appeared that the value of the building was negligible and the site value only, which had rather more than doubled since 1879, could be obtained. In October 1921 the Standing Committee held its first meeting in its own Board Room since July 1916.

The work of the charitable side went on steadily during the war years but many plans for extending missionary work were inevitably postponed, and the chief emphasis was laid on providing books for the armed forces. So the Society resumed the work which it had done in the days of Marlborough, Nelson and Wellington.

The Stepney Training College never recovered from the shock given by the war, when it was practically empty of students, and had to be closed at the end of 1924, when the building was sold. St Katharine's College continued full and by 1922 had 128 girls being trained as teachers; in 1919 £12,000 was set aside for extensions. The money voted to Medical Missions was spent almost entirely on training doctors and the difficulties of the work began to be apparent. In such a time of unsettlement it was easy for a young man or woman to lose the sense of vocation during the five or six years of training, or marriage would make it impossible to go abroad, and so it became necessary to insist on guarantees of repayment from parents or others if the candidate failed to serve for three years in the Mission Field. Enforcing these guarantees was a thankless task that fell to the General Secretary; sometimes the debt had to be written off as irrecoverable.

A useful piece of work was started in 1916, that of providing literature for the blind. The chief publication was *The Church Messenger*, a monthly magazine which had a circulation of about 150 copies and being passed from one person to another was probably read by about 500 people. A few books were printed from plates, but in the main the work consisted of making copies by hand. There were a large number of volunteers, who had to be trained and their work corrected at headquarters. After the 1939–45 war the work was handed over to the Royal National Institute for the Blind, which promised to continue its special Church character. By that time the Society had found recruitment of volunteers almost impossible under the new conditions.

Three changes in internal administration may be noted. In November 1915 the first woman was engaged on the staff; and in 1919 women were admitted as full members instead of being merely "lady sub-scribers". In the same year it was decided to spread legacies over ten years, one-tenth of the amount received being taken into current account each year.

On Monday, 11 November 1918 at 11 a.m. maroons announced the signing of the Armistice. Trafalgar Square witnessed a good-tempered riot, being thronged by crowds who had left their work. The Society's staff watched the scene from the windows of St Martin's vicarage and went home, no more work being possible. That afternoon the manu-script of a thanksgiving service for use on the following Sunday arrived from Lambeth Palace. Considering the atmosphere of the time and the universal depletion of staffs by the influenza epidemic it was remarkable that by Thursday copies had been printed and despatched to every parish in the country—a feat which was repeated in 1953 when a book of Prayers in a beautiful binding was printed and bound within a few days for presentation to the Queen for her coronation.

By 1920 the world had quietened down sufficiently to allow the Lambeth Conference of Bishops of the Anglican Communion to meet. Many of the visiting bishops came to the S.P.C.K. with their plans for meeting the piled up needs of their dioceses, which were assisted so far as resources permitted.

The Society's publishing was in a poor way in 1914. The Editorial Secretary was old and absent from the office a great deal; no respon-sible person could answer letters in his absence, indeed all activity ceased for three months in the summer. A business manager began his work in January, but with instructions to make no changes until the Secretary retired at the end of the year, by which time the manager was serving in the Army. The year witnessed a considerable output of new publications, 141 in all, excluding almanacks, magazines, and year books, but most of them would have fallen into Charles Lamb's category of "biblia a-biblia". Since the successful days of the nine-teenth century great changes had taken place in the interests of the reading public. For example, in 1869, according to *The Publishers' Circular* of 1870, 4,969 new books were published, of which 30% were new editions, about a quarter of the present output. Of these, Theology and Religion accounted for 1,049, Fiction 464, Educational Books 478, Arts and Sciences 343. Religious publishing was of course handicapped by this shift in public interest. But even in its own sphere the S.P.C.K. published few important books. Controversy, though sometimes regrettable, at least keeps interest alive, and it was the settled policy to avoid controversial books. The yearly turnover had steadily fallen, at a time when similar businesses were expanding, and had reached the low limit of £60,000. The three bookshops (head-quarters, City of London, and Brighton) relied almost entirely on S.P.C.K. books, those of other publishers being admitted very sparingly.

The business consisted in the main of Day and Sunday School prizes, Bibles and Prayer Books, and a parish magazine inset, all of which were destined to receive hard blows. The choice of books for school prizes had been largely in the hands of the clergy, who were accustomed to order from the S.P.C.K., since the contents could be relied on to be innocuous, if not actually edifying. For financial reasons, and also because Sunday Schools were depleted and reformers condemned introducing the element of competition, the demand for prize books fell greatly. The parish magazine inset, which some years before had reached a circulation of 700,000 and was now about half a million, was almost killed by the impossibility of getting enough paper during the war. And the S.P.C.K.'s pre-eminence in selling Bibles and Prayer Books depended on the willingness of the General Fund, and the ability of its clerical members, to spend large sums on free or assisted distribution; in any case the Society was a middleman, not the pri-mary producer of Bibles, Prayer Books, and the more popular hymnals. The inactivity of the editorial department (in 1915 not a single new book was being written for the Society, which was entirely dependent on such manuscripts as should be offered) and the vulnerable nature of its chief selling lines left it in a weak position to withstand the shock of war. In 1909 a blow had already fallen in the shape of a fire, which destroyed half the stock; much of the rest was damaged and sold as salvage to enterprising traders, who furbished it up and supplied it at cut prices, thus harming the ordinary trade of the Society. On the other hand, the new Secretary in 1915 found a most loyal and hard-working staff, who responded in an admirable manner to the demands made on them by war conditions.

A Committee of Inquiry into the publishing operations of the Society appointed in 1914 reported that the simultaneous care of editorial business, staff management, and the marketing of books was beyond the powers of one man and recommended the appointment of a business manager, which was made. Another recommendation arose out of complaints about the nature of S.P.C.K. publications. It was stated that the "advanced school" of Churchmanship provided the main body of book-buyers and that the Society was losing business owing to the colourless character of its publications. It was thought sufficient to say that the rules provided the remedy; the members were entitled to elect to the Committees whom they pleased and they were invited to use their powers. A contested election followed, as a result of which the Standing Committee was reinforced by a number of High Churchmen, who proved a great addition to the counsels of the Society. And the Tract Committee, as it was then termed, received two new members, who had a mandate to represent the Anglo-Catholic standpoint. In 1915, after considerable discussion, it was agreed to advertise the new policy of publishing for the two chief schools of thought not by any pronouncement but by commissioning two Communicants' manuals, representing the Anglo-Catholic and Evangelical schools, the Committee agreeing in advance to pass whatever was recommended by those members who would use the books as fairly representing their views. This is all a long time ago, but the present generation may be interested to know the difficulty involved in changing the ways of an old Society. For some years the acceptance of a book with definite teaching produced a demand for another book on the same subject written from a different standpoint "to redress the balance", with the result that a number of unwanted books were published. On one occasion a crowded agenda was deferred until the next meeting while the propriety of publishing a tract was debated. It happened to be anonymous and the Committee felt that the Society was responsible for every sentence. On another occasion the putting into Braille of a single hand-made copy of a desired book, without a corresponding one on the other side, which had not been asked for, occupied most of an afternoon. So strictly did the Committee interpret its duties that no book or tract could be removed from the catalogue except by a vote of the Committee originally responsible for it. Such rigidity, added to the difficulties of the war, made progress very slow.

A policy of broadening the basis of publishing was a long term one, not likely to produce appreciable results for some years. However, the war, which harmed the Society so much, supplied it with opportunities of proving its usefulness. The Archbishop of Canterbury (Dr Davidson), always a devoted friend, at the end of 1914 asked the S.P.C.K. to undertake the publishing of prayers to be used on the first Sunday in 1915. The prayers issued at the outbreak of war had been published by the Privileged Presses, the form emanating from the Privy Council. They expected to publish the new form, but the Archbishop maintained his right to send a form for which he and the Archbishop of York were solely responsible to whomsoever he pleased. The staff worked splendidly and circulated 2,970,000 copies in a few days. The idea that the S.P.C.K. was the best publisher for such things dates from this time. In 1916 the Society was invited to become the publisher for the so-called National Mission of Repentance and Hope. If tracts could have saved the Church they would have done so then. Over 300 different titles were issued and the total circulation exceeded 10,000,000. Some of the projects seem curious in retrospect. After a great many evangelistic papers had been issued, a demand arose for tracts on doctrine. Two series were planned at first, one edited by C. C. B. Bardsley, Secretary of the C.M.S. and afterwards Bishop of Leicester, the other by members of the English Church Union. A third series, edited by William Temple, intended to be more in accordance with modern thought, was added. Finally, High Churchmen who thought that the second series misrepresented their views called for yet another, which was edited by Canon Scott Holland. These tracts in all numbered 90; they had a small sale and did not justify the trouble taken over them. So a demand was made for a fifth series, papers on the Apostles' Creed, longer and better planned; they were published later in book form, with an Introduction by G. K. A. Bell, afterwards Bishop of Chichester. If they did nothing else, these National Mission publications gave the S.P.C.K. a chance of showing what it could do; the great mass of literature, peculiarly difficult to handle, was most efficiently dealt with by the depleted staff, largely in overtime.

The financial results of these years were very bad. Even had there been no war losses could not have been avoided. The stock was greatly overvalued, much of it having long ceased to sell and being yet valued at cost. The reserve against obsolescence was £1,000 in 1914, about 2%

of the total. But the war caused very heavy loss. To begin with, stock to the value of about £10,000 had to be scrapped in 1916, since there was no room for it in the new warehouses—the real value was problematical. Paper was severely rationed, and of the small amount allocated to the S.P.C.K. in 1917 half had to be used to keep the parish magazine going. Several cargoes of paper, imported from Canada as part of the ration, were lost by enemy action and no allowance for this was made in the next allocation. Towards the end of the war publishers had to yield up a large proportion of the metal locked up in their stereo-plates and blocks. A minor cause of loss was the existence of a good many children's picture books and a few adult books printed in Germany, which had to be destroyed, so unpatriotic was it thought to sell anything of enemy origin.

Paper was so bad that war-time books had little chance of sale after 1919. Not that this mattered much, for reading in these years was largely of war books, for which in 1939-45 there was little demand, the preference then being for anything to take the mind away from the war. To add to the difficulties, overhead expenses went up greatly owing to the division of the business among different buildings. The result of all this was that in 1919 the Society had to make a new start. The "back list" was worth little, and new stock had to be made at the very high prices then obtaining.

As the Religious Literature Committee (the new name of the Tract Committee), whose members felt acutely how unimportant many of the earlier publications had been, faced the problem of "putting the Society on the map", they naturally began to plan worthwhile works of scholarship. Neither they nor the newly appointed Editorial Secretary had the requisite technical experience, and their efforts nearly resulted in disaster. A great many manuscripts had been kept back by their authors until the cessation of fighting, when it was hoped things would be easier. The Committee did not like to refuse good books and took many of those offered. As it turned out, the years 1919–21 were exceptionally difficult. Prices soared, and when they fell precipitously in 1922 the books produced at peak prices had to be reduced in order to compete with the later ones. Further, with the impoverishment of the clergy and the shift of purchasing power to new classes, the criteria of pre-war success no longer applied.

The concordat of 1915 was loyally observed by the Committee, with a bias towards caution. But the old tradition of interference with authors lingered on, and the Secretary often had to induce them to accept corrections desired by one perhaps not very well-informed member. The Committee's task was complicated by the existence of a large body of subscribers, mainly elderly men, whose instincts were conservative. Their efforts to improve the Society's books often produced letters from members announcing resignation as a protest against the publication of a book or tract, sometimes judged only by the reading of an unfavourable review. It was mortifying to be told that a bold policy was harming the missionary work of the Church by diminishing the income of the General Fund. Nor could the Committee claim that their books had reached a wide public. In the worst year, 1921–2, the loss was £17,786. We may say that the desired object of making the Society's name known in the literary world and attracting good authors was achieved, but at an unnecessarily high cost. After 1922 things began to improve, helped by a fall of £4,000 a year in overhead charges when the scattered parts of the Society had been reunited.

One way in which the new policy operated was the undertaking of publishing for outside bodies, chiefly Church Societies, which took responsibility for the contents of their books. This was sanctioned by the Standing Committee in 1917, with the proviso that the appropriate Committee kept a watch on the general tendency of the literature thus issued. As the books were generally published on commission for the outside Society it was possible for the S.P.C.K. to enlarge its turnover without risk of loss. The Report of the Anglo-Catholic Congress of 1920 was the first noteworthy example of the new policy. Also, many important works of scholarship were published at the cost of the authors, in whole or in part. Once more, losses were avoided, but it is impossible in this way to earn the normal publisher's profit.

Nothing has been said so far about the General Literature Committee, which for a number of years tried to maintain and improve upon the traditions they had inherited. They found themselves handicapped by the imprint S.P.C.K., which was unsuitable for, say, a book of popular science. The imprint "Sheldon Press" was therefore devised, the name being that of the parish of which Dr Bray was Rector for so long. It did good service for a time, but when in the late '30s general literature was practically abandoned it ceased to be of much use.

Perhaps the Committee went on too long, but all concerned were reluctant to break an ancient tradition.

In two directions a beginning was made in building up two lines of business which now form a large part of the Society's turnover— selling other publishers' books, and export. The former was negligible in 1914. The theory was that the Society was directly responsible for all books displayed in its shops, so, as an inheritance from the past history of two centuries, a Committee had to sanction them. A special Committee for the purpose had recently been discontinued, its functions devolving on the Religious Literature Committee. The result was disastrous. Customers asking for a new book could not be supplied because it was still *sub judice*. Sometimes it was months before a report was received. However, in 1914 the situation was regularized by opening an annexe to the shop for these books, kept separate from those of the Society, and before long the Committee was content to leave the selection to the Secretary, who was instructed to bring before them any doubtful case. So cautious was the Committee that the common practice of putting a list of books "by the same author" at the beginning of a book was frowned upon and in November 1915 allowed on condition that the Secretary read the books listed and satisfied himself as to their teaching.

It is difficult today to realize the suspicion that existed then of books with Anglo-Catholic or Modernist tendencies. Only gradually did the view prevail that customers should be trusted to know their own minds and not be treated like children. The turning point was the Lambeth Conference of 1920, when the S.P.C.K. ran a bookstall at the Palace, where the Bishops could buy the latest books on the subjects they were discussing. It was recognized that to say that priests and laymen should not be allowed to see the books displayed for the guidance of the Bishops was absurd. Naturally, proper caution has always been observed and books, for example, attacking the Anglican position have never been stocked but only procured for the convenience of customers.

Export sales in 1914 amounted to about £1,000 a year out of a turnover of £60,000. Great efforts were now made to procure agencies for the sale of S.P.C.K. books abroad. The Church depots, which went back to the old days of District Committees of the S.P.C.K., had almost everywhere died out and a new start was necessary.

Wherever possible Church agencies were used, but each case was considered on its merits and a well-known American general publisher was engaged for the United States. It was difficult at first for the Committee to realize the magnitude of the discounts needed if British books were to reach the overseas public at a reasonable price.

As one example of the enterprise shown by the Committee at this time we may cite the founding of the Uganda Book Shop in 1920. The S.P.C.K. agreed to pay two-thirds of the salary, allowances, and passages of a manager and his wife, who was to open a bookshop at Kampala, the diocese to find the remaining one-third. In 1926 the original premises had been bought, and enlarged to five times their size, a large turnover had been built up, and twelve branches founded. The S.P.C.K.'s contribution was never called upon and its share of profits had been all put back into the business or given to the missionary work of the diocese. The Society's help being no longer needed, the diocese henceforward was solely responsible for the shop.

Before leaving the war period it is worth noting how the Society's old publications proved useful in unexpected ways. There was a considerable demand for books in South African languages for the Black Labour Corps in France; also for Maori Prayer and Hymn Books for New Zealand troops fighting there; and even for Malagasy ones for French Colonial soldiers and Cree for Canadian.

In 1918–19 the Society published a number of Reports arising out of the follow-up work of the National Mission. That on the Teaching Office of the Church made far-reaching recommendations for the development of the S.P.C.K. to serve the Church more effectively. The Society appointed a Committee to consider these suggestions, the conclusions of which involved a considerable development that for financial reasons could not at the time be carried out. But the ideals were not forgotten, and in one way or another practically all the suggestions have come to fruition, though in different ways from those first contemplated.

The years that followed up to the outbreak of war in 1939 saw little change in the activities of the General Fund, the income of which from donations and subscriptions remained round about £20,000. As personal subscriptions decreased, parochial gifts increased; this meant that more people were interested, but to collect a given sum of money was more expensive when the donors were numerous and the amounts small than when, as of old, many people subscribed their guineas as a matter of course. The cost of organizing therefore tended to rise, and has remained a cause of anxiety. Grants to schools and church building in the Mission Field continued. The world-wide economic distress meant that in countries dependent on their primary products the Churches were less able to be self-supporting and asked for larger grants, which the Society was rarely able to give. It became the policy to give priority to training persons over putting up new buildings. In practice it was difficult to cut down old-established grants to schools and colleges according to the Society's policy, which had always been to start new work and not to guarantee continued help after it should have got on its feet. One continuing grant of £200 a year for scholarships at native seminaries and girls' schools and £150 for boys' scholarships actually went back to the days of the East India Mission. A noteworthy donation was £5,250, spread over a number of years, for the endowment of the sees of Calcutta, Bombay, and Madras, to make up for the loss of State help. Medical Missions took a large share of the free income. The average number of doctors in training was 60, and in 1939 the amount voted was £7,162.

Owing to the fluctuations of Government policy, dictated by economic difficulties, the Board (now Ministry) of Education insisted that 160 students were the irreducible minimum for a Training College, and St Katharine's College was enlarged to hold that number, besides being greatly improved. (Between the two wars capital outlay of about £64,000 was incurred on the College, of which half came from the sale of St John's College, Battersea.) In fact, the College was allowed to take only 140 students, a figure cut down later to 129.

The care of the archives was a concern to the Committee. Preliminary work was done between 1927 and 1931 and then stopped for lack of funds. In 1934 the Pilgrim Trust came to the rescue with a grant of £400 a year for three years, to pay the salary of an archivist and the cost of necessary binding and repairs. In 1937 the Trust made a further grant to finish the work, the purpose of which was to make the archives accessible to students. Other matters of domestic interest included alterations in the Rules. The Foreign Literature Committee, instead of being nominated by the Archbishop of Canterbury, was to be elected in the same way as the other Committees. And the rule concerning Episcopal Referees was reworded: in future no complaint regarding religious publications would be considered unless it was made by three members of the Society; it was to be laid before the Standing Committee, which would consult the Religious Literature Committee and then decide whether it should go before the Referees; if it did go, their decision was to be final. In the years 1915 to 1944 no formal reference to the Bishops was made, though the advice of individuals among them was occasionally sought. In 1937 a compulsory pension scheme for the staff was adopted; the older members were allowed to contract out, with the expectancy of a pension similar to that given in the Civil Service.

The Publishing Department had many years to go before it reached a measure of stability. The inter-war period was one of widespread unemployment and political upheavals at home and abroad. One difficult time was in 1926, the year of the General Strike and the almost complete stoppage of coal-mining for seven months. However, in that year S.P.C.K. published a noteworthy book, *Essays Catholic and Critical*, edited by Dr E. G. Selwyn. It was hard for the Society to make even a start in getting well-known authors, for they naturally did not want to desert their publishers, who in some cases had bound them to offer their next three books. Given the chance to choose, an author preferred a good general publisher who would not desire to alter his manuscript to a Society whose Committee might demand changes in his opinion unwarranted. There was also an impression that a general publisher could reach the general public better than a religious one, and it took some years to convince authors that they could get as much, sometimes more, in royalties from the S.P.C.K. But, if the Society took the initiative and planned a composite book of essays, this objection did not apply. Plans were being made for some more ambitious volumes than the original *Essays*. The Reverend Charles Harris, a scholar with great powers of initiative and organizing, induced the (English) Church Union to take up the publishing of important books in conjunction with the S.P.C.K. This resulted in a number of good books, notably the *New Commentary on Holy Scripture*, edited by Bishop Gore, which appeared in 1928 and had a remarkable sale. *Liturgy and Worship* (1932) was also a great success. Another venture, in 1929, was the refounding of the Church Historical Society of the 1890's, on different lines. It was to be affiliated to S.P.C.K. and its purpose was to publish (a) works of research in Church History, the publication of which is desirable but impeded by economic difficulties; (b) works of historical scholarship which may from time to time seem especially to concern the Anglican Communion; (c) popularizations of such works of research and historical scholarship. A stately library of books has been built up with a relatively small expenditure of money and has been much appreciated.

A publishing feat to be proud of is the Report of the 1930 Lambeth Conference. A fairly big book, it was passed for press on the Tuesday after the Conference ended and copies of the book were in the book-shops on the Thursday, to be ready for publication on Friday.

The financial blizzard that began in America in 1929 and reached Britain the following year nullified the Society's efforts to get its business operations on a sound basis. The Publishing Department had been assisted in 1925 by the scaling down of the capital on which interest was paid to the General Fund from £70,000 to £25,000. It was originally a paper figure and had long ago been repaid out of profits, so this seemed an act of justice; besides, the capital no longer existed.

By 1932 the losses, which for a time had been practically eliminated, had mounted to about £4,000 a year. This was most serious, for all resources were exhausted. There was a suggestion of abandoning publishing and being content with a bookshop for Prayer Books, etc., but it was decided to try once more. The business manager was retired on a pension, full responsibility being put on the Editorial Secretary; the staff was drastically reduced, and the Southwark warehouse sold, with the result that some stock had to be destroyed, there being no room to house it at headquarters. Also the shop in the City of London was closed. However, there was no hope in a policy of retreat, and in the year 1933 the Society opened a new shop in the Precincts of Canterbury Cathedral, which made a profit in its first year and provided experience on which to base further ventures. By 1939 shops had been opened at Bournemouth, Bradford, Cardiff, Sheffield, and Worcester, and headquarters had taken over from local Committees the management of shops at Bath, Exeter, and Liverpool. The financial results of the combined publishing and bookselling began to improve and by 1939 the finances were much better. Substantial progress was also made overseas, where the Society had shops at Dar-es-Salaam, Johannesburg, and Salisbury (Southern Rhodesia), and a small venture at Singapore.

The editorial department continued to be busy, and in 1939 the new works listed in the Annual Report amounted to 407: including 102 books at 1s. and upwards, 112 pamphlets and tracts, and 146 publications of the Foreign Literature Committee. Many of these last were published overseas, and only voucher copies were received at the head office, which however had to supervise the operations of the diocesan Committees to whom were entrusted these publications of the S.P.C.K. In 1938 it was decided to reduce to a low minimum the non-religious books at home.

The fortunes of the Society in the 1939–45 war can be briefly told. After September 1938 many London businesses arranged for alternative premises outside what was expected to be the bombing area, but in the case of the S.P.C.K. the difficulty of moving great quantities of stock seemed insuperable, so it was decided to remain. Eventually 47 of the staff were called up and some of the women went to various forms of national service. The first impact of war was disastrous to the business, and the cost of providing an air raid shelter and of insuring against war damage was a heavy burden. Later in the war stock to the value of about £5,000 had to be destroyed owing to a Government order that nothing inflammable be kept in top floors, there being no room for it elsewhere in the house. So large a building could not be adequately blacked out and the staff had therefore to go home at 4 p.m. in the winter months, which made it hard to get through the work. They, including the newly engaged members, responded splendidly to the demands made on them, and the Society came through the war better than had been feared.

On 11 September 1940, the house was hit by an incendiary bomb, which started a fire. The hoses were at work for about six hours and great damage was done to the stock. Many weeks passed before the roof was repaired and still further damage was done by rain. For some six months the staff were engaged largely in clearing up the mess and preparing a claim for damages. The branches went on normally, except for Liverpool, which was totally destroyed; Sheffield also suffered damage.

The General Meeting was suspended, the Standing Committee taking over its functions. The Committees carried on as usual, though occasionally executive action had to be taken by the Secretaries, to be confirmed by Committee later. St Katharine's College was moved in

January 1941 to Babbacombe, Devon, where accommodation for 100 students was found in hotels; the Tottenham building was occupied by 300 evacuees from Gibraltar, brought to London as a precautionary measure. The training of new medical missionaries came to an end.

The publishing of new books presented an unexpected problem, on the solution of which the experience of the first war threw little light. Whereas in 1914 war was a new and shattering experience diverting all minds to its problems, this time our people had for some years been living in an atmosphere of crisis, which had been reflected in the output of books, and there was little demand for war books. Not till June 1940, "their finest hour", the time of the evacuation from Dunkirk, did a demand for religious books develop, which proved a continuing one. The difficulties of supplying it were great, but by way of compensation old books came into their own and publishers' shelves were denuded of stocks. Unexpectedly, therefore, the financial results of the war years were good, and by the end of 1944 the losses of the pre-war years were largely retrieved.

The paper ration during a large part of the period was $37\frac{1}{2}\%$ of the amount bought by publishers in the twelve months preceding the outbreak of war, an arrangement which helped those who had bought heavily in anticipation of war; and 18% for periodicals. The paper was of much better quality than in the closing part of the first war. The amount available for new books and reprints was about as much as could be used, since printers worked under great difficulties and had moreover to give priority to the innumerable orders from Government departments. The S.P.C.K. was handicapped in taking advantage of such opportunities as existed at home, since it held that missionary work came first and devoted about half its paper ration and printing facilities to foreign literature. The Paper Control was sympathetic to these needs and on several occasions gave special licences for them, as also for the various services put out by authority. Concentration on export added to the troubles because so many cargoes were sunk.

Pursuing a policy of faith, the Society opened several new branches and also acquired premises for opening shops after the war. It also bought The Challenge Limited, a small business for producing and selling religious pictures, and the Talbot Press, Saffron Walden. The latter could not be reopened until 1945, when it began a useful career in the Society's service.

The writer of this book was nominally responsible for the conduct of business during this period, but the actual work was done by Mr E. W. Bishop, who from 1945 was the Society's Financial Secretary, and whose indomitable courage, skill, and faith enabled the S.P.C.K. to face post-war problems with confidence.

15
Epilogue

T HE WORD EPILOGUE suggests the end of a story, and that, in a sense, is the subject of this chapter. For although, looking back from 1959, it is clear that an epoch ended in 1939, in 1945 it was by no means yet certain what this would involve. Even a decade later parts of the process of ending were still going on.

In the meantime, as had been the case after 1918, the inevitable aftermaths of modern war—false stabilization, fictional expansion— made it difficult to discern the true shape of the epoch that was already beginning. Yet, even during the war, the Society had begun to rethink its policy so as to deal more effectively with the problems of a new world. A striking example of this is that in 1943 the Archbishop of Canterbury, William Temple, was able to announce the formation of an official Church of England Film Commission, an experimental body, which would be housed and financed by the Society. From this may be dated the Society's express mandate to promote Christian Knowledge, not only through printed literature and pictures but also through such other means of communication as film and filmstrip. For such reasons it is possible, in 1959, to see both 1939 as the beginning of an end, and 1958 as the end of a beginning. If the past twenty years are the Epilogue to Volume I of the Society's History, 1699–1958, they are also the Prologue to Volume II which, whether it covers a quarter of a millenium or not, will, we may trust, be by no means the last volume in the series.

In 1943, as it became clear that the turning-point of the war had been reached and passed, the author of this history decided that he would not himself attempt to guide the Society's publishing and bookselling a second time through the transition from war to peace. On 31 December 1944 he attended his office for the last time, having serenely initiated his successor as Editorial Secretary against such a background of flying bombs as might almost be said to constitute, and very nearly became, a baptism of fire.

In 1945 the Society was, on its business side, most obviously faced with the short-term problems common at that time to all publishers: how to settle down with a staff of servicemen returned to conditions unlike those they had previously known; how to produce books at all with the prevailing licences, controls, and government priorities; how to make the right decisions in a time of great uncertainty. Business itself was helped by full employment and a rising scale of earnings, so that a large section of the public could pay the increased price of books, if they really wanted them; by the great increase of educational facilities and libraries; above all, by the continuing interest in theology.

At the same time, it was becoming clear that, so far as the Society's General Fund was concerned, a long-term policy had to be worked out. The General Fund could not expect an income two to three times that of 1939, which would be needed if an equivalent amount of work was to be done. A rethinking of the Society's aims was becoming urgent. The rival claims on the generosity of Church people were many and exacting. The rebuilding of bombed buildings, the cost of which nearly always exceeded the official compensation, the raising of clerical stipends, the starting of Church work in new housing areas, the maintenance of Church schools, the general acceptance of the view that the diocesan quota was a first charge on parish funds, and the great needs of the Societies primarily responsible for missions overseas —all these combined to put the claims of the S.P.C.K., as previously understood, in the background. The Society had weakened its appeal by spreading itself over too wide a field. It must concentrate on its main tasks, literature and education. It must go back to Dr Bray's original design, as limited by the foundation of the S.P.G.: *propaganda*, promoting knowledge of the faith.

There were further complications, secondary perhaps, but none the less real: complications of structure. Before 1939 the policy of the Society had theoretically resided in the hands of its members, through the monthly General Meetings, even though in practice it had for many years been difficult to obtain the required quorum for these, and the Standing Committee had in fact become the policy-making body. During the war, however, the regular General Meetings had been suspended. Now it had become clear that they could never be restored. The days when the members of a large Society could meet in sufficient numbers to represent the Society realistically were, indeed, long past. But what would make the Standing Committee competent to conduct the Society's affairs? Again, the Society's publishing—now in size its most important activity—was at that time entrusted to two Statutory Committees, one for Foreign Literature, one for Religious Literature. By the Constitution, two members at least of each of these committees had to be members of the Standing Committee. But even if it was possible to find members both capable of giving expert advice to a statutory committee and able to spare the time to attend the Standing Committee, and even if they always attended, the links between the policy-making Standing Committee and the executive Statutory Committees were perilously slight. Comparatively little of the business of the Standing Committee was concerned with publishing and bookselling, and on the whole this reflected the interests of its ordinary members. Moreover, there was a multiplicity of further sub-committees, whose particular business monopolized the interest of some of their members. It was easy for the wood—the Society's over-all policy—to be lost sight of for the trees.

Again, for many years the Society had had two Secretaries. From 1945 there were three with full Secretarial status—the General Secretary, the Editorial Secretary, and the Financial Secretary. Although they met frequently and co-operated fully, it was inevitable that each saw the Society's tasks from the point of view of the work for which he himself was responsible. None of them had responsibility for overall policy. There was no officer taking thought for the wood as a whole.

The 250th Anniversary of the Society's foundation was celebrated during the year from Founders' Day, 8 March 1948 to Founders' Day 1949. The celebrations were planned with imagination. There was an opening Meeting on 8 March at the Mansion House. On Sunday 18 April and the neighbouring Sundays sermons were preached for the Society in nearly half the parishes in England. A pilgrimage was made on 1 May to Chirbury in Shropshire, where Dr Bray was baptized, and another on 15 June to Llandowror, Carmarthenshire, where Griffith Jones was once Rector. On 28 May the Charity Schools Service formerly held in St Paul's Cathedral was recalled by the assembling of 3,000 children in the Cathedral. On 29 June nearly half the Bishops of the Anglican Communion, present in London for the Lambeth Conference, attended a Thanksgiving Service in St Paul's. From 19–31 July a Pageant of Pilgrim's Progress, arranged by Hugh Ross Williamson, with music arranged and directed by Sir Malcolm Sargent, with Robert Speaight, Barry Jackson, and Jack Hawkins, was generously presented by the *Daily Telegraph* in honour of the Society's anniversary. In September a service was held at Sheldon, of which Dr Bray had been rector, when only half of those who wished to attend succeeded in entering the Church; and another at St Botolph's without Aldgate, where he had been vicar. And so the celebration proceeded until its end on 8 March 1949.

It was at the meeting at the Mansion House on 8 March 1948 that the Archbishop of Canterbury presented a statement of policy which marked the beginning of the changes completed in 1958. Simplicity of appeal to the parishes was necessary. The S.P.C.K. had accumulated a number of odd jobs, some of them the main concern of other Societies. There was a general desire for the rationalizing of Societies and their work. The S.P.C.K. would therefore concentrate on education and literature, the former being defined primarily as the training of clergy and teachers overseas, the latter including all kinds of aids to education, such as pictures and films. Grants in future would be more selective, some being larger and many of the small ones being dropped. The spiritual care of emigrants would continue, and the Society would not "abandon the traditional readiness to give immediate help to the Church in any unseen eventuality".

This policy involved giving up the Medical Missions after more than 70 years. The work was coming to an end in any case, for in 1947 no new application had been received from any European student. It was therefore decided to leave the training of doctors to the Societies which had provisionally accepted them and were expecting them to serve later; in this way continuous pastoral care during training could be better given. Also the Braille work was taken over by the Royal National Institute for the Blind, and the endowment of bishoprics overseas ceased to be one of the Society's objects.

Further changes followed. The biggest was the bringing of St Katharine's College, Tottenham, into line with other Church Training Colleges. From 1952 onwards, while the Society remained Trustee of

Birmingham Post

"250th Anniversary . . . celebrations were planned with imagination"

"The Society's headquarters was moved . . . into a church"

the property for the purposes of a Training College, control of the College itself was transferred to an independent governing body, on which the S.P.C.K. was represented. Henceforward the Council of Church Training Colleges was responsible for capital development within the limits of what is made possible by central church funds and the equivalent Government grants to meet them. The Society's outstanding task was to provide an assembly hall, using a legacy left for this purpose by Prebendary G. H. Perry, which by the time it could be spent had with accumulated interest reached the figure of £28,000. This Hall was completed in 1955 and opened on 27 June by the Minister of Education, Sir David Eccles.

The whole story, however, is not one of withdrawal. There was no question of giving up the Society's work on the high seas, for emigration, which had ceased between the two wars, had revived greatly in the post-war years. Indeed, this part of the Society's work developed considerably; more priests were available for appointment as chaplains than at many periods in the past, and thanks in particular to the energetic co-operation of the Australian Government and the Church in Australia, few migrant ships sailed without a chaplain.

Meanwhile, the number of bookshops overseas was increasing. Mr E. W. Bishop, the Financial Secretary, accompanied the S.P.G. delegation to the West Indies in 1946, and as a result a chain of bookshops was set up in the Islands, British Guiana, and British Honduras. After some growing pains, it was found possible to staff them with nationals. This chain of bookshops constituted the first efficient bookshops in the area, bringing literature to places where it had previously been obtained only with the greatest difficulty, and before long handling a very large proportion of all the books distributed in the Caribbean. Shortly afterwards, the Society took over bookshops in Rangoon and Baghdad, and extended its bookshops in Tanganyika. The bookshops in Rangoon and Baghdad remained fully in the Society's ownership only for some ten years, for the growing difficulty of owning a trading activity within a country outside the British Commonwealth eventually made it necessary to place them under local ownership, though, at the time of writing, both are still proud of their connection with the Society. But during those few years, the experiment was fully justified by the extent of the literature, including Christian literature, which the Society was able to distribute by this means. It was a significant example of Christian energy and perseverance at a time when Asia was hardening itself both against the West and against the Christian religion.

As recorded in a previous chapter, in February 1949 the Reverend James Stuart went to Delhi as Editor of the S.P.C.K. in India. This was a veritable landmark in the Society's history. At last the hopes and plans that had for many years been frustrated by failure to find a competent man began to bear fruit. Almost at once Mr Stuart began to build up a careful programme of publishing in the chief Indian languages, and set to work to gather round him the band of translators necessary for this purpose. In 1952 he was joined by Mr John Finch, who opened the Society's first bookshop in India, at Delhi.

Some examples of the new policy of making substantial grants for educational work of primary importance may be given. In 1949, £2,400 a year for three years was voted to pay the fees of priest-students from overseas for a year at St Augustine's College, Canterbury, £2,400 being at that time five-sixths of the Church of England share of the annual cost. Since then this grant has twice been repeated, though now the Church of England draws on other sources for a greater share of the increased cost. In 1945–6, £1,500 was voted to the Southern Sudan for a Divinity College at Mundri, to which a number of further grants were subsequently made. In 1947, £500 was granted to Codrington College, Barbados, a sum increased to £750 per annum at the time of writing. Later, £2,450 was granted to found the College of St Patrick, Gwelo, Southern Rhodesia—which might almost be called a S.P.C.K. College—and £2,000 for the Anglican Hostel of St Peter at Singapore; also £250 for an educational adviser in the new diocese of Basutoland, and two grants of £500 each for a Board of Theological Advisors for the Province of West Africa. More recently, the Society has become accustomed to make grants towards the stipends of teachers in theological colleges overseas. At the time of writing the greatly increased cost of living in all parts of the world, by forcing the Society to increase the value of its bursaries and scholarships, has caused it to cut down the number of its larger grants for education.

In 1947 the Church of South India came into being, and several dioceses which had been closely connected with the Society in the past, and had derived much help from the Society, ceased to be dioceses of the Anglican Communion and in some cases were divided up into new dioceses. The Society continued, however, to give what help it could. It gave warning that its existing grants must be tapered off over a period of five years, and at the same time announced that it would make grants towards the expenses of ordinands from the Church of South India at Anglican Theological Colleges, and provide literature for use in South India. Its book-grants for ordinands in this area continued as before.

The formation of the Church of England Film Commission, in 1943, has already been reported. A Committee of the Society had previously explored the ground thoroughly, and given advice both on the choice of films and on technical matters connected with their presentation. In 1948 the Film Commission, to which the Society had made a grant of £10,000 for production, released a film, *Your Inheritance*, which set new standards in religious film production, and constituted a permanent addition, of considerable value, to the resources of Anglican teaching films. But it was still too early, in the history of the non-commercial use of films, for religious films of this kind to be produced with any hope that they would pay for themselves. A film made by the Society in 1948, as a souvenir of the Lambeth Conference, was, however, a financial success. In 1948, the Archbishop of Canterbury announced that the Church of England Film Commission, which had been purely experimental, was dissolved. Instead, a Church of England Film Council would be set up, and the S.P.C.K. was invited to become the Executive Film Agency of the Church. This offer was accepted, and since then, in addition to its grant for production, the Society has been voting up to £2,000 a year for office expenses. Thus fully charged with a new responsibility, the Society set energetically about the production of filmstrips, at the same time taking steps to make the Church in the parishes aware of the potentialities of film and filmstrip techniques in the service of the Church. The remarkable increase in the use of films and filmstrips for this purpose owes not a little to the Society's efforts, while again and again filmstrips produced by the Society have led the way in the development of this medium.

In 1949 a further responsibility was undertaken by the Society. For many years the Religious Drama Society had been associated with the S.P.C.K. The Religious Drama Society, however, is an inter-denominational body, and it was felt that the time had come for the Church of England to have some more official connection with this increasingly important work. It was decided that this could be achieved by affiliation between the S.P.C.K. and the Religious Drama Society. Since then the two Societies have worked even more closely together, and the S.P.C.K. has contributed £1,500 per annum to the R.D.S.

Meanwhile, the number and the trade of the branch bookshops were steadily growing. In 1945 there were 18 bookshops in the British Isles, with a turnover of £158,000; in 1958 31 bookshops with a turnover of £529,600. In 1953 efficient distribution of the vast output of Coronation literature was ensured by their existence. The Branch Managers' Conference had been revived, on a much larger scale. It now took the inside of a week and was held, for some years at Farnham Castle, then at a number of Training Colleges. Daily services, including the Eucharist, were sung; and there appeared to be a remarkable growth not only in professional *expertise* and friendship among the managers and headquarters staff, but also in understanding of the Society's purposes, and keenness to fulfil them. In 1955 a joint conference of the Society's Diocesan Organizing Secretaries and Bookshop Managers was held at Bishop Otter College, Chichester, and led to much closer co-operation between these two sides of the Society's activities in the dioceses. From this time it began to be generally recognized that the provision of bookshops to serve the dioceses and parishes by supplying the literature the Church requires, and by bringing Christian books to the notice of a wider public, is itself missionary and evangelistic work. It was now beginning to be possible to describe all that the Society was doing as one concerted activity, every part of which exists to promote Christian knowledge.

This integration of the Society, as it came to be called, was assisted by the revision of the Constitution, which was effected in two stages, in 1950 and 1955. Government by monthly meetings of the Society was abolished. An Annual General Meeting is to be held within the Octave of St John Baptist's Day, 24 June, and provision is made for Special General Meetings, as may be necessary. There are three Committees, Finance, Home, and Overseas, the majority of whose members are elected by the Annual General Meeting. The general administration of business is vested in these Committees. Together with the President, the Treasurers, and certain co-opted Vice-Presidents, the elected members of these Committees form the Governing Body, which retains the constitutional functions of the Standing Committee. This arrangement secures that those responsible for the Society's policy are themselves closely acquainted with at least one side of the Society's work.

At the end of 1954 Canon L. E. Parsons retired from the post of General Secretary, having done much to forward the new plans. It was decided that he should not be replaced, and for a short time the Reverend F. N. Davey, who had been Editorial Secretary since the end of 1944, acted in a dual capacity. By the new Constitution he was appointed Director of the Society. In view of the terms of the Society's incorporation it was, however, necessary that the Society should continue to have two Secretaries. The new Constitution therefore provided that, as well as the Director, the Deputy to the Director should rank as a Secretary. No Deputy Director was actually appointed until 1958, when Mr E. W. Bishop, who, as Financial Secretary, had secretarial rank, retired after 50 years service with the Society. With the appointment of Mr A. K. L. Stephenson as Deputy Director the new Constitution came fully into operation.

Before this, a most striking and inspiring event had taken place, symbolizing a new epoch in the Society's history. The Society's headquarters was moved from Northumberland Avenue into a Church. The move was dictated by necessity. The cost of remaining in the region of Government offices, banks, and shipping firms, with the inevitable high rates doomed soon to soar far higher, was becoming excessive. It could not be right to use such a valuable site for storage purposes, as for the most part it was being used. Nor was the office accommodation suited to the enlarged staff. The decision was therefore taken to sell, first the freehold, later the leasehold, and to seek other premises. A warehouse was built at Saffron Walden in Essex, near the printing press, and a shop was found at No. 322 Regent Street. The Church of Holy Trinity, Marylebone Road, London, N.W.1, was secured as headquarters. This is a masterpiece of Classic architecture, designed by Sir John Soane, and consecrated in 1828. Owing to the shift of population and other causes it was no longer required as a parish church. It was skilfully adapted by Mr Cecil C. Handisyde, to provide a chapel holding 200 people, the organ being enlarged and thoroughly modernized. A large room, called the Ante-Church, was constructed, for meetings of the Society, exhibitions, and bookstalls;

also a film-theatre, many offices, and a canteen. The large crypt or basement was racked for storing stock. The parish and benefice of Holy Trinity had been united, by an Order in Council, with the parish of St Marylebone, and the church designated for charitable and educational purposes. By a declaratory deed of the Bishop, it is now vested in the London Diocesan Fund as custodian trustees, and the S.P.C.K. as administrative trustees. The Society formally took possession of the Church on 28 October 1956, when the Bishop of London blessed the various parts to their new use. Dr Wand, the previous Bishop, to whom the Society owed so much for his skilful Chairmanship of the Standing Committee in the post-war years, preached the sermon, saying that in this age of specialization the Society must canalize its efforts in the chief aim of publishing and distributing Christian Literature. "I believe that, in a place of this kind, those who worship here will find their work and prayers united. Their whole life will become one great *Gloria* to the Lord."

"When a man hath finished, then he is but at the beginning." Those who are at present working for the Society would be the last to think they have solved their problems. They will be confronted by many difficulties, but the experience of two and a half centuries shows them that difficulties are generally surmounted by the old Society. It is doing its work, if not more vigorously than ever before, at least with more accurately directed aim. The yearly contributions from its supporters are now over £30,000, apart from legacies. And the combined publishing and bookselling operations are approaching £1,000,000 a year. When all allowance has been made for the changed value of money, this is a big advance on the £60,000 of 1914. Future progress will depend not only on skilful direction from the top, but also on gaining recruits for the staff, whether in London or elsewhere, who will regard the work as a rewarding and desirable form of Christian service.

Appendix A

THE S.P.C.K. IN IRELAND AND SCOTLAND

THE STORY of education in Ireland during the eighteenth century is melancholy indeed; it laboured under the weight of an impossible task, that of maintaining schools by which to establish the ascendancy of a Protestant minority. The Irish Charity Schools began in imitation of the English ones, the first being founded in Dublin in 1704; by 1717 there were fifteen in Dublin alone. A few noblemen and great landowners wholly maintained schools on their estates and some were supported as in England, but the conditions that made for success in England did not exist, for there was practically no pious middle class to which to appeal. In 1717 the scattered efforts were focused by the foundation of a Dublin Society for Promoting Christian Knowledge for "the more general establishment of Charity Schools". These by 1725 numbered 163, with 3,000 pupils. Then progress ceased. The poverty of the Anglican clergy and the number of parishes one man had to serve in order to get a living wage made supervision by them impossible. The well known William King, Archbishop of Dublin, would not support the movement, which he condemned as based on intolerance, and in most of the country the illegal Roman Catholic schoolmasters drew away the potential pupils. The schools tended to die out unless they were supported by endowments.

In 1733 the Government intervened and granted Letters Patent for the establishment of the Incorporated Society in Dublin for Promoting English Protestant Schools. This step was greeted with enthusiasm. The schools were expected to be a bulwark against Popery, which in the popular mind was associated with disloyalty, and to teach habits of industry and piety. Parliamentary grants were made, beginning with £1,000 a year and working up to an average of £3,500 in 1750–60, and nearly £20,000 in the opening years of the nineteenth century. The schools were intended to be homes of industry and the children were boarded, often away from home. The masters exploited and neglected the children and the Charter Schools, as they were called, being virtually under no supervision, became a scandal, which was at last exposed by the great John Howard, who visited Ireland four times between the years 1782 and 1788. The system was an example of mismanagement carried to an

219

incredible pitch. Responsibility rested with the central body and with the local Committees and each could put the blame on the other. Meanwhile the Catholic "hedge schools" carried on their work of education with the support of the mass of the population; even Protestants used them in preference to the detested Charter Schools.

In 1792 three ex-scholars of Trinity College, Dublin, met on 9 October at the house of one of their number, William Watson, a Dublin bookseller, and began the Association for Discountenancing Vice and Promoting the Knowledge and Practice of the Christian Knowledge, now called Association for Promoting Christian Knowledge, or A.P.C.K. for short. In 1800 it was incorporated by Act of Parliament and the membership had grown to over 1,000. It received substantial Parliamentary grants. After 25 years it had helped to found and maintain 250 schools, attended by Protestants and Roman Catholics (the latter were not taught religion except at the parents' request); had founded a training college for teachers; and had done much to circulate Bibles and other books. It became the official publisher and bookseller to the Church of Ireland and, though the directly educational work has passed into other hands, it has to this day carried on its beneficent work on lines parallel with the London Society.

The English Society was in close touch with the Irish and its report of 1822 records a gift of £1,000 to enable its Irish sister to resume distribution of books for gaols, schools, hospitals, and workhouses. A further grant of £1,000 was made in 1836 to ease the difficulties of the Irish Society, caused by the withholding of payments to the clergy, its chief supporters.

Scotland, as is well known, established a national system of education long before England. But behind the Highland Line conditions of squalor and ignorance existed which horrified the progressive Lowland Scots and touched their consciences. In 1707 the Assembly of the Church of Scotland appealed for help to found a Society to Propagate Christian Knowledge in the Highlands and Islands. A patent incorporating the Society was obtained in 1709. From the first its affairs were managed centrally and with great care and economy. Collections were received from the churches and a Royal Bounty assisted the cause. The schools were supplementary to the parish schools, being placed in remote places, and were not to relieve the parishes of their obligations. The schoolmasters were examples of heroic devotion. The Scottish S.P.C.K. was no longer required when a national system of education was fully developed, and came to an end soon after 1880.[1]

---

[1] The story of Ireland and Scotland is told by Dr M. G. Jones in *The Charity School Movement*. The account of the A.P.C.K. is based on a pamphlet by Dean D. F. R. Wilson called *A.P.C K* (1942).

The London Society in February 1910 agreed not to correspond with the Scottish Society on the ground that it was a private body, the Scottish one being incorporated. At a meeting on 10 November 1709, an address to Edinburgh was deprecated for the same reason and because the step would be inconsistent with "the humility and modesty that have hitherto been such remarkable ornaments of this Society".

Appendix B

PITCAIRN ISLAND

THE SOCIETY possesses the Pitcairn Island Register, which it published in 1929, edited by Sir Charles Young. The Register, which begins with January 1790 and ends at February 1854, contains births, deaths, and marriages, a chronicle of important events, a list of current prices, and another of the ships that called at the island from 1823 to 1853; also prayers by John Adams. The Reverend T. B. Murray, Secretary of S.P.C.K., received the book from G. H. Nobbs, missionary to the island, and a friend of his. There are also three volumes of the proceedings and correspondence of the Pitcairn Island Fund Committee, which was founded in 1852 to provide funds for Mr. Nobbs' passage and clothing for the islanders. The Committee, which was drawn mainly from that of the S.P.C.K., may be regarded as an unofficial offshoot of the Society. The last meeting was held apparently in 1858 and the surplus funds seem to have been handed over to the Government of New South Wales.

H.M.S. *Bounty*, a vessel of 215 tons, sailed in 1787 for Tahiti to collect bread-fruit and other plants for the West Indies, commanded by William Bligh. After twenty-three weeks in Tahiti the ship had reached the neighbourhood of the Tonga Islands when a mutiny occurred, provoked perhaps by the severity of the Commander. The leaders were Fletcher Christian and John Alexander Smith, who lived to be known as John Adams, the patriarch of Pitcairn. Bligh and eighteen others were cast adrift in an open boat, which eventually reached Timor. Of these, twelve got to England with the news. H.M.S. *Pandora* was sent to Tahiti, whither the *Bounty* had returned, to arrest the mutineers, of whom fourteen were captured. However, the ship was wrecked on the Great Barrier Reef and four of them were drowned; of those who were brought back to England, three were executed. Nine of the mutineers who evaded capture sailed from Tahiti, with Tahitian wives and ten other Tahitians, and came to Pitcairn in 1790. They burned their ship, in order to conceal their identity.

Pitcairn is in the East Pacific opposite Chile and a little south of the Tropic of Capricorn; the mutineers found it uninhabited. By the end of 1791 only four male adults were left, owing to fighting between the English and the

Tahitians, and by 1800 Adams was the only survivor of the original sailors. The island was "discovered" by a British ship in 1814, which found a population of forty, of whom eight were original settlers, one man and seven women. John Adams, who possessed a Bible and Prayer Book, constructed a religion from them and converted the island. The S.P.C.K. was in touch with it from 1819 and sent books. Two sailors joined the settlers in 1823, one of them, John Buffett, becoming the schoolmaster. In 1831, the inhabitants, by then numbering 87, were removed to Tahiti, where they suffered from ill health, and decided to return almost at once. A chief magistrate was appointed in 1838 and the island became a protectorate of Britain. G. H. Nobbs, inspired by what he had read, set out to find it in 1838 and made the care of the islanders his life-work. He came to England in 1852 and was ordained by the Bishop of London, returning to the island as S.P.G. missionary. Next year the population, now 168, petitioned the Government to remove them to Norfolk Island, which was done at a cost of £5,580. However, a number drifted back. The story illustrates the growth of population in conditions of great hardship. The islanders later became Adventists.

Appendix C

SECRETARIES OF THE SOCIETY

Appointed		*Appointed*	
1699	John Chamberlayne	1869	John Evans
1702	Humphry Wanley		Henry Swabey
1708	Henry Newman	1870	Henry Swabey
1743	THE REVEREND★		J. M. Fuller
	Thomas Broughton	1875	Henry Swabey
1777	Michael Hallings		Edmund McClure
1785	George Gaskin	1890	A. J. Carlyle
1823	William Parker		Edmund McClure
	W. H. Coleridge	1891	W. Osborn B. Allen
1824	William Parker		Edmund McClure
	A. M. Campbell	1910	G. L. Gosling
1830	William Parker		Edmund McClure (*to*
	E. J. Burrow		*Christmas* 1914)
1831	William Parker	1915	G. L. Gosling
	George Tomlinson		W. K. Lowther Clarke
1842	William Parker	1944	G. L. Gosling
	T. B. Murray		F. N. Davey
	John Evans	1945	L. E. Parsons
	J. D. Glennie		F. N. Davey
1843	T. B. Murray		E. W. Bishop, Esq.
	John Evans	1955	F. N. Davey (*Director*)
	J. D. Glennie		E. W. Bishop, Esq. (*Finan-*
1860	John Evans		*cial Secretary*)
	J. D. Glennie	1958	F. N. Davey (*Director*)
1868	John Evans		A. K. L. Stephenson, Esq.
	J. D. Glennie		(*Deputy Director*)
	Henry Swabey		

★ *From this date the office was held by ordained ministers.*

Appendix D

LEGACIES OF £10,000 AND UPWARDS, WHICH HAVE BEEN BEQUEATHED TO THE SOCIETY

			£
1799	Baron Vryhouven	(Stock)	75,334
1818	Francis Thomas, Earl of Kerry	(Stock)	10,200
1819	The Reverend E. Parkinson		20,000
1824	The Reverend Richard Wilkes		10,500
1843	Robert Lowrey, Esq.		14,500
1859	The Reverend Henry Stonhouse	(Stock)	12,000
1868	Miss Ann Lockwood	(Stock)	28,000
1899	The Reverend L. C. Bathurst	(Part Stock)	13,231
1903	Lt-Col. Temple-West		30,545
1906	Edward Baker, Esq.	(Part Stock)	13,623
1913	Thomas Stephen Whitaker, Esq.		10,724
1915	The Reverend E. F. Cave-Browne-Cave	(Part Stock)	26,716
1918	The Reverend C. C. Collins		15,040
1922	Henry Herbert Wills, Esq.		16,871
1935	The Reverend Prebendary G. H. Perry		21,660
1937	Miss Mary Anna Brown		12,289
1951	Mrs Susan Murray Genevoix	(Part Stock)	16,240

Appendix E

S.P.C.K. BOOKSHOPS

Home	*Opened*
London:	
Great Queen Street	1836–79
S.P.C.K. House, Northumberland Avenue	1879–1916 & 1918–56
Queen Victoria Street	1880–1938
68 Haymarket	1916–18
64 New Bond Street	1918 only
69 Great Peter Street (taken over from the National Society)	1943
322 Regent Street	1956
Brighton	1880
Bath (opened by local committee about 1820)	1920
Canterbury	1932
Exeter (taken over from local committee)	1932
Liverpool (taken over from local committee)	1934
Sheffield	1936
Bradford	1936
Bournemouth	1937
Cardiff	1937
Worcester	1937
Ipswich	1940
Salisbury	1941
Newcastle-on-Tyne	1943
Gloucester	1945
Wakefield	1946
Chester	1946
Lincoln	1946
Edinburgh	1947
Jersey	1947
Peterborough	1947
York	1947

S.P.C.K. BOOKSHOPS

Home	Opened
Bristol (opened by local committee 1813)	1948
Darlington	1949
Truro	1950
Ely	1950
Northampton	1953
Durham	1954
Chichester	1957
Stevenage	1958
Manchester (still administered by local committee)	1814

Overseas	
Johannesburg	1937
Salisbury, Southern Rhodesia	1937
Dar-es-Salaam (taken over from U.M.C.A.)	1938
Singapore (2 shops)	1939
Baghdad (now locally owned)	1946–57
Isfahan	1946–51
Rangoon (administered by S.P.C.K. Burma from 1957)	1947
Trinidad:	
Port of Spain	1947
Tobago	1955–8
Grenada, Windward Islands	1947
Georgetown, British Guiana	1947
Bridgetown, Barbados	1947
St John's, Antigua	1947
Kingston, Jamaica	1947
Belize, British Honduras	1947
Nassau, Bahamas	1947–51
Tanga, Tanganyika	1948
Lindi, Tanganyika	1950
Zanzibar	1952
Delhi	1953

Index

Aaron, Pastor, 65, 69
Abraham, Rev. C. J., 167
Abyssinia, 118
Account of the Charity Schools, 24, 33
Account of the Religious Societies, 2, 4
Act for the Better Preservation of Parochial Libraries, 79
Act for the Better Propagation of the Gospel, 56
Act of Uniformity, 110
Adams, John, 222f.
Additional Curates Society, 155
Adelaide, 163
Africa, 128f., 163
—, East, 120, 129f.
—, South, 149, 168
—, West, 214
Africa Company, the, 97f.
"African Princes", 96f.
Afrikaans, 113
Agencies, for bookselling, 202
Agents, 24, 30
Aldgate School, 35
Aleppo, 116f.
Alexander, Bishop, 179
Alford, Dean, 176
Allen, Rev. W. O. B., 112, 224
All Souls', Langham Place, 182
A.L.O.E., 126
American Episcopal Church, 115, 127
— Mission, 12
Amharic, 118f.
Anand, John H., 126
Andrewes, Bishop Lancelot, 180
Anglesey, 55
Anglo-Catholic Congress Report, 200
Annapolis Library, 77
Anne, Queen, 6, 15, 26, 113
Annual Dinner, 90
— General Meeting, 149, 216
— Meeting, 151f., 164
— Report, 31, 89, 114
— Sermon, 28, 31, 92, 156

Annual (Anniversary) Service, 29f., 49, 93, 146ff., 148, 211
— Subscription, 14, 23
Antigua Bookshop, 227
Anti-Infidel Committee, 179
Anti-Roman Catholic Literature, 85
— — — Measures, 92
Antioch, Patriarch of, 116
Apocrypha, Issue of, 105, 109, 172, 177
—, Translations, 109
Apprenticing of Charity School Children, 48ff.
Arabic, 91, 116ff.
Archbishop's Examination in Religious Knowledge, the, 160
Archbishop's Mission to Assyrian Christians, 164
Archives of the S.P.C.K., ix, 203
Arian Controversy, 3
Armenian, 119
Army, books for the, 171
Ashley, Lord, 174
Ashton, Thomas, 37
Asia, 214
Associates of Dr Bray, 8f.
Association for Promoting Christian Knowledge, 220
Assyrian Christians, Archbishop's Mission to, 164
Athens, 111f.
Auckland, N.Z., 163
Augsburg, 136
Austen, Jane, 188
Australia, emigration to, 167f., 213
Authors, 175, 183, 186f., 200, 204

Babbacombe, 207
Baghdad Bookshop, 129, 213, 227
Bagot, Bishop Lewis, 32
Bagster, Samuel, 111
Bahamas Bookshop, 227
Baker, Edward, 225
Bampton Lectures, 179

Bangor, 80, 133
—, Bishop of, 32, 80, 176, 181
Banks, Sir Joseph, 99
—, Robert, 21
Barbados, 156, 214
— Bookshop, 227
Bardsley, Rev. C. C. B., 198
Barnes, Archdeacon, 125
Barrington (Cambs.), 39
—, Mr, 41
Barrow, Isaac, 84
Bartlett's Buildings, 16f., 86, 89, 153, 188
Basket, Mr, 103, 117, 170f.
Basutoland, 214
Bath, 44, 52, 142, 144
— Bookshop, 205, 226
— and Wells, Bishop of, 102
Bathurst, Rev. L. C., 225
Battersea, 161
Beaumaris, 57
Bedell, Bishop, 114
Bedford, Arthur, 95, 100
—, Duke of, 46, 117
Belize Bookshop, 227
Bell, Bishop G. K. A., 198
—, Dr, 156f.
Bellamont, Earl of, 78
Bengal, 64, 69, 71, 74f.
Bengali, 124
Berlin, 94
Besant, Walter, 186
Bevan, Madam, 58
Beveridge, Bishop, 81
Beverley, 34, 50, 133
Bicentenary of the S.P.C.K., ix, 154
Bible, Commentary on the, 177
—, distribution of the, 109f., 170ff.
—, publishing of the, 170ff.
—, translation of the, 109f.
— and Religious Tract Society, 75
Birkenhead, 167
Birmingham, 100, 180
Bishop, E. W., 208, 213, 217, 224
— Otter College, 216
Bishop's College, Calcutta, 76, 119, 126
Bishopsgate School, 49
Blake, William, 33
Blewbury (Berks.), 45
Bligh, William, 222
Blind, Literature for the, 194

Block Grants, 150
Blomfield, Sir Arthur, 161
—, Bishop C. J., 116, 150
Blue Coat School, 42
Blundell, Mr, 48
Board of the S.P.C.K., 149, 153, 172
— Schools, 160
Böhme, Rev. A. W., 61
Bolzius, Rev. J. M., 136ff.
Bombay, 67, 69, 74f., 97, 203
— Committee, 125
— Education Society, 125
Book Grants, 215
— of Common Prayer, 82, 119, 170
— Societies, 182
Bookrooms, 126
Bookselling, 142ff., 192, 201
Books for Charity Schools, 50f., 181
Bookshop Managers' Conference, 216
Bookshops, 129f., 179, 196, 201f., 205, 213, 216, 226f.
Bookvans, 130
Boone, Rev. J. S., 189
Borneo, 128
Boston (U.S.A.), 51
Bosworth, Dr, 113
Botany Bay, 96
Bounty, H.M.S., 222
Bounty, Queen Anne's, 132f., 140
—, Royal, 117, 132f.
Bournemouth Bookshop, 205, 226
Bowles, Mr, 98
Box (Wilts.), 39
Bradford Bookshop, 205, 226
Braille literature, 194, 197, 212
Bray, Elenor, 5
—, Goditha, 5
— Libraries, 78
—, Rev. Thomas, ix, 3, 5ff., 11ff., 21ff., 42, 56, 59, 63, 68, 77ff., 86, 97f., 200, 210f., 224
—, William, 5
Brazil, 115
Brentford, 24, 42
Bridges, Mr, 24
Bridgetown (Barbados) Bookshop, 227
Brightman, Dr F. E., 112
Brighton, 51, 147, 150
— Bookshop, 196, 226
Bristol, 21, 95, 100, 141, 181
— Bookshop, 227

Bristol Charity School, 46, 53
British and Foreign Bible Society, The, 104, 109, 171
British and Foreign School Society, 157f.
British Guiana, 213, 227
— Honduras, 213, 227
Broadhinton School, 36
Bromfield, Mr, 13, 51
Broseley (Salop), 138
Brougham Commission, 156
Broughton, Rev. Thomas, 18, 155, 224
Brown, Miss A., 225
—, Rev. David, 72
Browne, Edward, 114
Buffet, John, 223
Building Grants, 151, 163f., 203
Bulletin Anglican, 108
Burgess, Bishop Thomas, 82
Burkett, Mrs, 53
Burma, 129
Burnet, Bishop Gilbert, 9, 36, 38
Burnett, Thomas, 36
Burnside, Rev. F. H., 154
Burrow, Rev. E. J., 224
Burton, Dr, 176
Bury St Edmunds, 39, 41
Business Manager, 195, 205
Butler's Analogy, 126, 179

Caernarvon, 57
Cairo, 118
Calbo, A., 111
Calcutta, 72, 74f., 119, 124, 152f., 162, 203
— Committee, 124
Calderon, Rev. Juan, 115
Cambridge Brotherhood, 126
— University, 34f., 62, 106, 119, 135
— — Library, 174
— — Press, 107, 170
Campbell, Rev. A. M., 224
Campe, Pastor, 60
Canada, 108, 112, 116, 163, 167f.
Canterbury, Archbishop of, 7f., 89, 93, 117, 121, 132, 141, 152, 157, 159, 168, 173, 176, 182, 189, 198, 203, 212, 215
— Bookshop, 205, 226
Cantonese Prayer Book, 128
Cardiff Bookshop, 205, 226
Carey, William, 53

Caribbean, 213
Carlisle, 133
—, Bishop of, 79
Carlyle, Rev. A. J., 224
Carmarthen College, 96, 159
— Library, 80
Carolina, South, 134
Caroline Divines, 180
Carpenter, Canon E. F., 112
—, Mr, 100
Caslon, William, 117
Catalogue, S.P.C.K., 85, 184f., 192
Catechetical Lectures of Dr Bray, 5, 22
Catechetical Libraries, 14
— Schools, 11ff., 21
Catechisms, 83
Cave-Browne-Cave, Rev. E. F., 225
Cawnpore, 124
Central Board of Finance, 155
Ceylon, 70, 74, 125
Challenge, Ltd., The, 207
Chamberlayne, Edward, 15
—, John, 13, 15, 26, 132, 224
Chandler, Dean George, 182
Chandos, Duke of, 97
Channel Islands, 107
Charitable Trustees Incorporation Act, 192
Charity Commission(ers), 50, 154
— Schools, 10, 12, Ch. 4, 87f., 93ff., 101f., 148f., 156f., 170, 181, 211
— Sermons, 35f., 53
Charles II, 1, 20
—, Prince of Denmark, 66
Charter of the S.P.G., 7
— Schools, 219f.
Cheap Repository Tracts, 81
Chelsea College, 161
Chester, Bishop of, 14, 22, 101, 110, 143
— Bookshop, 226
—, Maryland, 51
Chetwood, Dean, 38
Chichester, Bishop of, 13f., 89, 97, 146, 156, 182, 198
— Bookshop, 227
— Charity School, 53
—, Dean of, 23, 32, 182
— Depot, 146
Childs, Rev. T. C., 166
China, 127f.
Chinese, 128

Chirbury, 5, 211
Chislehurst, 35
Chisleton, Mr, 25
Chittagong, 124
Christ Church, Newgate Street, 30
— —, Walcot, Bath, 99
Christian, Fletcher, 222
Christian Evidence Committee, 179
— Literature Society, Madras, 126
— —, Shanghai, 128
Christian Schoolmaster, The, 40, 42f., 50f.
Church, L. F., 134, 136
Church Army, 162
— Assembly Council for Foreign Rela-
    tions, 108
— Authority, 93
— Building Society, 155
— Historical Society, 204f.
Church Hymns, 178
— life, 99
— Literature Committee, China, 128
Church Messenger, The, 194
— Missionary Society, 75, 118, 122,
    165, 198
— Missions to Jews, 119
— of England Council for Common-
    wealth and Empire Settlement,
    168
— — — Film Council, 215
— — — Film Commission, 209, 215
— — — Year Book, 154
— of India, Pakistan, Burma, and
    Ceylon, 126
— of Scotland, 92
— of South India, 123, 127
— Publishing Society, Tokyo, 127
— Schools, 146, 160, 181, 210
— Training Colleges, 160, 212
— Union, the, 204
— Year Book Committee, 154
Churchmanship, 82
Churton, Archdeacon Edward, 155
Circular Letters, 14
Circulating Schools, 55, 58
Cirencester Blue Coat School, 42
City Bookshops, 196, 205, 224
— Churches, 3
Civil War, 1, 20
Clarke, Rev. A. T., 72
Clement, Mary, 55f.
Clergy Correspondents, 14, 80, 143

Clergy Mutual Assurance Society, 153
— Orphan Corporation, 147
Clerkenwell, 25
Clerks, 17
Cleveland, 155
Clive, Robert, 69
Clothing, of Charity School Children,
    46ff., 53f.
Cnattingius, H., 63, 72
Codrington College, Barbados, 214
Coghan, Mr, 23
Colchester, Col. Maynard, 10ff., 14, 21,
    54, 57
Colebath, Dr, 34
Colenso, Bishop, 149
Coleridge, Bishop W. H., 89, 139, 156,
    182, 224
Coleshill (Warwick), 26
College of St Mark and St John, 161
Collins, Rev. C. C., 225
Colombo Committee, 125
Colonial Bishoprics Fund, 163
Colonies, Education in, 153
Colston, Mr, 46, 53
Commissioners for Pious Uses, 35
Commission publishing, 200
Committee for Propagating Religion
    in India, 15
— of Correspondence, 141, 144
— of Council of Education, 158f., 192
— of General Knowledge and Educa-
    tion, 159
Committees for Literature, 148
— in India, 75
Commonwealth, the, 1, 12, 20, 56
Communion Manuals, 83f.
— Money, 35
Compton, Bishop Henry, 6f.
Conference of British Missionary
    Societies, 129
Confession, 84
Confirmation Manuals, 83
Congregatio de propaganda fide, 59
Congregationalists, 177
Constantinople, 119
Constitution of the S.P.C.K., 6, 87f.,
    211, 216f.
Convocation, 3, 8, 110, 154, 159
Co-operation with other Societies, 143
Copenhagen College of Missionaries,
    60, 67, 70

Coptic, 119
Copyrights, 186, 191
Corporation for the Propagation of Christian Knowledge, 7
— Society, 51
Correspondence, Committee of, 141, 144
Corresponding Members of the S.P.C.K., 14, 22, 25, 88, 93, 141ff., 148
— Society, 58
Cosin, Rev. J., 180
Costing, 190f.
Costs, of Schools, 40
"Country Priests", 73
Cowie, L. W., ix, 16
Coxon, Mr, 139
Cragg, Rev. Kenneth, 118
Crane, Mr, 97
Cranmer, Archbishop, 123
Cranston, Rev. James, 100
Cree, 202
Cuddalore, 64, 68f., 71
Curricula, in Charity Schools, 42f.
Cutts, Rev. E. L., 164

Dacca, 124
D'Allone, 8
Dampier, Bishop, 141
Danish, 112
— West Indies, 112
Dar es Salaam Bookshop, 129, 205, 227
Darlington Bookshop, 227
Davey, Rev. F. N., 217, 224
Davidson, Archbishop Randall, 121f., 198
Davies, Rev. G. C. B., 140
—, Sir Leonard, 56
Deal Library, 78
Deanery Libraries, 77
Debtors, Assistance to, 90
Delagarde, 18
Delagoa, 97f.
Delhi, 214
— Bookshop, 126f., 214, 227
Denne, Archdeacon, 17, 65, 68, 90, 135
Depots, 145, 201
Deputy Director, 217, 224
Dickens, Charles, 166
Diego, Pastor, 69
Dinapore, 124

Diocesan Committees, 141f.
— Grants, 150
— Organizing Secretaries, 216
Director of the S.P.C.K., 217, 224
Directors of Georgia, 9
Discipline in Charity Schools, 43
Discounts, 142f., 190f., 212
Disney, Mr, 99
Dissenters, 1f., 12, 28, 57, 92, 100, 158, 174, 182
Dissenting Academies, 20
District Committees, 110, 124, Ch. 10, 149, 152, 157, 174, 181f., 192, 201
Distribution of Literature, 126, 143ff., 150, 213
Doctors, training of, 163f., 212
Dod, Mr, 188
Dodd, A. H., 55
Donations, 148, 154
Doncaster, 21
Douglas, D. C., 16
Downing, Joseph, 81
Driver, R. S., 177
Dublin, Archbishop of, 219
— S.P.C.K., 219
— University Press, 107
du Fresne, Mr, 133
Dupleix, General, 69
Du Quesne, the Marquis, 17
Durham, 141, 150
— Bookshop, 227
Dutch, 112f., 116
— East Indies Company, 74

Earnings of Charity Schools, 45
East Africa, 120, 129
— India Company, 66f., 69f., 72, 74, 97, 114, 123, 125, 153
— India Mission, Ch. 5, 91, 93, 148, 203
— Indies, 87
Eastern Orthodox Church, 119, 123
Ebenezer (Georgia), 136f.
Eccleshall (Staffs.), 45, 48
Eccles, Sir David, 213
Ecclesiastical Establishment in British India Scheme, 74
Edburton (Sussex), 21
Edinburgh Bookshop, 226
— House, 129
Editorial Department, 206

Editorial Secretary, 185, 190, 195, 199, 205, 210f., 217
Education, 19f., 156
— Act 1904, 146; 1870, 159
— of Ordinands, 96, 163, 212, 214f.
— Society, 75
Edward VI, 20, 107
Edwards, A., 56
Elizabeth I, 2, 21
Ellerton, John, 178
Ely, 34, 141
— Bishop of, 100, 141
— Bookshop, 227
Emanuel, Don, of Minorca, 99
Emigrants, 151, 165f., 212f.
Enabling Act, 154
Endowment of Sees, 151, 162f., 203, 212
Endowments, 20, 34
English Church Union, 198, 204
—, Simplified, 130f.
"Enthusiasm", 85
Episcopal Referees, 176, 178, 180f., 203
Eskimo, 130
Ethiopia, 118f.
European Language Translations, 108
Evangelicalism, 150, 180
Evans, Mr, 51
—, Rev. John, 224
Evelyn, John, 10
Every, George, 3
Ewhurst, 35
Ewing, Mrs, 190
Examination of Charity School Children, 52
Exeter, 26, 34, 51
— Bishop of, 139
— Bookshop, 205, 226
— District Committee, 146
Eye (Suffolk), 37

Far East, 127f.
Farrington, Mr Justice, 35
Fees in Schools, 45, 158
Feoffees, 80
Field, Dr F., 112
Film Commission, 209, 215
Films, 209, 212, 215
Filmstrips, 209, 215
Finance Committee, 145, 199f., 205, 210, 216
—, of District Committees, 143

—, of the East India Mission, 71, 91
Financial Secretary, 208, 211, 213, 217, 224
Finch, John, 214
Fines, 36
Finnish, 112
Flaxman, John, 71
Fleet Street Bookshop, 179
Fleetwood, Bishop, 84
Florida, 134
Folkestone, 21
Foreign Committees, 142
— contacts, 93
— Literature, Ch. 8, 207, 211
— — Committee, 109, 203, 206, 211
— Translation Committee, 108f., 121
Fort St David, 67, 69
— St George, 66ff.
— William (Calcutta), 69
Founders' Day, 152, 211
Founding of Bishoprics, 151
Fox, Mr, 170
Franke, Professor A. H., 13, 58, 60, 64f., 67
Frankfurt, 107
— on the Oder, 113
Frederick I of Prussia, 113
Frederick IV of Denmark, 59f., 62, 66f.
Frederick William I of Prussia, 60, 135
French, 107f., 116
— Proselytes, Ch. 9 (a)
Frend, Rev. Walter, 89
Frere, Bishop W. H., 122
Friedrich Werber Gymnasium, Berlin, 60
Fukien Prayer Book, 128
Fuller, Rev. J. M., 190, 224
Furness District Committee, 174

Gaelic, 92, 106f.
Gambia, 108
Gaskin, Rev. George, 18, 72, 139, 155, 224
Gateshead, 143
Gawthorpe, Mr, 102
Geister, Rev. J. E., 68f.
Genevoix, Mrs S. M., 225
General Fund, 191f., 200, 202, 205, 210
— Literature Committee, 109, 182, 185f., 200

General Meeting of the S.P.C.K., 76, 109, 141, 149, 172, 180ff., 189, 206, 210
— Secretary, 194, 211, 217, 224
George I, 15, 26, 30, 94f., 117, 132
George II, 135
George III, 30
George, Prince, of Denmark, 61, 63
Georgetown Bookshop, 227
Georgia, 8, Ch. 9 (b)
German, 113, 116
Gibb, Mr, 100
Gibraltar, 115, 156
—, Bishop of, 111, 156
Gibson, Bishop Edmund, 27, 41, 81
Gittisham (Devon), 102
Gladstone, W. E., 165
Glasbury (Brecknock), 46
Glasse, Samuel, 32
Glennie, Rev. J. D., 224
Gloucester, 32, 38, 100
— Bookshop, 226
— Cathedral Grammar School, 30
Goa, 61
Goddard, Dr W. S., 111
Godolphin, Earl of, 138
Good, Mr, 37
Gore, Bishop Charles, 204
Gosling, Canon G. L., 152, 224
Gosling's Bank, 76
Gouge Schools, 56f.
Governing Body of the S.P.C.K., 90, 216
Grammar Schools, 19, 22, 33, 57, 146f., 157
Grants, 149f., 161f., 203, 212, 214
— of Books, 95, 151, 215
— for Medical Missions, 163, 203, 212
— for new dioceses, 150, 162f.
— for publishing, 126f.
Gravesend Library, 78
Gray, A., 89
Great Dunham (Norfolk), 99
— Gransden (Hunts.), 27
— Peter Street Bookshop, 226
— Queen Street Bookshop, 153, 189, 226
— Suffolk Street Warehouse, 193, 205
Greek, 110f.
Greenock, 167
Greenwich Girls' School, 43

Grenada Bookshop, 227
Grey Coat Hospital, 21, 44
— — School, 34
Grocers' Company, 179
Gronau, Rev. I. C., 136f.
Gründler, Rev. J. E., 63f., 67
Guardian, The, 144
Guernsey, 107f.
Guilford, Lord, 9, 11ff.,
Gujerati, 125
Guyon, Madame, 81
Gwelo, 214

Hadleigh, 150
Hainton, G. H., 26, 43, 54
Hales, Robert, 94
Halle University, 13, 60, 64, 67f., 72f.
Hallings, Rev. Michael, 18, 224
Handisyde, C. C., 217
Hanover, 94, 136
Hanoverian Succession, 94
Harris, Rev. Charles, 204
Harrison, Rev. T., 147
Hartshorne, Rev. R. C., 138
Harvey, John, 21
Hastings, 100
—, Lady Elizabeth, 38
—, Marchioness of, 124
Hatton Garden, 89
Hawkins, Jack, 212
Hawtyne, Rev. J., 124
Hayley, Dean William, 14, 53
Haymarket Bookshop, 193, 226
Hayter, Bishop Thomas, 32
Hayward, S., 110
Heber, Bishop, 64, 75
Hebrew, 119
"Hedge Schools", 220
Hedingham, 51
Hereford, Bishop of, 105
Hickes, Dean George, 15
High Church Party, 26
Hildesley, Bishop Mark, 106
Hindi, 126
Hindustani, 68, 124
Hoare, Benjamin, 135
—, Henry, 91
Hoare's Bank, 76
Hobson, Rev. Edwin, 161
Hodges, Dr Moses, 36
Holidays, in Charity Schools, 41, 54

Holt, Rev. Arthur, 51
Holy Trinity Church, Marylebone, 217
Home Committee, 216
— Organizing Committee, 154
Honeycott, John, 25f.
Hong Kong, 128
Hook, Dr, 158, 176
Hooke, Justice, 7, 9ff., 23, 51, 56, 89, 91
Horneck, Dr A., 3, 79
Horsley, Bishop Samuel, 33, 81
Horst, Mr, 72f.
Horsted Keynes (Sussex), 39
Hospitals, 141f.
How, Bishop Walsham, 177f.
Howard, John, 219
—, Mr, 65
Howley, Archbishop, 180
Huguenots, 107
Hull, 112
Huron, 163
Hutchinson, Dr, 41
Hutton, John, 42, 100
Hymns, 177f.
— Ancient and Modern, 178

Imitation of Christ, The, 177
Income, 23f., 154, 202, 218
Incorporated Society in Dublin for Promoting English Protestant Schools, 219
Incorporation, 87
Independence, American war of, 138
India, 116, 123, 126, 152
Indian Mission, Ch. 5, 93, 150, 152
— S.P.C.K., 126
Infidelity, measures to counter, 179
Inspectors of Schools, 23, 160f., 184
Instructions for the Protestant Missions . . ., 64
Insurance, 23
Ipswich, 39
— Bookshop, 226
Iraq, 164
Ireland, 219
—, Church of, 220
Irish, 106
— Charity Schools, 219
Irthlingborough School, 45
Isenberg, Rev. K. W., 118

Isfahan Bookshop, 227
Isle of Man, 106, 133
Islington, 39
Islip, 34
Italian, 113f., 116

Jablonski, 113
Jackson, Barry, 212
Jacobite Rebellion, 26
Jacobitism, 95
Jacobson, Dr, 110
Jamaica Bookshop, 130, 227
James I, 106f.
Japan, 127
Japanese, 127
Jennings, Mr, 27
Jersey, 107f.
— Bookshop, 226
Jerusalem, 118
Jewel's Apology, 114
Johannesburg Bookshop, 129, 205, 227
Joint Stock Companies, 23
Jones, Griffith, 17, 58, 62, 104, 211
—, Dean John, 57
—, Rev. John, 96
—, M. G., 28f., 55, 220
—, Mary, 103
Jubilee, 152

Keble, Rev. John, 176
Keith, George, 11f., 21
Ken, Bishop Thomas, 82, 84, 178
Kensington, 37
Kerry, Earl of, 225
Kettlewell, Mr, 78, 84
—, Mrs, 79
Keys, prayer for the House of, 106
King, Mr, 134
—, William, 219
King's College, London, 155, 182
Kingston, Jamaica, Bookshop, 227
Kirby-on-Bain, 99
Klein, F. A., 117f.
Knapp, Professor, 72
Knebworth, 183
Kohlhoff, Rev. J. B., 64, 70
—, Rev. J. C., 64, 73
Krapf, Rev. J. L., 118
Kurdistan Expedition, 119

Labourdonnais, 69
Lambeth Conferences, 121, 195, 201, 205, 212, 215
— Palace, 112, 117
Lancaster, 157
Lane, C. A., 191
—, Mr, 140
Lang, Archbishop Cosmo, 151
Language Problems, 120
Latin in Schools, 19
— translations, 110
Laud, Archbishop, 112
Launceston, 39, 44
Lay Correspondents, 14
— Readers, 162
Laymen's Libraries, 77
Lea Marston, 5
Leason, John, 52
Leeds, 144
Leek (Staffs.), 146
Legacies, 34, 86f., 96, 154, 213, 225
Leicester, Bishop of, 198
Levertoff, Rev. P. P., 119
Lewes, 146f.
Libraries, 9, 13f., Ch. 6(a), 125, 159
Lightfoot, Bishop, 151
Lincoln, 25, 133, 141
—, Bishop of, 27, 31, 171, 179
— Bookshop, 226
Lincoln's Inn, 7, 89
— — Fields, 153
Lindi (Tanganyika) Bookshop, 227
Literature Committees, 148
— for special classes, 84, 181
Literary Committees, 149
Littledale, Dr, 113
Liturgical Committee of the Lambeth Conference, 122
Liverpool, 34, 48, 144, 166f.
— Bookshop, 205f., 226
Llandaff, Bishop of, 117, 176
Llandowror, 17, 58, 211
Lloyd, Bishop William, 54f.
Lockwood, Miss A., 225
London, 3, 23ff., 30, 34, 36ff., 45, 167
—, Bishop of, 6, 8, 18, 23, 26f., 93, 95, 100, 132, 142, 150, 155, 173f., 176, 218
— Diocesan Fund, 218
— — House, 79
— Life Association, 153

Lotteries, 100, 132
Lowrey, R., 225
Lowther Clarke, Canon W. K., 209, 224
—, Sir Thomas, 88
Luscombe, Bishop, 108
Lutheran Churches, 113
— Clergy, 75
— Missions, 63, 75
Lütkens, Chaplain, 59f.
Lysius, Pastor, 60

Mackworth, Sir Humphrey, 9, 11, 56, 78
Madagascar, 108
Madras, 64, 67ff., 74f., 156, 203
— Committee, 75, 124f.
— Diocesan Press, 125
Madura, 61
Maidstone, 62, 147
Major S. D., 99
Malabar, 64, 123
— Church, 123
— Committee, 61
— Mission, 97
Malagasy, 202
Malta, 117
Maltby, Bishop, 150
Maltese, 114
Malthus, 89, 156, 182
Man, Isle of, 106, 133
Managers' Conference, 216
Manchester Bookshop, 227
Mandarin Prayer Book, 128
Manners Sutton, Archbishop, 157
Mansion House Meeting, 211f.
Manuals, 83f.
Manual Work in Charity Schools, 44f., 48f., 53
Manx, 106
Maori, 202
Marathi, 125f.
Markham, Mrs, 177
Marlborough, 39
Marrison, Rev. G. E., 61
Marsh, Professor H., 30, 156f.
Marshalsea Prison, 95, 193
Martin, Mr, 62
—, Rev. John, 67
Marton (Salop), 5
Martyn, Mr, 13
Mary, Queen, 107

Maryland, 6f., 12, 51f., 78
Mauritius, 107f.
Mayo, Rev. R., 91
McClure, Rev. E., ix, 11, 21, 87, 185, 224
Medical Missions, 163f., 194, 203, 212
— Missionaries, training of, 163f., 194
Meerut, 124
Meetings of the S.P.C.K., 12, 89f.
Melbourne, 163
Membership of the S.P.C.K., 88f., 148
Members' Prices, for books, 142
Methodists, 177
Methodist Societies, 4
Metropolitan Board of Works, 153f.
Middleton, Bishop T. F., 74f., 162
Milan, 114
Mines Adventure, 9
Ministry of Education, 192, 203
Minutes of the S.P.C.K., 22
Missionary Grants, 124, 162f.
— Projects, 96
— Society, of the Church of England, 75
Missions to Seamen, 162
Monk, Bishop J. H., 33
More, Hannah, 81
Mullins, Mrs Esther, 126
Münch, Minister in Augsburg, 136
Mundri (Bishop Gwynne College), 214
Murray, Rev. T. B., 190, 222, 224
Muslims, Literature for, 116, 118f.
Muss-Arnolt, W., 106
Mussoom, James Macquillan, 97f.
—, John Chaung, 97f.

Name of the S.P.C.K., 86
Nantes, Edict of, 132
Naples, 114
Nare, Mrs, 70
Nassau, 163
— Bookshop, 227
Natal, 149
National Mission of Repentance and Hope, 198
— Schools, 53, 157
— Society, 75, 146, 152, 155ff., 181, 184
Navy, books for the, 171
Near East, 110f., 116, 118
Neath, 37, 39, 56, 133
Needham, Mrs, 34

Negri, Solomon, 117
Nelson, Robert, 14f., 26, 52, 78ff., 82, 84, 181
Nestorians, 164
Net Book Agreement, 146
New Bond Street Bookshop, 226
New Brunswick, 112
Newbury, 48
Newcastle, 170
— Bookshop, 226
Newfoundland, 16
New Jerusalem, 61
New South Wales, 124, 222
New York, 78, 112
New Zealand, 163, 167
Newland (Glos.), 35
Newman, Henry, ix, 16ff., 27, 37ff., 44, 49, 62, 64ff., 78, 80, 87, 90, 93f., 132f., 135, 137f., 188f., 224
Newman, J. H., 176
Newton, Sir Isaac, 133
Nicholls, Dr Samuel, 32
Njanapiragasam, "Country Priest", 73
Nobbs, Rev. G. H., 222f.
Non-jurors, 3
Norfolk Island, 223
Norman, Clerk, 18
Norris, Canon, 160
—, H. H., 75, 141f., 189
North Boughton, 45
— China, 128
North, Robert, 36
—, Sir Francis, 9
Northampton Bookshop, 227
Northumberland Avenue, 151, 153, 193, 217, 226
Norwich, 141
—, Bishop of, 32, 62, 135
Nottingham Presbyterians, 117

Oath to the Crown, 95
Oecumenica, 108
Oglethorpe, General, 134, 138
Office of Works, 193
Oliver, J., 58
Orders and Rules for the College of Missionaries, Copenhagen, 60
Ordinands, Education of, 96
Ordination of Missionaries, 64
Organizing Department, 154
— Secretaries, 154, 216

Orwell, 34
Osterwald, Dean J. F., 94
Otter, Bishop William, 156, 182
Oundle, 79
Over Whitacre, 5
Overseas Bookshops, 129, 205, 227
— Committee, 216
— Publishing, Ch. 8
Owen, Dr H., 91
Oxford, 34, 110, 116
—, Bishop of, 49, 102
— University, 179
— — Press, 107, 116, 122, 170, 192

Packets, 91
Padwick, Miss Constance, 118
Paley, Mr, 92
Paley's *Evidences*, 115
Palestine, 118
Palmer, Mrs, 62
Pamlico Library, N. Carolina, 77
Pandora, H.M.S., 222
Paper, 199, 207
— Control, 207
Parish Authorities, 23
Parker, James W., 176, 182f.
—, J. M., 192
—, William, 224
Parkinson, Rev. E., 225
Parnel, Archdeacon, 52
Parochial Libraries, 13, 77ff.
Parsons, Canon L. E., 217, 224
Pasche, Chaplain, 64
Passengers Act, 167
Patrons, of Schools, 157
—, Society of, 30
Payment to Authors, 187
Penitentiaries, 142
Penn, William, 12
Pennsylvania, 12, 104
Pensions, for S.P.C.K. staff, 204
Penwell, Marmaduke, 97f.
Perceval, Lord, 97, 133
Percivall, Samuel, 62
Perry, Prebendary G. H., 213
Persecution of Protestants, 135
Persia, 116
Persian, 126
Peterborough, Bishop of, 31, 156
— Bookshop, 226
Petit, Rev. Paul, 162

Petitions, 152, 159, 180
Philadelphia, 51
Philipps, Sir John, 13, 40, 57
Philips, Bishop John, 106
Phillpotts, Bishop Henry, 140
Piedmont, 114
Pilgrim Trust, 203
Pilgrims, Tax on, 153
Pimlowe, Rev. A., 99
Pitcairn Island, 124, 222f.
— — Fund Committee, 222
— — Register, 222
Plantations, 6, 8, 13, 80
Platts, A., 26, 43, 54
Plays and Players, 100
Plutschau, Rev. Heinrich, 60f., 66
Plymouth Library, 78
Pococke, Professor Edward, 116
Pohle, Rev. Christian, 73, 75
Poland, 119
Policy, 91, 93, 148ff.
Polish, 114
Pondicherry, 60, 69
Poplar, 95
Port Chaplains, 168
Port of Spain Bookshop, 227
Porteous, Bishop, 82, 126
Portuguese, 61, 65, 68, 114, 116
Pott, Archdeacon, 141
Potterne (Wilts.), 170
Powys, Sir Lyttleton, 35
Practising Schools, 158
Prayer Book, Issue of, 82, 109f., 119ff., 170ff.
— — Publishing, 170ff.
— — Revision, 120ff.
— — Translation, 109f., 119ff.
Prendergast (Pembs.), 40
Prerogative Office, 91
Presbyterians, 12, 117
President of the S.P.C.K., 152, 216
Presses, Privileged, 104, 107, 170f., 198
Preston Committee, 157
— National School, 158
Price, Sir Thomas, 5
Prices of books, for members, 142
Priestley, Joseph, 89
Printers, 117
Prisoners, discharge of, 90
Prisons, 95, 141f.
— Bill, 153

Private Devotion, 84
Privileged Presses, 104, 107, 170f., 198
Prize Books, 196
Proselytes, French, Ch. 9 (a)
Protestant Episcopal Church in the
U.S.A., 115, 127
— Missions to the East Indies, 62, 87
Provincial Libraries, 77
Psalms and Hymns, 178
Publication, the S.P.C.K.'s first, 13
Publishers to the S.P.C.K., 176, 182f.,
188
Publishing, 80, 91, 173f., 196
— Department, 154, 204f.
— Grants, 126f.
— Policy, 91, 197f., 207
Punjab, 125
Punjabi, 126
Pupil Teachers, 160
Puritanism, 28
Pusey, Dr E. B., 109, 112

Quakers, 11f.
Qualifications, for teachers, 37f.
Quebec, 107
Queen Anne's Bounty, 132f., 140
— Victoria Street Bookshop, 226
Quincy, S., 138

Rajanaiken, 69
Ranelagh, Earl of, 36
Rangoon, 129
— Bookshop, 213, 227
Rawlins, Prison Chaplain, 95
Raynes, Mr, 38
Readers, Lay, 162
— , publishers', 184
— , school, 184
Recommendation of MSS., 184, 187
Recruitment of Teachers for Charity
Schools, 37
Red Maids' School, 21
Referees, 174ff., 180f., 203f.
Reform Bill, 181
Reformation, 19, 180
Reformers, 19
Refugees, 115, 135f.
Regent Street Bookshop, 217, 226
Rejection of MSS., 187
Religious Drama Society, 215f.
— Literature Committee, 199ff., 204

— Societies, 2, 15, 23, 36, 80, 101f.
— Tracts, 172
— Tract Society, 81, 143
Remuneration of Authors, 186f.
Repository, 79
— Tracts, 81
Reprints, 185
Residing Members of the S.P.C.K., 14,
88f.
Restoration, the, 1, 3, 20, 56, 85
Revision of Tracts, 179f.
Reunion, 94
Richmond, Duke of, 53, 146
—, James, 37
Ripley, 102
Rivington, John, 188f.
—, Septimus, 189
Rochester, 78
—, Earl of, 81
Rose, Rev. H. J., 150
Ross, 39
Ross Williamson, Hugh, 212
Rotterdam, 136
Royal Bounty, 117, 132f.
— Geographical Society, 119
— Institute of British Architects, 154
— National Institute for the Blind, 194,
212
Royalties, 186
Rules and Orders for Charity Schools,
24, 27, 38, 43, 49
— of the S.P.C.K., 90ff.
Russia, 116
Russian, 115

Saffron Walden, 207, 217
St Andrew's, Holborn, 29f., 34, 86
St Andrew's, Holborn, Workhouse
School, 43
St Ann's, Aldersgate, 35
St Anne's, Blackfriars, 39
St Augustine's College, Canterbury,
214
St Botolph-without-Aldgate, 8f., 212
St David's, 33, 96, 158
St Dunstan-in-the-West, 21, 51, 90
St Dunstan's Coffee House, 16, 89
St George's, Southwark, 24
St Giles-in-the-Fields, 34, 53
St John's (Antigua) Bookshop, 227
St John's College, Auckland, 163

St John's College, Battersea, 161, 203
St Katharine's College, Tottenham, 161, 194, 203, 206, 212f.
St Katherine-by-the-Tower, 35
St Margaret's, Westminster, 35
St Martin's, Scilly, 139
St Mary-le-Bow, 30
St Mary's, Devonport, 166
St Mary's, Scilly, 138ff.
St Michael's School, Bristol, 102
St Neot's, 36
St Patrick's College, Gwelo, 214
St Paul's Cathedral, 29f., 90, 152, 211f.
St Paul's Chapter House, 89
St Paul's, Covent Garden, 30
St Paul's, Sheffield, 178
St Peter's Hall, Singapore, 214
St Sepulchre, Holborn, 29
Salaries, of S.P.C.K. staff, 15ff., 23, 189f.
—, of teachers, 37ff.
Salisbury Committee, 142, 147
—, Bishop of, 32, 36, 38
— Bookshop, 226
— (Southern Rhodesia) Bookshop, 129, 205, 227
Salmon, Mr, 62
Salzburgers, 134f., 137
Sargent, Sir Malcolm, 212
Sartorius, 67ff.
Satteyanaden (Sattianden), " Country Priest ", 73
Saturday Magazine, The, 182f.
Savannah, 137
Savoy Chapel, 3, 133
Scarborough, 36
Scholarships, 203
School Boards, 159
— Books, 128, 184
Schoolmasters, 28, 37f.
—, Society of, 39f.
"School Pence", 45, 158
Schools, Charity, Ch. 4
—, National, 53, 157
Schultze, Rev. B., 67ff.
Schwarz, Rev. C. F., 64, 68ff., 75
Scilly Mission, Ch. 9 (c), 150
Scotland, 170, 220f.
—, Church of, 177, 220
Scott, Bishop C. P., 128
Scott Holland, Canon H., 198

Scottish S. P. C. K., 87, 220f.
Scougat, H., 41
Secker, Bishop Thomas, 49
Secretaries of the S.P.C.K., 15, 211, 217, 224
Selwyn, Dr E. G., 204
Serbian, 115
Serfogee, Rajah, 70f.
Sermon, Annual, 28, 31, 92, 156
Service, Annual, 29f., 49, 93, 146ff., 148, 211
Seychelles, 107
Shaftesbury, Earl of, 174
Sharp, Archbishop of York, 113
Sheffield, 178
— Bookshop, 205f., 226
Sheldon, 5, 8, 42, 97, 100, 212
— Press, 200
Sherlock, Dean Thomas, 32
Sherow, Captain, 97f.
Short, William, 26
Shrewsbury, 34, 40, 48
Shrivenham, 41
Shute, Rev. Henry, 17, 89, 91
Sierra Leone, 165
Silesia, 114
Simeon, Charles, 150
Singapore, 128, 214
— Bookshop, 128, 205, 227
Singing in Schools, 41
Sinhalese, 125
Sion College, 6, 77, 89
Skate, Mr, 24
Smalridge, R., 79
Smith, Augustus, 140
—, H. M., 122
—, John Alexander, 222
—, R., 41
—, W. H., 145f., 191
Soane, Sir John, 217
Social Conditions, 100
Socialists, 180
Societies, 1f., 10, 36, 87, 92, 101f., 152
Society for Education, 36
— for the Propagation of the Gospel, 7f., 14, 59, 61, 63, 72, 75f., 87, 92, 136, 146f., 152f., 155, 189, 210, 213, 223
— for the Reformation of Manners, 1, 10, 15, 87, 92, 101
— of Authors, 186

Society of Patrons, 30
— of Schoolmasters, 39f.
— to Promote Christian Knowledge in the Highlands and Islands, 220
Somers Town, 115
Sons of the Clergy, 87
Sophia, Princess, of Hanover, 94
— Hedwig, Princess, of Denmark, 66
South, Dr, 34
South Africa, 168
— African Church, 149
— American Missionary Society, 115
— Carolina, 134
— India, 69, 74, 114, 125
— —, Church of, 123, 127, 214
— Sea Islands, 99
Southampton, 51, 167
Southern Sudan, 214
Southwark, 24
S.P.C.K. Burma, 129
— House, 151, 193, 226
— India, 126
— Near East, 118
Spanish, 115f.
Speaight, Robert, 212
Special General Meetings, 216
Standard Bank of South Africa, 193
Standford (Berks.), 42, 100
Standing Committee of the S.P.C.K., 76, 109, 144, 172ff., 183, 186, 194, 197, 200, 204, 206, 210f., 217f.
— Rules and Orders of the S.P.C.K., 90ff.
Stanhope, Dean George, 31
Statutory Committees, 211
Steere, Bishop Edward, 128
Stephenson, A. K. L., 217, 224
Stepney Training College, 162, 194
Stevenage, 183, 227
Stevenson, Chaplain at Madras, 66
Stoke Newington, 155
Stonhouse, Rev. H., 225
Strand, 30
Stroud, 37
Stuart, Rev. J. D. M., 126, 214
Stubbs, Rev. Professor, 110
Subscribing Members of the S.P.C.K., 88f.
Subscriptions, 14, 22, 24f., 34, 89, 143, 148f., 154, 202f.
Subsidies for Literature, 129

Sullivan, Arthur, 178
Sunday Schools, 28
Swabey, Rev. Henry, 224
Swahili, 120ff.
Swedish, 112, 116
Sykes, Professor Norman, 81
Syllabus in Charity Schools, 50f.
Syrian Church, 123

Tahiti, 222
Tait, Archbishop, 168
Talbot, Bishop William, 32
— Press, 207
Talbott, James, 42
Tamil, 61, 65, 68, 125
Tanga Bookshop, 227
Tanganyika Bookshops, 213, 227
Tanjore, 69ff., 73f., 76
—, King of, 70
Tatam, John, 100
Tate and Brady's Psalms, 171
Taylor, Joseph, 44
Teachers, in Charity Schools, 37ff.
Telugu, 68, 125
Temple Gairdner, Canon, 118
— School, Bristol, 53
—, William, 198, 209
Tenison, Archbishop, 5, 74, 93, 112f.
Thanksgiving Fund, 152
— Services, 195, 212
Theological Advisors for West Africa, 214
— Colleges, 150, 163
Thetford, 35
Thomas, Francis, Earl of Kerry, 225
—, John, 32
Thompson, Rev. H. P., ix, 5, 12, 98
Thoresby, Ralph, 8
Tillard, William, 91
Tillotson, Archbishop, 82, 180
Timor, 222
Tindal Hart, A., 55, 113
Tinnevelly, 163
Tischendorf, Mr, 175
Tiverton, 38
Tobago Bookshop, 227
Tomlinson, Bishop George, 111, 114, 156, 224
Tonga, 222
Tottenham, 161, 207

Tract Committee, 109, 172ff., 178, 181, 183, 197, 199
Tracts, 81, 172, 198
—, revision of, 179f.
Tracts for the Times, 150
Training Colleges, 150, 158f., 162f., 194, 203
Training of Teachers, 38, 102
—, vocational, in Charity Schools, 51
Tranquebar, 60f., 65, 67ff., 74f.
Translation, problems of, 105, 108, 110f., 128, 131
Travellers, 192
Treasurers, 91, 191f., 216
Treasury, 158
Tresco, 138, 140
Trevelyan, G. M., 28
Trichinopoly, 70, 73, 75
Triebner, Mr, 138
Trinidad Bookshop, 227
Trinity College, Dublin, 220
Truro, 95
— Bookshop, 227
Trustees for Georgia, 134
— for the Maintenance of Ministers, 56
— of Charity Schools, 22, 27, 30f., 33, 37
— of the S.P.C.K., 192
Tucker, Joseph, 32
Turin, 114
Turkish, 119
— Empire, 110, 116, 164
Turner, Bishop, 153
Twogood, Captain, 97
Two-hundred-and-fiftieth Anniversary celebrations, 211f.
Twyford, 133

Uffington (Lincs.), 44
Uganda Bookshop, 202
Ukrainian, 115
Ulrichskirche, Halle, 60
Uniformity, Act of, 110
Uniforms in Charity Schools, 46, 53
United States of America, emigration to, 167
Universities Mission to Central Africa, 123
University of Dublin Press, 107
Upton-upon-Severn, 41

Urdu, 125f.
Urlsperger, 136

Van de Water, 117
Van Mildert, H., 141
Van Vryhouven Trust, 154, 225
Vaud, 114
Velimirovitch, Nicolai, 115
Vepery, 71
— Press, 124f.
Verelst, H., 134
Vernacular School Books, 128
Vice-Presidents, 216
Victoria, Queen, 176
Visitation of Schools, 23, 43
Voting, in S.P.C.K. Committees, 149

Wake, Archbishop William, 8, 27, 31, 61, 64, 68, 82, 93f., 99
Wakefield, 39, 177
— Bookshop, 227
Wales, 25, 55f., 80, 96, 103ff.
Walker, Rev. Samuel, 95
Wand, Bishop J. W. C., 218
Wanley, Humphrey, 15, 224
War Damage, 193, 206
Ware, 50
Warre Cornish, F., 103
Warwick, 36, 46, 48
Waterland, Dr, 38
Watson, Joshua, 75, 141f., 155, 158, 189
—, William, 220
Webster, A. B., 155
Wellington, Bishop of, 167
Wells, 102
Welsh, Rev. J. W., 166f.
— Literature, 103ff.
— Schools, 55
Wesley, Charles, 137f.
—, John, 2, 18, 89, 137f.
—, Samuel, 4
Westbury Court, 10
— on Severn School, 54
Westcott, Dr, 175f.
West Indies, 87, 115, 163, 213, 222
— — Bookshops, 129, 227
Westminster, 30, 133
Weston, Bishop Frank, 122
Whateley's *Evidences*, 114, 126
Wheeler, Rev. Maurice, 30
Whitaker, T. S., 225

White, Blanco, 115
—, Gilbert, 89
— Kennet, Bishop, 22, 31
Whitefield, George, 2, 85, 89, 137f.
Whole Duty of Man, The, 36, 51, 54, 82, 94
Wilberforce, Bishop, 118
—, William, 74, 152
Wilkes, Rev. Richard, 225
Wilkins, Dr, 97, 117
William III, 2f., 8, 113, 132
Williams, Archbishop John, of York, 115
—, W. M., 58
Wills, H. H., 225
Wilson, Arnold, 100
—, D. F. R., 220
—, Bishop Thomas, of Sodor and Man, 62, 84, 106
Wilton Road, 193
Winchester, 141f.
—, Bishop of, 135, 176
Windsor, 36
Winlaton (Co. Durham), 36
Wisbech, 40, 44, 50
Wisdom, Mr, 44
Witham, Mr, 91
Woburn, 46
Wolverhampton, 37
Wood, Miss Elsie Anna, 118
Woodly, Mr, 139
Woodward, Dr, 4
Worcester, Bishop of, 14, 36, 54, 101

— Bookshop, 226
— Schools, 54
Wordsworth, Christopher, 75, 141f., 155
Work, in Charity Schools, 44f., 48f., 53
Workhouses, 141, 171, 176
Workhouse Schools, 49f.
Working Schools, 44
Worlington, 35
Wotton-under-Edge, 37, 174
Wright, E. G., 57
Wynch, Mr, 65

Yarpol (Hereford), 40
Yates, Mr, 13
Year Book of the Church of England, 154
Yelvertoft (Northants.), 42
Yeovil, 37
Yonge, Charlotte, 177
York, Archbishop of, 117, 151, 178, 198
— Bookshop, 226
Young, Sir Charles, 222
Yugoslavia, 115

Zante, 111
Zanzibar, 122f.
— Bookshop, 227
Zealand, Bishop of, 60
Ziegenbalg, Bartholomew, 60f., 64, 67
Ziegenhagen, Mr, 135
Zwiffler, Mr, 137